W. C. E. (William Charles Edmund) Newbolt

Speculum sacerdotum

Or, the divine model of the priestly life

W. C. E. (William Charles Edmund) Newbolt

Speculum sacerdotum
Or, the divine model of the priestly life

ISBN/EAN: 9783741183102

Manufactured in Europe, USA, Canada, Australia, Japa

Cover: Foto ©Andreas Hilbeck / pixelio.de

Manufactured and distributed by brebook publishing software (www.brebook.com)

W. C. E. (William Charles Edmund) Newbolt

Speculum sacerdotum

Speculum Sacerdotum

OR

THE DIVINE MODEL

OF THE

PRIESTLY LIFE

BY THE REV

W. C. E. NEWBOLT, M.A.

CANON AND CHANCELLOR OF ST. PAUL'S CATHEDRAL,
SELECT PREACHER BEFORE THE UNIVERSITY OF OXFORD, AND EXAMINING
CHAPLAIN TO THE LORD BISHOP OF ELY

"Si quis auditor est verbi et non factor, hic comparabitur viro consideranti vultum nativitatis suæ in speculo; consideravit enim se, et abiit, et statim oblitus est quis fuerit."

THIRD EDITION

LONDON
LONGMANS, GREEN, & CO.
AND NEW YORK: 15 EAST 16th STREET
1894

All rights reserved

TO THE REVERED MEMORY OF

HENRY PARRY LIDDON

IN WHOSE BRILLIANT GIFTS

HIS FRIENDS STILL LOVE TO TRACE

THE POWER OF

"THE PRIEST IN HIS INNER LIFE."

"Amo te, mi frater, amantem Paulum."

PREFACE TO THE THIRD EDITION

THE kindness with which this book has been received both by the Clergy and by the Press, makes it necessary once more to insist on the point that if a preacher does not lower his doctrines to the level of his own attainments; so, on the other hand, he must not be regarded as having mastered the difficulties which he knows to be incident to his profession, if he attempts to set them forth before his fellow-labourers. For, apart from a temptation to exaggeration and unreality which belongs to subjects of this kind, there must always be a fear lest they prove to be the writer's own condemnation. "Thou therefore which teachest another, teachest thou not thyself?"

There is nothing which seems to require notice, in the criticisms passed on the book, except the statement of one of the daily journals, that it is here suggested that "the only way of forgiveness is by Absolution." As the Reviewer has not even read the title-page, ascribing it, as he does, to another author, it is, perhaps, needless to say that there is no such teaching even in suggestion in the addresses, to one who will take the trouble to read them.

I wish to express my great indebtedness to an old friend and parishioner, who has added this to his other kindnesses—that he has enabled me to correct certain faults of expression, and textual errors, which, I hope, will make this edition more accurate and complete.

W. C. E. N.

3, AMEN COURT,
   Michaelmas, 1894.

PREFACE

THE first eight of these addresses are published as the fulfilment of a promise made a few years ago to His Grace the Lord Archbishop of York, then Lord Bishop of Lichfield, on the occasion of the first diocesan Retreat given in that city. Since that time it has been found possible to complete the series, and they are put forth, such as they are, as a small contribution to the higher side of the ministerial work, in which it would seem there is more room for the expression of some simple thoughts than there is on the side of the well-occupied field of pastoral work.

It need hardly be said that the title, which is taken from the *Instructio Sacerdotum* in the old Service-books, refers to the inspired words of S. Paul,[1] which form the basis of these addresses, and not to the addresses themselves, for which, indeed, an apology would be due, were it not

[1] 2 Cor. vi. 4–10.

amply understood that such words as these are not delivered as from a master to pupils, who have much to learn; but as from one who, from a painful experience, knows something of the difficulties and failures incident to a great profession such as the Priesthood, and ventures to put them down to see if he can help others.

This book, it should be further added, is not a printed edition of well-used matter, but has been carefully rewritten, and in most cases enlarged and expanded. If it has been difficult to escape repetition, this, apart from any natural poverty of resource, has been owing in a great measure to the fact that the Apostle views the same thing from so many sides, that to expand his thoughts is necessarily to traverse ground which has been trodden before.

In spite of all their imperfections, however, these addresses are submitted to the kindness and forbearance of those whose lives are a constant exposition of the inspired words of the Apostle, in the ranks of the Anglican clergy.

W. C. E. N.

3, AMEN COURT,
    Christmas, 1893.

CONTENTS

CHAPTER		PAGE
I.	God's Ministers	1
II.	Endurance	14
III.	Work	28
IV.	Watchfulness	40
V.	Self-Denial	54
VI.	Purity	67
VII.	Knowledge	81
VIII.	Long-suffering	94
IX.	The Gentle Life	109
X.	Spirituality	123
XI.	Love	138
XII.	Truth	152
XIII.	Power	167
XIV.	Controversy	181
XV.	Success	195
XVI.	Reputation	210
XVII.	Suspicion	224
XVIII.	Obscurity	238
XIX.	Death	254
XX.	Chastisement	269
XXI.	Sorrow	283
XXII.	Poverty	296
XXIII.	Self-Surrender	309

CHAPTER I.

GOD'S MINISTERS.

" What we are comes before what we do."

Θεοῦ διάκονοι.
("The ministers of God."—2 Cor. vi. 4.)

Ἐν παντὶ συνιστάντες ἑαυτοὺς ὡς Θεοῦ διάκονοι. (He does not say διακόνους.) "As the ministers of God should do." S. Paul is on his defence, and he is treading on delicate ground. The Corinthian Church to which he is writing is restless, suspicious, and disrespectful. It is always a distasteful task to a sensitive man to defend himself; more especially to one who sets his mission and his work on a much higher level than his personal claims, and cares for success as the victory of truth, more than for the reputation which in vulgar gratitude it offers in payment to the workman. But this is not the first nor the last time when we must own our indebtedness to an apology. More than once it has happened that the insidious piercings of the enemy, in the endeavour to rend the shell which covers a man's life, have only resulted in the formation of that delicate and beautiful pearl, which marks the point where malignity tried to penetrate, and the dignity and beauty with which a true nature rose to meet it.

S. Paul in this passage sets out with his own hand the distinguishing marks and characteristics of the priestly life. "You suspect me; you would pierce and shatter the shell which masks my life? Very well. This is what I am; attack this; penetrate here. It is the only defence I offer; what I strive to be in my ministrations, what by God's grace I am." So that we may almost say that we have in these verses a portrait of himself, by himself—a true *speculum sacerdotum*, into which a priest may look for instruction, guidance, and rectification of life; an ideal portrait of what a priest ought to be; painted, it may be, in strong colours, with features which stand out in high relief; a portrait neither attractive to look at nor easy to copy; a portrait at once unexpected in its details and startling in its suggestions. And yet, inasmuch as we believe that the Holy Ghost has deigned to guide the hand that drew it in, it is at least, we may believe, true; and further, deserving of the most careful study in those who aspire to follow his footsteps, as the servants of God and the instructors of men.

Now, there are two words which stand at the head of this passage, which may be taken as giving the summary, the general expression, the completeness of the whole portrait, and they are Θεοῦ διάκονοι.

Look at it altogether, piece in the different elements, the suffering inflicted from without, and the discipline imposed from within, action, passion, grace, precaution, equipment, the paradoxes of God's providence; and you will find this as the great χαρακτήρ, stamped upon the whole. "The minister of God." This is, after all, only that which any minister of God should be able to do—to commend himself in the unmistakable colours which distinguish such a service from all other, and to recognize in the rough handling of the world the training of an Apostle.

Now, of course, there are many ideals short of this in putting forward self. Time was when a man went from college to encounter the difficulties of ministerial life, and to develop his capacities, pre-eminently as a gentleman; to add a desirable acquaintance to the society of the neighbourhood; to be a good man to ask out to dinner, or to associate with the squire. Time was when a man went from college to make himself acceptable in the character of a scholar; to view everything from an intellectual standpoint, and to mingle in parochial affairs and personal difficulties, tinged with that complexion and absorbed in those pursuits, in the abundant case of a neglected parish Time was when a man went to commend himself by conducting his actions as a pioneer of improvement. a martyr, if need be, to sanitary reform, to intellectual culture, and material improvement. All, be it noticed, excellent ideals in their way—ideals which one can so easily bring one's self to believe are most suited to the circumstances of the case, and most congenial to the feelings of those with whom we have to do. A man may so easily bring himself to believe that he is putting forward his best self, his self of influence and of power, by being in society a man of society, in touch with the world; or that a learned leisure is of infinite profit in an age prodigal of energy, and a spendthrift in immatured schemes; or that the position of respect which he holds on Boards and Committees does show that, after all, more than anything else, men appreciate the clever administrator and the good man of business. But there is a startling amount of the spirit of the old prophet still in the world. He draws the man of God down from his high ideal; he brings him back; he makes him eat bread and drink water in the forbidden place, and return by the prohibited way. He makes him break his vow, and lose his high ideal, and then mourns over his inconsistency, and laments his downfall: "Alas, my brother!" Look again, is there not a wistful longing for something higher? Does not Herod respect and admire the steadfastness of S. John Baptist, even while he is keeping him in prison? Does not Ahab have a sort of lingering respect for Micaiah, uncompromising and unyielding though he be? Is there not a fascination about a S. Paul which even Felix and Agrippa cannot resist? "As ministers of God." This is, after all, what men want. This is the clerical self which most commands respect. Think only of such various and separated instances as Savonarola, John Wesley, and the Père Lacordaire; and then, as we recognize the fascination of a high ideal, let us ask ourselves whether on the lowest ground it does not answer to be what we profess to be, ministers of God; and put forward a self which commands the respect due to that honoured title.

"As ministers of God should do." What does this mean, then? Simply that we should come to our people as messengers from another world; messengers from God. There is a beautiful description of a picture of S. Michael in our National Gallery. "His triple crest unshaken in heaven, his hand fallen on his crossleted sword, the truth-girdle binding his undinted armour; God has put His power upon him, resistless radiance is on his limbs; no lines are there of earthly strength, no trace on the divine features of earthly anger; trustful and thoughtful, fearless but full of love, incapable except of the repose of eternal conquest, vessel and instrument of omnipotence, filled like a cloud with the victor-light, the dust of principalities and powers beneath his feet, the murmur of hell against him heard by his spiritual ear like the winding of a shell on the far-off seashore."[1]

So the minister of God, being a messenger from another world, bears upon him something of the radiance of the beauty from which he comes.

I.

And, first of all, he comes from a world where God is ever working in love, where benevolence never ceases, and mercy never grows tired, nor tenderness grows cold. "My Father worketh hitherto, and I work,"[2]—it is the very motto of Heaven. And so

[1] Ruskin, "Modern Painters," vol. ii. § ii. ch. v. p. 216.
[2] S. John v. 17.

God's minister, who is frequently taken by his prayers to the court of heaven, whose most frequent utterance lifts him at once in addressing his Father into the blessed surroundings of that holy place, finds that heaven means a region of active love. It is a thought which may well stagger us, the ceaseless round of the activity of God. Think of all the lives which are being lived in dependence on His never-ceasing providence, twining and intertwining their destinies in the mystery of free-will, yet never swerving from the line of predestination. Think of one single life only, our own: as we remember the history of its formation and the construction of its character, we see how patiently and unceasingly God has worked upon it, and the marvellous intricacy of adjustment, and the strange fragments and jagged ends out of which it has been built up. "Just as you look at the crest of the alp from the far-away plains over which the light is cast, whence human souls have communion with it by myriads, if you approach it, the glory of its aspect fades into blanched fearfulness, its purple walls are rent into grisly rocks, its silver fretwork saddened into wasting snow; the storm-brands of ages are on its breast, the ashes of its own ruin lie solemnly on its white raiment." Ah, yes! we know too well the history of the construction of our own character. And what He has done with us, He is doing with the teeming myriads who throng the world. The very sparrow as it falls is marked by His calculation. The lilies in their royal robes are part of the ritual of the earth, which perpetually does

Him homage. A minister of God goes backwards and forwards as it were from the centre of life, which sets all these things in motion, and sustains them; and therefore, as a natural result, he will of necessity be thoughtful; there will be a σεμνότης about him which is not gloom, and an earnestness which is not cant. He will be trying more and more, gently, quietly, naturally, to make men realize the end of life and its responsibilities; the meaning of what God is doing for them, and how they must work together with God. He will feel and know that men are losing terribly and bitterly the good out of life; that God is near them and they know it not, around them and they perceive Him not. He will have to go to men who seem turned loose into a world which they do not understand, and tell them there is something better than the nearest public-house, something more elevating than the nearest entertainment-booth. Architecture in the churches, history in the streets, art in the galleries, beauty in the hills, health in the fresh air, botany in the fields, geology in the stones, and God everywhere. *Sursum corda* will be the message of his life and the summons of his presence; he will lift flippancy into reverence, controversy into thoughtfulness, frivolity into practical life. He will note the faintest glimmer of religion, the simplest foothold on which to climb up to God. The waterpots of stone at the marriage feast, the few loaves in the wallets of the Apostles, the simple provision in the hands of the lad, so many materials for miracles, so many openings leading up to the glory of God. Zacchæus in the tree, the penitent on the ground, S. Matthew at his desk,—he notes them all. If it be true that we are living at a time of much frivolity, when the stream of life runs too quickly to be deep, too full of froth and foam to be lasting, all the more need is it that the minister of God should be a minister of seriousness, reality, and thoughtfulness. The saying of Louis XIV. to Massillon is well known: "Mon père, j'ai entendu plusieurs orateurs dans ma chapelle. J'en ai été fort content. Pour vous toutes les fois que je vous ai entendu, j'ai été très mécontent de moi même." It is a true comment on a faithful ministry.

II.

Once more, the minister of God goes backwards and forwards from a world of redeeming love; from the home of the Good Shepherd, Whose feet are bleeding, and Whose hands are scarred by the cruel thorns which He has disentangled from the lost sheep. He comes from the home where the lost coin reposes, scarcely yet freed from dust, which the sweeping and toil of the Church has recovered. He comes from the home where the father of the prodigal waits for his repenting and returning son; the same tender God Who followed poor S. Peter out into the night, to drive him in again by his tears; the same patient love which brought Saul, blinded and powerless, to grope his way back into life; the same forbearing patience which restored S. Mark to usefulness and duty. There, where the earthquake has torn up the ground, or the lightning scarred the cliff, or the torrent swept over the smiling plain, He is gently weaving over it the graceful cloak of verdure or clothing the gash with colour, or restoring the drenched earth with healing sun; everywhere opposing Himself to the awful waste, the wear and tear of sin.

It is wonderful to notice, as we pass up and down the parish, how God waits and waits, and follows, and lingers, and at last secures the wandering sheep. Perhaps all is severed which bound him to God, but one tiny thread, a memory of the past not quite obliterated, a warning buried beneath the rubbish of frequent falls, a talisman of goodness retained out of the wreckage of a fair life. So that the minister of God must needs be the minister of redeeming love. He finds that more than half the difficulties which he encounters spring from the taint of sin. That proud temper, which scornfully rejects all overtures, and rudely turns you from the door—which thwarts, and opposes, and ridicules, and insults, is often merely a display of restlessness, which has its root in irreligion. There is a sore within, a deep-seated prayerlessness; and prayerlessness is the *insomnia* of the soul, and the soul which has lost its peace in God is restless and irritable. That young man who looks so wistfully at you, is scanning your sincerity; he has been struggling a long time with a desperate sin. Can you help him? Do you know? Do you care? Are you a minister of God, or just another clergyman going his rounds? He soon finds out. "Come, see a Man, Which told me all things that ever I did: is not this the Christ?"[1] You can trust a man who seems to know your case, who will not hurt you by clumsy handling.

Certainly the minister of God, with the atmosphere of heaven upon him, can never despair. He can never say of any case, "It is hopeless; it is a case for the magistrates, for the police, not for me." Has Christ given him up? Has his guardian angel given him up? Perhaps it will not be until he is crucified by some accident, or caught up on the elevation of a sickness; but yet he may enter Paradise first, if he can but catch sight of the Lord to Whom your sympathy has pointed him. It has been beautifully said, "There is hardly a roadside pond or pool which has not as much landscape in it as above it. It is not the brown muddy, dull thing we suppose it to be. It has a heart like ourselves, and in the bottom of that there are the boughs of the tall trees, and the blades of the shaking grass, and all manner of hues of variable pleasant light out of the sky. Nay, that ugly gutter which stagnates over the drain-bars in the heart of the great city, is not altogether base. Down in that, if you will look deep enough, you may see the dark serious blue of the far-off sky, and the passing of pure clouds. It is at your own will that you see in that despised stream the refuse of the streets or the image of the sky." The minister of redeeming love must go about like his Master, as one

[1] S. John iv. 29.

who "is come to seek and to save that which was lost."[1]

III.

Yet, again, the minister of God comes from a world of sanctifying love. It is all-important to remember this. We are not making experiments; we are not dealing with unknown cases; we are not patching up wounds which we do not understand, with a treatment which we do not appreciate. He Who knew what was in man left us, for our help and cure, the Catholic Church—old remedies, slow and painful, but effectual. Would that we were more faithful in the use of them! Original sin, with its taint and malignity, does need Holy Baptism. Actual sin is forgiven and its chain snapped off by Absolution. The weakness of our nature, too feeble to stand alone, is braced and supported by Confirmation. There is growth and sustaining power in Holy Communion. Do we, as the ministers of God, know how to use these things? Have we tried their edge? There is no liberality in substituting untried remedies of human invention which happen to be in the fashion, for the tried remedies of God which happen to be unpalatable. We must not be ashamed to tell Naaman to go and wash seven times in the river Jordan, if he will be cleansed from his leprosy; nor desist for his rage, nor give in because he threatens to go elsewhere. We must not be ashamed to proclaim that we hope to subdue the vice and overthrow the ramparts of sin

[1] S. Luke xix. 10.

in our towns, simply by walking round it with the sevenfold procession of grace. No, there is no liberality in distracting a poor sufferer by ill-considered advice, or evenly balanced advocacy of opposing remedies. We shall not cure a man who lies desperately ill by telling him that allopathists, homœopathists, herbalists, faith-healers, and all quacks, are either equally good or equally useless; but we shall feel it necessary to diagnose his case, and act carefully and with the utmost accuracy of treatment. Much more, when we are dealing with a man's soul we feel it must not be trifled with or treated inconsiderately. If we come from the God of sanctifying love, we feel that we come from a God Who has given His Son to die for us, and to rise again for our justification.

Ministers of God—men from another world! How can this be? Every one has felt what a different thing it is, either in some record of missionary enterprise or tale of geographical research, if, instead of reading a dry record, or hearing the narrative of those who have received it second-hand, we encounter a man who has been on the spot, and comes to us with all the freshness of detail which only a personal knowledge can bestow. Then there are a hundred interesting facts and graphic touches which he is able to impart, which give at once a different complexion to the whole narrative. In like manner we must come to our people from another world, as men who have been there. As we have stood on the shore watching the incoming tide, we have seen how it surrounds at first a patch of sand here, a heap there, a litter there, and then gradually spreads with a steady flow all around, until the whole surface is covered with its bright fresh waves. So, if we do but open our hearts to the inflow of Divine love, all will soon be covered by the gathering tide. There are patches of our life covered by it already, where the Holy Eucharist lies deep and still, the daily meditation ripples over our heart, and the Daily Office pours along its wave of devotion. If we interpose no barrier, our points of religious earnestness will meet in a sea of Divine love, whose bright surface reflects the sun, and covers over the cracked and barren sand of a worldly life. Surely our people may well demand this of us, that we should be in frequent communication with God; that we should linger long and frequently in the atmosphere of heaven, that we may come forth to meet God's discipline and the world's assaults as ministers of God should do.

CHAPTER II.

ENDURANCE.

"Hopes have precarious life;
 They are oft blighted, withered, snapt sheer off:
 But faithfulness can feed on suffering,
 And knows no disappointment."

Ἐν ὑπομονῇ πολλῇ, ἐν θλίψεσιν, ἐν ἀνάγκαις, ἐν στενοχωρίαις, ἐν πληγαῖς, ἐν φυλακαῖς, ἐν ἀκαταστασίαις.

("In much patience, in afflictions, in necessities, in distresses, in stripes, in imprisonments, in tumults.")

WHAT a list we have here! What a strange badge of ministry, these various forms of suffering imposed from without!

Did Saul think of this, as he looked out into the future at Tarsus, and imagined himself, it may be, a great man in the days to come? Did his learning, drunk in at the feet of Gamaliel, shape itself into a hopeless antagonism to his spiritual and intellectual environment? When he started off that day, in the full glow of religious enthusiasm and frantic zeal, along the Damascus road, laying, as he thought, all the forces of his being at the disposal of truth, did he think that 'the Truth" was going to ask for a patient, afflicted, straitened, troubled, beaten, fettered messenger? Did Jesus meet him for this, in the blinding flash and overwhelming utterance which crushed him to the earth? Yes, the great mould had been prepared, into which all the molten impetuosity of his fiery life was to be run. Ananias points to it; it was the offer he had to make to him, with his newly found eyesight, on his spiritual birthday—"I will show him how great things he must suffer."[1] And now there is enshrined that name, under the bright badge of the cross, above the roar and bustle, the business, the wealth, the intellect, of London—S. Paul's. But it was the name of one who in his lifetime pointed out, as the first field of ministerial exercise, the distinctive badges of his ministry, much patience, afflictions, necessities, distresses, stripes, imprisonments, tumults.

When the bishops were assembling for the great Council of Nicæa, we are told that the confessors among them, who had survived the last and worst of the persecutions, came like a regiment out of some fearful siege or battle, with the scar of torture, the marks of suffering imprinted on them.[2] And sometimes, as we sit in the quiet of our room, or in the peace of a retreat, and meditate plans of campaign, or sharpen our weapons before the battle, we wonder, if we are spared another ten or twenty years, whether any of these marks will be upon us, as we step into line, where our comrades have dropped out in death, or come tottering in, worn out in mind and body,

[1] Acts ix. 16.
[2] See Stanley, "Eastern Church," vol. i. lect. iii. p. 96.

faint, disappointed, hard-hit, weary, yet still resolute. The Visitation as it comes round, the Diocesan Conference, the clerical meeting, are too often like the famous "roll-call" after Inkermann, with its shattered, broken line of wounded, maimed, and sickly heroes, each *non indecoro pulvere sordidus*. Here are some stern marks of the ministry which we do not always like to look upon.

I.

What does it mean? It means discipline. There stands, in the forefront of the grim list, that ominous and yet grand word, ὑπομόνη. Did he look back to the time when Saul—his old self—was brought in crushed and quivering, with all his great powers, like machinery out of gear, aimlessly beating the air, as yet undisciplined, untrained, unspiritualized, to be twisted back, shaped, and hammered into "the minister of God"? Many rough lines must come away; perhaps some lingering taint of former years. Was the temper under control? Was his heart single? Was his obedience unflinching? What was the thorn in the flesh? Why was it left there? All this list of sorrows meant, no doubt, the perfecting of the instrument, the shaping of an Apostle, the making of the minister of God.

It is a hard matter to face a training like this. We would serve the strongest master—stronger than worldly ambition, stronger than passion—but we did not calculate that the Holy Child would weigh us down. The waves mount higher, the storm waxes fiercer, and our tread becomes more difficult, the burden more intense, as we stagger forward, trying to bear Christ. It is hard to acquiesce patiently, as He looks at us in all our strength and vigour, and says, "Verily, verily, I say unto thee, When thou wast young, thou girdedst thyself, and walkedst whither thou wouldest: but when thou shalt be old, thou shalt stretch forth thy hands, and another shall gird thee, and carry thee whither thou wouldest not."[1] It is hard to feel the "much patience," and keep quite still, as blow after blow seems to shatter a life's work. It is hard to acquiesce in the "affliction" of reiterated disappointment and resolute distress. It is hard to stand bareheaded and shivering in the driving storm and pitiless blast of "necessities." "Distresses" find out the weak place in the armour and dart in upon the heart with mental anguish, intellectual perplexity, spiritual dimness, physical weakness, the dull gloom and fog of earth's unrelieved miseries; "imprisonments" forbid our escape from uncongenial surroundings, the "few rustics," the commercial vulgarity, the refined scepticism, the cold contempt, the controversial bitterness, "the parish where we have no sympathy;" unpopularity lashes with its "stripes;" opposition terrifies with "tumults."

All this list of misery represents trouble inflicted from without, and there is no sacrament so difficult to receive in a worthy spirit as the sacrament of suffering, which God distributes to us through the hands of our fellow-men. "Let us fall now into the

[1] S. John xxi. 18.

hand of the Lord; for His mercies are great: and let me not fall into the hand of man."[1] It would seem to be a law of God's dealing with His people, that those who come nearest to Him, and aspire to any special work in His kingdom, must submit to the constant discipline of suffering, the thwarting of the will which might assert itself against His plan; the cleansing away of even those defilements which, unnoticeable in ordinary men, are serious defects in a courtier, and breaches of the etiquette of heaven. If the ordinary Christian feels that he must turn an attentive ear to his Lord's voice—" Take up thy cross, and follow Me "—much more must he who aspires to a place in His hierarchy approve himself by self-discipline as the minister of God.

II.

But these are not the contents of a torture-chamber of mere ministerial discipline, an unproductive tread-mill of hard routine, an arbitrary task, which might easily be removed. It means more than this; the intense difficulty of conveying truth to a fallen and unwilling world. It always has been so, and there seems no indication of a change; truth demands its martyrs. It is true of discoverers, who have seen ahead of their times, and proclaimed truth too suddenly to those who, sitting in intellectual darkness, only felt it to be a painful flash, an irritating confusion, rather than a productive illumination. It

[1] 2 Sam. xxiv. 14.   [2] S. Matt. xvi. 24.

has been the case with many reformers of crying abuses. The touching biography of the great Lord Shaftesbury exhibits the extraordinary phenomenon of one carrying through Parliament improvements and schemes of philanthropy, which are now recognized as the A B C of common humanity, with every form of opposition, obloquy, and scorn at the hands of tender-hearted and generous men, who yet resented the intrusion of new features into a routine which roused no dangerous activities, and conflicted with no strong interests. Much more has this been the case, and is now, with those who are the pioneers of religious truth. Unpopularity seems a trivial thing on paper, but it may become a real martyrdom. It may sour a man's kindliest energies. And when we talk of popularity, we must not bring before us the man who loves display in his sermons, or the homage of his flatterers, or the incense of the praise of those who think he can do no wrong. Most men must confess, and without shame in the confession, that it is pleasant to be thought well of, to be loved and welcomed. So that one singularly endowed with the gift of a keen insight into human nature has said, "Do we not feel that we are apt to think of ourselves as others think of us? and that, not by a rational act of judgment, but by a mere passion yielding to an impression from without. Let people around us think poorly of us, and we think poorly of ourselves. The opposition to surrounding influences taxes one's self-reliance. Hence it is that, as an ordinary rule, it is not good for a man either to live with or even see much of another who habitually depreciates him; such intercourse tends to lower his spirits."[1] And yet is not this the lot of many a parish priest?—despised until he feels himself despicable, laughed out of his enthusiasms, hardened by unthinking, indiscriminate opposition into unsympathetic, unloving selfishness, until his very religion bristles with defiance, and the hard dislike is met with a religious self-pleasing which does not even aim at edification. Each fresh complaint, each fresh alienation, is met with scorpions instead of whips.

With some people there is a craving for tenderness. The experience of a parish priest, who had to cast away his much-cherished popularity in going against the evil lives and low standard of the parish, has been beautifully described in a well-known story. "With a power of persistence, which had been often blamed as obstinacy, he had an acute sensibility to the very hatred or ridicule he did not flinch from provoking. Every form of disapproval jarred him painfully; and though he fronted his opponents manfully, and often with considerable warmth of temper, he had no pugnacious pleasure in the contest. It was one of the weaknesses of his nature to be too keenly alive to every harsh wind of opinion; to wince under the frowns of the foolish; to be irritated by the injustice of those who could not possibly have the elements indispensable for judging him rightly; and with all this acute sensibility to blame, this dependence on sympathy, he had for years been constrained into a

[1] Mozley, "Lectures on the Old Testament," p. 43.

position of antagonism. He had often been thankful to an old woman for saying, 'God bless you,' to a little child for smiling at him; to a dog for submitting to be patted by him." This craving for sympathy, for kindness, if it be a fault, surely is a very slight one. It carries with it deep pain, and many a heartache, as the word has to be spoken, the action done, the concession refused, at the price of a present smile, but of future remorse, and what has been described as "the untold anguish of a dishonoured conscience."[1] And yet how frequently and how unexpectedly the decision has to be made! Need Daniel carry his opposition so far as to kneel down, when he is thwarting the wishes of the king, in putting up his petitions to God? There is nothing essential in a posture, or vital in a mere piece of ritual. Is it worth while to throw away his splendid position and his great influence with the king for an irritating detail and an ostentatious item of defiance? Is it necessary for S. John Baptist always to allude to the king's private disgrace? It might ruin his chance of ultimate influence, and establish an irritation, and preclude all hopes of future usefulness; it might be even thought unmannerly, as well as unstatesmanlike, to persist in a protest, wearisome from its monotony, ineffective from its constant repetition, "It is not lawful for thee to have thy brother's wife."

If I refuse an invitation to dinner on Friday, or on a Vigil, the world will not understand it, my host will think me unfriendly, my neighbours will think me

[1] Bishop of Winchester, "Pastoral," 1892, p. 6.

ostentatious, and many will view me with suspicion; and my influence will be gone, while I have been sticking out for a trifle, and putting fasting, or one form of it, above charity.

Yes, it is hard to bear the cold looks, the impatient scorn, the smart epigram, the cheap wit, the falling away of friends, the collapse of support, the withdrawal of subscriptions, the letter to the newspaper, the harsh names, the ungenerous suspicions. And, perhaps worse than all these, is the sense of loneliness, which has crushed many a man to the earth. To stand alone argues self-reliance; it may mean self-conceit. We mean it for steadfastness of purpose; is it obstinacy? We are standing out for principle; does that mean love of our own way? And there pours in from every side the pitiless refrain, Why do you refuse to act like other people? Why? Because we have caught a glimpse of the higher peak, white and glorious against the unclouded blue; because the mists, as they drive down the mountain-side, have parted just for a moment, and showed us the path, wet and slippery, fossed with precipices, battlemented with crags, and swept with the storm, but still a path, and above it the blue sky. Why? Because we have heard just for once the celestial harmony sighing in upon the wind, and we cannot rest until it becomes louder, so that others may hear it too. Why? Because we have felt the Presence, mysterious and awful, not as a victory in argument, or a thesis in disputation, but the pressure of a hand when we had almost gone, a firm support when our treadings had well-nigh slipt; just a light in the darkness, a face out of the gloom. And we crave with all our hearts to make others feel, and others know; to make them look up from their controversies, and their party-books, and their views, and their opinions, and just for once to see, for once to hear, and to say, as the one thought which has swallowed up all else, "O my God, Thou art true; O my soul, thou art happy!"[1] Why? Because we have climbed to the foot of the Cross, and have laid there our sorrow and our sin. We know what that Hand did for us; we can feel thrilling through every fibre of our being the marvellous relief, and the intense mercy of His voice, "Neither do I condemn thee: go, and sin no more."[2] And we want to tell others of the great things He has done for our soul. We know something of what worship means, as its voices sweep down to earth across the crystal sea; and we long to make others feel it too, to lift up their hearts to God above. But we shrink back; it seems impossible. "Let us alone." "These that have turned the world upside down are come hither also;"[3] "This fellow persuadeth men to worship God contrary to the Law;"[4] "We have heard him speak blasphemous words."[5] It seems as if we were rousing men out of a sound sleep, only to impatience, irritation, and incredulity. Having eyes, they see not; having ears, they hear not. But patience! It is only just above them; have patience a little

---

[1] Hooker, "Ecclesiastical Polity," v. 67. 12.
[2] S. John viii. 11.   [3] Acts xvii 6.
[4] Acts xviii. 13.   [5] Acts vi. 11.

longer, and they will all begin to climb. First one, and then another, until by degrees the whole parish is lifted up. But there was a time when we were quite alone, and it was lonely indeed.

And further, we must not shrink from coarse opposition of a violent kind. The literal prison has only during the last few years ceased to be the punishment of zeal, which incurred suspicion, or ran counter to popular prejudice. The world is not converted yet, nor does it own the easy yoke of Christ. Sin has still to be grappled with, twisted tightly round every form of unbelief and misbelief, and, alas! orthodoxy too. At any moment it may be ours to face almost in any parish the popular tumult, "Great is Diana of the Ephesians!" and the popular protest, "Our craft is in danger."[1] But how is he behaving as a minister of God should, who does not know how to commend himself, "in stripes, in imprisonments, in tumults"?

III.

And this list means further, with all its gradation of troubles, self-sacrifice. Here is the forgetfulness of ease and self-enjoyment, which will take the parish priest round day after day, in all weathers, wet or fine, cold or hot, waiting for his opportunities, tender and sympathetic, a friend in trouble, a welcome sharer in every simple joy. Here is the spirit of devotedness, which will make the refined scholar

---

[1] Acts xix. 27, 28.

enjoy the daily teaching of simple country children in the early morning hour, whose leisure to him at least is golden; or give up the well-earned rest and opportunities of the evening to the training of the choir, the lecture, or the class. Here is something of the affliction of their desolating sorrows shared in, in all its hopelessness, poverty, and gloom. Here is the necessity of their hard lot realized in the self-denying simplicity of home and daily food. Here the distress patiently listened to, passes over on to the shoulders bowed to bear another's burden, and becomes his own. Here is the imprisonment to work, which makes a man cheerfully recognize that his own parish is his first work, and not the excitement of itinerant preaching, and spasmodic or sporadic work in other fields of labour. The temple has to be built, and his contribution to the structure to be prepared in the depth of the quarry, or in the shades of the forest; to neglect it means a blank space in the wall, or an incongruous ornament where a buttress was needed, or a finial in the place of a foundation. The imprisonments of God are the opportunities for careful and individual work. Here, too, will be the marks of close rooms, and fetid alleys, and fever-poison, risked with unflinching courage, as a simple duty. Self-sacrifice has ever been a great force in the world, and men are won by the Cross who are repelled by the power of wealth, the brilliancy of culture, the strength of resource. The great French novelist asks with some touch of exaggeration, "How can a man incessantly, both night and day, come into contact with distress, misfortune, and want, without having a little of that holy suffering, the dust of toil? Can we imagine a man sitting close to a stove, and not feeling hot? Can we imagine a workman constantly toiling at a furnace, and having neither a hair burned, a nail blackened, nor grain of soot on his face?" Certainly luxury, indolence, ease, will sit badly on one who is brought into contact with the want and starvation of suffering humanity.

And who would shrink back? Christ has asked for more than this. He has asked for martyrs in all ages, and in all ages He has found them. Look at the African missionary, driven home to breathe after the gasping fever; his sole wish is to get back again. Look at those labouring among the teeming populations and close streets of London and our large towns; they seldom seem happy elsewhere. There are bright views, and refreshing breezes, and pleasures unlike anything else to be found on those wind-swept heights by the hardy mountaineer, as he climbs on over snow and rock and ice, with benumbed fingers, weather-beaten brow, and aching feet. He never thinks of turning back; he would not for the world be one of that idle throng hanging over the village bridge, or watching listlessly through the telescope. He is ever seeing fresh beauties unfolding before him. He sees the Alpine flower "among the rack of the higher clouds, and howlings of glacier winds, piercing through the edge of an avalanche," in the wondrous mysteries of the lonely height. He sees skies such as no one else does, and exults in the simple exhilaration of ever getting higher and higher. Would S. Paul, after all, have changed this weather-beaten life, and all he had seen, and all it had taught him, for the old life of Saul, with its culture and prospects of success? The priest's life may be a hard one, but it "is as the shining light, that shineth more and more unto the perfect day."[1]

[1] Prov. iv. 18.

CHAPTER III.

WORK.

> "To our own nets ne'er bow we down
> Lest on the eternal shore
> The angels, while our draught they own,
> Reject us evermore."

> "I must accept what I cannot do, or get done, or hinder, as soon as I have done all that is possible; then it is not negligence, but simple submission to the will of God."

Ἐν κόποις.
("In labours.")

IN a room well known to many generations of young men, there used to hang a photograph of the great Bishop Wilberforce, under which was written the one word κόπος: as if this were the designation of all others which summed up the indomitable energy, resource, and ceaseless activity of that wonderful man. S. Paul puts it here first, among the marks of the ministry burnt in as it were on his life, with his own hand, ἐν κόποις. And any thinking man must, as life goes on, have forced upon him more and more the dignity of labour, its beauty and necessity. What fascination is it which makes us inspect with wondering eyes those huge masses of iron and steel, with their gliding wheels, and shooting straps, and puffed-out jets of steam? It is the nicety and finish of their working, which gives, as it were, a living character to that which in itself is an ungainly mass of metal. Coming higher, it has been exquisitely pointed out that beauty and labour are closely connected. "So far as I know," says a deep observer, "there is no beauty in any slothful animal; but even among those of prey, its characters exist in exalted measure upon those that range and pursue, and are in equal measure withdrawn from those that lie subtly and silently in the covert of the reed or fen." He would say, a slothful animal is an ugly animal. Coming higher, is true beauty to be seen in its highest form in the calm, unemotional, smooth, sensualized mask of some stately Apollo; or rather in the lined, torn, and furrowed marks, cut into what is called expression, in features even ugly and misshapen individually, yet lit up with the inner glow of a life's work? Coming higher still, what is the secret of attraction in a priest, of a legitimate attraction which wins hearts through the man to God? Is it, first and foremost, the splendid genius, the high honours, the fervid eloquence, the fine voice, the agreeable companionship? Is it not rather the living message, whose rugged periods are eloquent with the facts drawn from many a hard day's work in the parish; whose voice has in it some of that sympathetic ring which has cheered the sinner with comfort, and spoken peace to the dying, and hope to the weary? Men get tired of Admirable Crichtons; they ostracize Aristides simply because they are wearied of hearing his praises. The aggressive genius provokes comparisons; but they do respect hard work. Ἐν κόποις. Here is a mark of the minister of God, within reach of all. "My Father worketh hitherto, and I work."[1] Whatever else he may be, the priest who neglects to work is not the minister of God. For "if labour is the glory of humanity, idleness is death anticipated."

And yet there is no profession, at least among the learned ones, so exposed to dangers in respect of κόπος, as that of the priesthood. And this in two directions. The priest may be the idle, inert mass as of a machine not in motion. One of whom the Spanish proverb speaks, when it says, "The devil tempts man; an idle man tempts the devil." Or he may be a machine and nothing more, like the slave of the ancient world, ἐμψύχον ὄργανον—a tool which is alive, but still only a tool.

I.

Now, first of all, there stands out clearly looming before us the danger of idleness in its barest and simplest form—a danger by no means imaginary, but real and pressing. In ordinary cases, the parish priest is not recompensed for his work, or paid in proportion to his work, as a doctor or barrister is paid. If he neglects his duties, his stipend, such as it is, still comes in. If his church has been emptied by

[1] S. John v. 17.

his neglect, it still comes in. If his school is unvisited, and the school-bell, as it calls together the children to receive knowledge, finds him, who should be the chief regulator and distributor of that knowledge, in bed or at breakfast; if it passes out of his hands altogether, and godless education settles down over the parish, to be the curse of ages yet unborn; if his church is shut up from Sunday to Sunday; if his people are unvisited; if he languidly complains of his intense fatigue after " three full services on Sunday;" if he never opens a book, or if he spends his time at lawn-tennis parties, or away from the parish;—still the stipend comes in. What chance is there, for the man who has not learned to love work, to see its dignity and importance and absolute necessity? Without this, he will but drift, and drift, and ultimately settle down on a very low level indeed, another Demas who forsakes the side of a hard-pressed friend through love of this present world.

Are there, then, any safeguards of work, which may serve to keep us from falling away? There are sundry monitors which appeal to those that have ears to hear, and sundry considerations which may serve to quicken our activity; among which, first of all, we would place the appreciation of the value of time. So many things might bring this before us. See how men economize its fleeting moments, as it speeds along, its hours, its minutes, its seconds, as if to try and stay it as it passes.

> "O precious hours! O golden prime,
> And affluence of love and time!

> Even as a miser counts his gold,
> Those hours the ancient timepiece told—
> Forever,—never!
> Never,—forever!"

A child must, as a matter of course, have his day mapped out for him, or he will waste it all. But as he gets older he learns to do this for himself, and by degrees to recognize the tremendous responsibility of unoccupied moments, and hours of leisure from fixed work. And so we have to learn more and more the value of spare time; to ask ourselves, What does God mean me to do with a privilege so great? What would Franklin have done with it, as he sat up during whole nights to study science, in the years of his weary drudgery as an apprentice? Times of quiet, lulls in the storm of life, the undisturbed monotony of a peaceful routine, carry with them great responsibilities. Because time is the great preparer. David at the sheepfolds is learning to shepherd Israel; S. Paul, pinned down to the soldier that kept him, is being held still to write his Epistles, and thereby to evangelize the world; the weariness of a long convalescence is the conversion of S. Ignatius Loyola. Those whom it has been customary to call "the lazy monks" preserved for us, during rude ages of bloodshed and idle activity, the priceless monuments of literary antiquity. A brook is a lovely, fertilizing thing as it gushes along in its ceaseless flow; the flowers dip their heads in it; the insect-life sports in it and around it; the birds fly down to sip from it with uplifting head; and men are refreshed by it, as it babbles by in its hurrying course. The strong river is a grand thing as it sweeps along, watering fields, bringing commerce to towns, and rushes away to its embrace with the sea. But there is also a force in that quiet lake, that reservoir of stored strength, with its calm expanse, fed by the rain from heaven, and the streams which trickle down the mountain-side. Underneath its calm surface there is going out the life and health of some great centre of commercial activity. So God, in His good providence, may mean our lives to gush along like the brook, with deep pools here and there, even if its general course be the shallowness of rapid movement. He may so order that our activity be that of the strong river, and take us past the great seats of learning and worldly business. Or He may call us to be the calm reservoir in the mountains, in the leisure of a country parish, in the prolonged responsibility of a quiet life.

And therefore a second safeguard of work at once suggests itself, which is—rule. If we would keep our hand on time we must learn to live by rule; otherwise it will surely flit away, we know not how, we know not where, and its golden opportunities be lost to us. How shall we guard, for instance, against the encroachments of the daily death which we call sleep? We cannot leave to chance, or pure inclination, the hour for rising in the morning, or the hour for going to bed, that we may be able to rise in good time for the morning's work. It seems a little thing, in speaking of work, and yet it is the foundation of our rule. The day takes its shape from the morning. The late rising means hurried prayer, and hurried prayer means an irritable soul, a soul deprived of nourishment and rest. The first hours of the day run one into another, and the confusion of the morning extends itself to the afternoon, and is felt throughout the day. More than this, the body feels that it has won a victory, and like a bully is proud of its own powers for evil; it was but half an hour in bed, but the will has lost its spring, and the day's work its soundness; and irritation and discomfort witness to its power to annoy, while they are the earnest of future victories. But more than all, the best things are gone. The manna lay round the host in the early morning; the sun is up, it has melted away. He was there standing by the shore as the day broke over the lake, to bless the weary fishermen. S. Mary Magdalene has found Him early, while it is yet dark. Early rising seems such a little thing. But can we leave it out of the purview of a life, whose minutes are to be accounted for before God? Rule will, then, serve to keep us in check all day. It makes us feel pre-eminently the value of punctuality. Napoleon is credited with saying that he lost his great opportunity at Waterloo because one of his generals was five minutes late. However this may be, how many active men in our large towns have given up attending early services because the clergy come in five minutes, ten minutes, or a quarter of an hour late? Time is money to a business man, and we owe to them the appreciation of the value of a minute, and the spectacle of accurately economized time. Rule will further help us to pick up the odd fragments of time, the five minutes when we are kept waiting; the remnants from big occupations. The pickings of a dust-heap are said to be of some value. The odd minutes of time discarded from occupation can be utilized in like manner by those who have the determination to do so.

A third safeguard of time might be found in a suggestion of a modern divine and writer, in what he calls the two questions; the first being, "What doest thou here, Elijah?" the second, "Wist ye not that I must be about My Father's business?"[1]

The one question "would keep us away altogether from many places, and would hasten our leaving many more." The other would help us ever to rise to, to return to, our own standard. To get on and up, higher and higher, past human sympathies, past the happy home, past the thoughts of this life, higher and higher up the steep path, ἐν κόποις.

II.

But κόπος is threatened with danger in quite another direction. There is a tendency with many people to thrust it out of its place, to make it an end instead of a mean. It is a mistake too commonly made to confuse labour with work, and to think κόπος the same thing as ἔργον. What a rush it is which is now hurling itself along the corridors of life! There is little rest even in pleasure, and recreations are elevated into a toil! And this spirit has penetrated largely into the

[1] Cardinal Manning "The Eternal Priesthood," p. 121.

clerical world. There are plenty of people who tell us that the recitation of the Divine Office is a sad waste of time, and services in church on week-days a diversion of energy from its proper channels into a pious idleness. There are men who hold up their hands in horror at young life and vigour being wasted, as they call it, on a country parish, or any trouble being expended in evangelizing a "few rustics." Men who will meet you with a perfect network of organizations, clubs, committees, guilds, associations, societies of all sorts. Men who do their reading in obedience to the rule of a society, who are temperate in virtue of an organization, pray in fulfilment of a pledge to a guild, evangelize the heathen according to the aim of an association, defend the Church, uphold the relation of Church and State, distribute charity, give alms in church, educate the poor, according to the bye-laws of some institution, not without manifold meetings and committees of management. All, it may be, excellent things in their way, but which certainly need watching, lest at times it should be impossible to see the building itself, by reason of the forest of scaffolding poles, and fragments of unfinished designs, and multiplied methods of spiritual architecture.

It is only too possible for these things to play sad havoc with the spiritual life of the priest. Your great organizer, for instance, has a meeting of the Diocesan Fund in the morning in the cathedral town; he has to attend a committee meeting of local charities in the afternoon; he must look in at a guild meeting, to see how things are going on, during the time when the curates are taking the evening service; and at night, if he can spare the time, there is a meeting of Church Defence in the public rooms, at which he must make a speech. And the poor woman with a sick child hesitates to approach so great a man for so trivial an object. And he does not know that, could he have gone with her, he would have found that the child was not baptized; he does not know that, if he had gone that night, he would have found the father nursing it; he does not know that the elder brother would have come in from work, rough and timid and suspicious; and that he would have found out from him, as the roughness wore off, that he wished to be confirmed, only he had been afraid to apply. He does not know that there would have been a man sitting by the door in church on the following Sunday, very shabbily dressed, and very unused to his surroundings, who had come there simply because he thought there must be some good in a parson who would turn out at night to see a sick child. But the great organizer has magnificently determined that the great thing to be aimed at is to discourage pauperism. And his might and his greatness, and the speeches which he made, may be read in the columns of a Church paper, but not in the hearts of his parishioners. Do not let us make a mistake, or be unfair. We must organize, it is obvious, that we may work; we must labour, that we may work; but do not let us idolize either. A priest can never give up his sacred functions, or become simply a man of business, delegating his spiritual work to subordinates. He must rather take care that he makes himself felt to the very finger-tips of his parochial organization. Curates, district visitors, masters, organists, church-wardens, lay-helpers, are not so many substitutes to relieve the *persona* of the parish of his work; they are rather representatives, delegates, helps for the better diffusing of the spiritual power and responsibility lodged in him by the authority of the Church, for the welfare of his parishioners and the advancement of God's glory, while, at the same time, we remember that the work of the priest is work of a very special kind. He must stand frequently in God's presence, if he is to bring forth any message to men. The Daily Services, the frequent Communion, the meditation in and devotional study of God's Word, are as essential to him as the fire and water are to the great engines which are to do the work of some complicated machinery. If he is to help his people, he must bring something in his hand out of the treasury; he must receive the Law at God's mouth, if he is to instruct the people. The great, the essential part of the priest's κόπος will, after all, be before the throne of God.

And then at the end the fire shall try every man's work of what sort it is, what he has built upon the One Foundation—whether it has been gold, silver, precious stones, or wood, hay, stubble; work that will perish, or work that will endure. It has been finely said, " When we are close to a cataract, we are dazed with the countless bewildering succession of hurried movements, in all variety, vastness, and rapidity of mutation. Myriads of lines of foam, and clouds of spray, and torn masses of ever-plunging water. But leave the cataract, and some miles away in clear weather look back. Far off in the lustrous distance you see one broad white unwavering ribbon or banner, nailed as it were to the steadfast rock of the mountain-side. And so our myriad thoughts and doings every day and night are our works, but all the hurry is lost in the retrospect from the awful distance of eternity. Each man's works have shrunk into each man's work,"[1] his κόπος into his ἔργον.

We may well pause and wonder whether God has any work for His priests to do beyond the grave. And yet it would seem that they whose lives have been so spent in giving out, and ministering to others, may need more of the calm preparation of the intermediate state for the perfecting of their own souls. And as the labourer who has toiled all day for his master, until his own garden is quite neglected, rejoices in the quiet evening to work for himself, and do what he can for his own flowers and herbs, with what strength remains to him; so the priest feeling, as he never did before, the unclean lips with which he proclaimed the king's message, the soiled feet dusty with life's mission, the heart bare and destitute of many of the finer virtues which have been trampled down in his busy life, may hail the peace and quiet in which his soul is being made ready, while he learns that all his own efforts and all his own merits are so much κόπος, which is after all of little avail, unless it be consummated in the ἔργον, which is the crown of the merits of Jesus Christ.

[1] "The Great Question," Bishop of Derry, p. 190.

CHAPTER IV.

WATCHFULNESS.

> ". . . once I looked on many men
> And spake them sweet and bitter speech, and heard
> Such secrets as a tempest of the soul,
> Once in a lifetime, washes black and bare
> From desperate recesses of shut sin."
>
> Ἐν ἀγρυπνίαις.
> ("In watchings.")

ONE of the hardest burdens which the ministerial life has to bear is the weight of responsibility, which is incident, of course, in varying degrees to any great profession.

Kinglake describes Lord Raglan taking his rounds in the awful snows of the Crimean campaign, with all that devolved upon a commander-in-chief heavy upon him, aggravated by home mismanagement and difficult allies. What a responsibility is laid upon a surgeon undertaking some first-class operation, in which his nerve and skill will be taxed to the utmost, while the life or health of a fellow-creature hangs upon his surgery! The judge, who has to shape a verdict, amid the pleadings of pity, or the obloquy of prejudice, or the clamour of popular feeling, knows the full weight of professional duty. And the minister of God no less, more especially in the case of those on whom ultimately the cure of souls rests, in the charge of a parish, or other position of authority. And so every earnest priest will know something of this ἀγρυπνία of which the Apostle speaks. He will know the impossibility of settling down quietly in what the outside world pictures as the cushioned ease of a comfortable living. He will know something of the unexpected dangers which constantly open up under his feet; he will know the weight of the people which he has to bear, and the names which stand out on his breast, even when he ministers before the Lord. He will know the difficulty of keeping things going, —the schools, with new educational requirements, shifting teachers, difficult parents, indifferent managers, and always at the end—no money. The choir, with two standards of excellence, musical and religious, who fail conspicuously in both; and here, again, the want of money. The clubs, with their heavy routine, worked it may be by kind friends, who in the end bring their confused accounts to the vicar to unravel, as the child brings her tangled skeins, in the story, to her fairy godmother; and here, again, there looms in the distance an appeal for money. The expenses connected with the maintenance of the Church and its services, ever appearing before the people as a tax which would gladly be dispensed with. And then the poor, whose wants he knows, and whose real welfare he feels bound to consult, now helping, now rebuking, the constant referee in their financial difficulties, cheered by their gratitude, wearied by their importunity, blamed by their unreasonableness. Many a priest who could have faced cheerfully the ordinary routine of his parish, has found himself quite broken down by the annual burden of a sum of money which must be raised to finance the current schemes of his parochial administration.

A man has not to go far in the priestly profession before realizing something of this ἀγρυπνία—a wakeful anxious watching—while other men seem at ease, and everything seems to smile on a profession which, viewed from the outside, looks so calm.

And we must notice that this is another of the self-imposed troubles. It is not that S. Paul is so pressed by the afflictions, the stripes, the imprisonments, and tumults which he endures, that he cannot sleep. It points rather to the man who sits up, watching and planning, while others sleep; the father sitting up to work for the household; the watchman on his tower looking out into the night to protect the sleeping and defenceless city; the man of science painfully snatching a secret with aching eyes and weary brain from slowly yielding phenomena; the nurse waiting by the sleeping patient to be ready to minister to his needs when he wakes to pain and to himself. It is a thought which we meet with elsewhere. "They watch for your souls, as they that must give account (αὐτοὶ γὰρ ἀγρυπνοῦσιν ὑπὲρ τῶν ψυχῶν ὑμῶν), that they may do it with joy, and not with grief."[1]

I.

It is a solemn thing to stand up in a congregation to offer up their service to God. It is a solemn thing to plead the merits of the great Sacrifice, and to come so near to holy things. It is a solemn thing to be placed in a parish, as the *persona*, the representative in spiritual things, entrusted with the Word and Sacraments. And, therefore, some at least of this ἀγρυπνία should be spent in the preparation of self for the daily duties of the priestly life. This is done by professional men who wish to succeed in their profession. How many long hours of practice are spent in producing the power which delights us with one song, it may be, at a concert! How constant and persistent is the study in sketching, anatomy, and composition to which an artist devotes himself in order to produce the power of gratifying the eye even with one picture! A life which is so much spent in public as that of the priest must have its inner side of preparation and watchfulness, its waiting upon God. Men have a right to expect it. "For their sakes I sanctify Myself."[2] We must faint and fail without it. "Without Me ye can do nothing."[3] The priestly life is not a thing prepared for by a year at a theological college, after which all the preparation

[1] Heb. xiii. 17. [2] S. John xvii. 19.
[3] S. John xv. 5.

is over. But it is rather a life which gives out while it takes in. The activity abroad means watchfulness at home. If we needed self-examination before our ordination, even more we need it afterwards; if we needed repentance and confession then, even more we need them afterwards, when a fresh area of responsibility adds a fresh circle of danger. If ever we needed the grace of our communions, now, since our ordination, we need it more than ever. The constant giving-out of self must leave us cold and bare, without constant replenishing from above. And, therefore, the light will be burning in the priest's window, it may be, late at night. He will be among the first to rise in the morning, to see that he has oil in his vessel with his lamp; to see that the buyers and sellers, once driven out, have not come back again into the temple courts. He will watch the old plague-pit, lest any "renewed deceit or wile of former sin" burst up again; any lingering taint of boyhood or youth reassert itself, or the limb once imperfectly set give way again in the weak place. He will constantly see, with earnest and searching care, that the channel through which so many of God's gifts flow to His people be clean, lest through him men abhor the offering of the Lord.

II.

Watchfulness in the priest will include, as a matter of course, observation and study. If we want a holy, we also want a learned, clergy. For if the wise and prudent are untouched by revelation, fools and slow of heart in belief cannot unlock its mysteries. There is no virtue in ignorance, just as there is no merit in unpreparedness. "He that hath ears to hear," still prefaces the communication of Divine knowledge. What should we think of a doctor who ignored scientific discovery, and made no effort to keep pace with anatomical research? or of a general who was totally unacquainted with modern tactics, or the shifting conditions of warfare? In like manner, the priest must keep his eyes and ears open, his mind informed, his powers of understanding quickened; more especially at a time like this, when first principles are challenged, and the waves of controversy seem eating into the very rock on which the Church is built. It can be nothing else than exasperating to a clever man, to hear some of the shallow sermons of the day, where dogmatism varies in inverse proportion to knowledge, or a flow of words is made to disguise the absence of thoughts. It is a serious thing to abuse a privileged position by offering words in the place of instructions and platitudes for dogmatic truth. Men have a right to expect that while they are working in the fields that we may be fed, or working in the shops that we may enjoy the benefits of civilization, or working with the brain that our property may be protected, our mind instructed, or our health preserved, we should be working too, to bring out from the treasure things new and old, to weigh the interests of men in the balance of the sanctuary, and put, if necessary, contemporary history under the fierce light of God's truth. Sermons on questions of the day are not what people want; they irritate; they suggest an unfair vantage-ground, where the pulpit suppresses argument, and the sanctity of the place forbids signs of dissent. They want the gospel, and plenty of it, as it throws its light on the passing questions of the hour, by keeping prominently before us the question of all days. "What men and women really want to hear about is God's truth and their own duty. They do not want to be gossiped to about what they can read in the newspapers, nor to have fragments of raw science skewered into the discourse to serve for teaching, perplexing most and irritating many."[1] The minister of God will never turn his church into a concert-hall, nor his pulpit into a lecturer's rostrum; but will remember that the peculiar function of a sermon is the religious treatment of facts in their bearing on religious life. And each of us has his message to deliver, each life its own message. When a man neglects his observation and study, it is a sentry neglecting his post, up to which creep the enemy unperceived and unhindered; no mere rock of dignity or privilege is going to keep them back. Perhaps what he would call the cackling of geese is the first sign of danger, and a popular outcry recalls him to his duty. Each parish is an outpost of observation which the enemy may seize, to use a mistake of temper, or error of doctrine, or viciousness of life, as a place of arms against the whole

---

[1] Bishop of Winchester, "Pastoral," 1892, p. 57.

Church. And hence the priest must watch. "I will hearken what the Lord God will say concerning me."[1] In meditation, he will know the aspect of the heavens; in reading, he will make himself conversant with the records of past experience; in observation, he will watch for the signs of attack. The pulpit, in which the minister of God finds such ample room for expressing himself, ought to be a far greater power than it is; and would be, if men first prepared themselves, and then prepared their congregation, and then their sermons, speaking God's message "as if they had something to say, not as if they must say something."

III.

But watchfulness is, after all, chiefly displayed in the individual care which the priest personally bestows upon the flock committed to him. The responsibility of the cure of souls is, and always must be, his main burden. "They watch for your souls, as they that must give account." And this is a responsibility which makes itself felt in many ways. Primarily, and in the most ordinary way, the people must be visited in their own houses. What a day that is when the parish priest sees for the first time the scene of his future labours! The church, with its history barely intelligible on the furrowed walls, wrinkled with age, and scarred with the marks of change and upheaval; the churchyard, with its

---
[1] Ps. lxxxv. 8.

tombs—the open pedigree of the principal inhabitants, whose names strike the eye with an unfamiliar significance and then fade away; the school, with its staring lines of inquisitive children, anxious to see the new clergyman, yet more anxious for the hour of finished work; the knots of idle people here and there, suspecting the truth, and glad of any fresh sensation of excitement; the shops, with the familiar advertisements in unfamiliar surroundings, and the old goods with new faces, like fellow-countrymen in a foreign land. Compare this scene, with the same surroundings, when you turn to leave them after ten years' work. The church now with its deep memories, the churchyard with its tender ties, the houses peopled with living records of a stern experience; the school, the streets, the shops, the houses—each with a silken cord of association bound round the heart. It will not be for long that the priest remains a stranger to the tragedies, the record of simple lives, the joys, the sorrows, the hopes and fears, which repose beneath the surface of the parish committed to his charge. He will have mastered thoroughly, before many months have passed, the history of every man, woman, and child committed to his care, as so many souls "for whom Christ died." At first all seems tangled and strange; a feeling of loneliness comes over him as he passes through streets where he knows nobody, and the houses and their contents are sealed mysteries. But by degrees it opens out; the opportunity long looked for comes at last. A child is ill, and absent from school; or an accident takes place; or the encouragement comes from the evident pleasure with which the most ordinary pastoral visits are received. Or it is a time of Confirmation, or a time of physical distress. Sooner or later the reserve is broken down, and the pure delight of rejoicing with them that do rejoice, and weeping with them that weep, makes him feel how foolish he was ever to despise pastoral visitation. But there are times when he calls out in despair, "I am spending my strength in vain. I was not ordained merely to go round as an afternoon visitor, or a parish gossip. I am making no way. Everything which is not directly spiritual must be so much wasted time and visiting among them." And then comes the temptation to withdraw into a fastness of what the world really means when it talks of sacerdotalism; not the application of priestly help, but the affectation of spiritual arrogance. There comes the temptation to throw over all the drudgery of this spade-work, and to heave up all the parish at once by the explosion of perpetual missions, which, after all, are only effective in carefully prepared soil. Nothing will ever quite make up for the neglect of parochial visitation on the part of those who once have realized that the whole parish is their charge, and that they must watch for all; not complacently regarding a few selected sheep of undoubted respectability, or mourning over a few typical instances of prominent rascality.

Apart from the general supervision of the whole parish in parochial visitation, there will be the special treatment of souls, touched by conscience, or burdened by sin, or oppressed with the difficulty of holiness, who will demand more peculiar care; who take the Prayer-book at its word, and say they cannot quiet their own consciences; they do require further comfort and counsel, and have come to seek Absolution. Here, of course, at once opens up a region of great responsibility. It is a time of much self-abasement. We feel too often, " Where that penitent is kneeling, there ought I to be kneeling in his place. I recognize all my old sins coming up, the same failings, the same difficulties, the same imperfections, and how little is my sorrow and shame in comparison with his." It is a time of some danger. Many a surgeon has been poisoned in performing an operation. It requires a very prayerful mind and carefully kept heart to hear unscathed this deadly tale of sin and woe. It is a time requiring some skill, some knowledge of conflicting duties, and the waywardness of the human heart, the tricks which Satan plays on the scrupulous, the counterfeits of penitence which he tries to set up, the depths of despair which he endeavours to establish. "He doth ravish the poor when he getteth him into his net."[1] More than all, it is a time of great tenderness. Then the priest feels he is face to face with a man's soul. It is no groping in the dark, without lantern or gleam; it is a definite dealing with the real wants of the inner life. "How can I help? How can I ease? How can I raise up?" Surely God has put this wonderful power into the hands of men, that sym-

[1] Ps. x. 10.

pathy may be joined with reproof, tenderness with severity; that the answer of a living voice may mee the faint pleadings of the soul, which longs for assurance of forgiveness, and the sense of pardon, and the ease of a load shared with a fellow-man.

But this by no means exhausts the individual cases which have to be dealt with. The boys and girls have to be watched as they grow up, and if possible started in life. The waywardness and perversity of sin has to be struggled with in many a stumbling soul. The awful strength of sin has to be felt, as the devil leaves only with difficulty and bruising, the life which he had so long possessed. Doubts must be grappled with; low conceptions of religion elevated; religious scruples dispersed; ungenerous suspicion baffled. And then the dying must be ministered to. The first death-bed which we were called upon to attend is perhaps still a very living memory. And every death-bed to which we minister brings us very near to stern and great realities. All these things the priest has to watch for. He must not mind putting off pleasant engagements to carry out some parochial responsibility. He must not mind being disturbed at all times, by those who come for advice and help. Nicodemus will still come by night, and not always at the most convenient time, to ask about his soul. And so the parish priest must make himself accessible, welcoming people to his study, not holding them at arm's-length in a parish room, as if he was afraid of his carpets, or did not care to welcome their society; recognizing cheerfully that what are trivial troubles to him, are often serious troubles to them. And that sympathy is never thrown away. He must welcome the sick call, and go again and again to minister to the sufferer, to pray with him, talk to him, soothe him, and be in every way his priest. He must not mind taking a great deal of trouble with the young, writing letters for them and about them, bearing patiently with them, correcting them, amusing them, making friends with them. They may seem to forget it all, to get rough and rude; but it is possible that he may lodge something in their hearts, which some day will push itself up, through the *débris* of their failures—something which will come back to them like a buried virtue, asserting itself in the end of the days.

Watchfulness! S. Paul knew the meaning of this. See him watching there, chained to his soldier. The helmet is like salvation, the breastplate is a lesson of righteousness, the shoes are the readiness of the gospel, the sword is the Spirit, the shield is faith. There is something to watch even in confinement.[1] See, now he is caught up to Paradise;[2] he watches there as he watched the Roman soldier, to his soul's health. See, he is disputing with the Jews; because he has seized the opportunity; he is helping the Christians; he sends for his parchments; he sees in every turn and twist of his life fresh openings for the gospel.

There is an opportunity everywhere, if we watch for it. And for these opportunities we shall be

[1] Eph. vi. 10, etc.   [2] 2 Cor. xii. 4.

judged. In some parts of England there is a custom, when the parish priest dies, of burying him with his feet towards the west, that at the Resurrection Day he may be able, as they say, to stand up and face his people. Some day most certainly we must face them, those for whom we have been watching; those for whom we have stood before God; those whose lives we have tried to keep as jealous guardians of a sacred trust. God grant that as we stand before them, and before God, we may be able to say, "Behold, I and the children whom the Lord hath given me."[1]

[1] Isa. viii. 18.

CHAPTER V.

SELF-DENIAL.

"Ubi jejunantem videt (diabolus) suspicatur Deum,
Dei filium confitetur."

'Εν νηστείαις.
("In fastings.")

WHEN S. Paul speaks here in the plural number of fastings, he has been thought to indicate various kinds of fasting, involuntary as well as voluntary, which had been his lot. Others will tell us that we are restricted, by the unvarying meaning in Holy Scripture of the term which he uses, to fasting in the ordinary sense of the word. However this may be, we cannot fail to remember him in the ship, amidst the howlings of the tempest and the tossing waves, unmoved, clear-headed, full of resource after a fourteen days' involuntary fast;[1] or to see him strictly mindful of the Jewish day of obligation, as his chronicler shows us when he says, "and when sailing was now dangerous, because the fast was now already

[1] Acts xxvii. 33.

past."[1] Or we think of him in the mental agony of that sightless crisis of his life, when for three days he did neither eat nor drink.[2] While he seems to open up to us the habitual discipline of his character, when he tells us of bruising his body, and keeping it in slavery, by the rigorous power of a self-imposed asceticism.[3] The Apostle could hardly have done what he did, had he not learned the discipline of the body.

Now, fasting occupies a very prominent place in the Christian life; while to the priest it is presented with even more persistency than to others, as something which he not only has to practise as a Christian himself, but also to teach others, as an integral part of the system which he is called upon to administer. For there is at least one fast-day in every week, and many others scattered up and down the Christian year, culminating in Lent and Good Friday. It is difficult to see how a loyal servant of the Church can neglect fast-days, or, if he recognizes the duty of labour and watching, can think himself at liberty to dispense with fasting. And, indeed, fasting is not an indifferent matter, which quietly subsides under disdain, or shrinks beneath cold neglect. It has a disagreeable way of asserting its importance, in places where we least expect it, and in quarters where it is anything but welcome. There is plenty of fasting abroad, only under another name. What are the many temperance and total abstinence societies, but systems of fasting of a rigorous kind in one department

---

[1] Acts xxvii. 9.   [2] Acts ix. 9.   [3] 1 Cor. ix. 27.

of bodily craving? What is the strict medical rule, and spare diet enforced under heavy penalties, but fasting as it were *ex post facto*, which has all the discomfort, without the sense of any religious obedience, being compulsory? The body, which might have been trained as a useful servant by timely discipline, is now under chains as a dangerous rebel. What might have been religious fasting is the degradation of moral punishment. And yet, if the priest is to be the mouthpiece of a loyally accepted message, the dispenser of a well-tested medicine, sooner or later he must ask himself the question—Why? Why should I not go to my people as the champion of a pure and healthy manhood? Why should I not be the example of the perfect man, in whom the whole being is harmoniously working, and not the emaciated skeleton of a mediæval picture? Why should I, with S. Francis of Assisi, look upon my body as the beast to be beaten and starved? Why should I not rather look upon it as the shrine of my inner self, in form, in function, in beauty, to be cherished, developed, and perfected? There is trouble enough in the world already; scourges brandished in the air ready to descend; cold and hunger, weariness and sorrow, which none can quite escape. Why should I not be happy while I can, without troubling myself about a practice which is rooted in Manichæism, and is the resource of fanatics?

There are many reasons why the priest should fast, of which it might be well to mention three.

I.

First of all, fasting comes to us on the authority of Christ Himself. Here we have set before us the image of the perfect Man; and the perfect Man fasted. Here we have the perfect Truth; and the perfect Truth said, "Then shall they fast in those days."[1] Nay, more; it is to be one of the distinguishing marks of His service. "If any man will come after Me, let him deny himself, and take up his cross, and follow Me."[2] The highest type of humanity, after all, is not some demigod crowned with roses; but it is one Whose head is crowned with thorns, Whose hands and feet are pierced with nails, over Whose head is written this legend, "acquainted with grief." It is not in ease that the highest joys and the highest types of humanity are to be found. It is to those who scale the mountains that is vouchsafed the vision of the glorious view, the breath of the pure air, the scent of the mountain-grass, and the rapture of their changing aspect and unfolding glory. It is to those who burrow deep into the earth that she gives up her treasures and her fruitful store. Ease is barren and lifeless. It is the manger-cradle which attracts its devotees, the cross of wood which entrances the world. Sacrifice is the great Christian lesson, and sacrifice makes us like Christ; Who, "though He was rich, yet for your sakes He became poor, that ye through His poverty might be rich."[3] How are

[1] S. Luke v. 35. [2] S. Matt. xvi. 24.
[3] 2 Cor. viii. 9.

we going to approve ourselves as the ministers of God, if we cannot do without our luxuries; and can only enter on the great campaign with all the paraphernalia of a soft voluptuousness, like an effete imperialism, matching itself with its carriages, its courtiers and its cooks, against the grim battalions, led by iron men? If dinner, for instance, is an insuperable barrier, which precludes all interruption. If a ceaseless whirl of society prevents our attending to the drudgery of detail, or the minutiæ of management. If the first question is, What will it cost me in time, trouble, or money? rather than, Is it right? ought it to be done? The time has passed when the clergyman was famous for his good dinners, or as the best judge of a glass of wine, or was well known on the hustings, or in the hunting-field, the theatre, or even the ball-room. But, for all that, it goes sadly against the grain, in view of the poverty, misery, and sin which surround him, in view of the battles to be fought and won, that he should in any way be an example of luxury, not of bearing the cross. A follower of the Crucified will certainly bear in his body the marks of the Lord Jesus, and those marks the stigmata of the Cross.

II.

But fasting comes to us, again, with the voice of authority. Its very name implies something observed or kept fast; a binding rule, an obligation laid upon us by an authority acting from the outside. Without assigning any reason, or asking our consent, the Church orders us to fast on certain days, of which Friday in each week is one. Here is no open question, or matter of no importance; but rather a weekly call at least from a quarter which we must respect, to put a restraint on ourselves in the matter of food and enjoyment. We are ready enough to keep the feasts; why are we not equally ready to keep the fasts, when both come to us on the same authority? It is a great thing to be thus disciplined; to be reminded, in spite of ourselves, of the obedience due to a commanding authority; while we remember what these fasts are to which the Church calls us. A Good Friday as well as an Easter Day in every week. A time of watchfulness and prayer before some high festival. The solemn time of ordination, with its devout preparation, set before us four times a year. The long retreat of Lent. The going out to Bethany before the Ascension with the voice of prayer and intercession on our lips. How blessed, how helpful, to be reminded of these things by a voice outside us, so that they should form an integral portion of our life!

A religious life which misses its fasting days must needs miss something of the fulness of the Church's teaching. The Christian year loses some of its veiling cloud and soothing twilight; the light of unshaded mysteries and unprepared-for festivals scorches the feeble soul, or at the best becomes a monotony of almost wearisome sunshine. Seeing what we are, the soul needs penitence and shade, and the clouds which burst into rain. A life which misses the shadow of the Cross, sees its finest virtues and its most delicate graces faint and flag for lack of shelter and healing gloom.

III.

Fasting appeals to us once more for a third and different reason. It has a very definite part to play in our difficult life. "I keep under my body, and bring it into subjection: lest that by any means, when I have preached to others, I myself should be a castaway."[1]

The priest must ever feel for himself the constant need of discipline. The part of our being about which he is more particularly busied is the spirit, the seat of God-consciousness, in which he himself has contact with God, and which he strives to keep open in others to heavenly influences. How can this be free, unless the body has been definitely subdued and curbed? S. Paul, with an estimate which we feel at once to be courageous and true, speaks of it as "the body of humiliation."[2] Courageous, because it requires some courage in a critic to suggest that a masterpiece is after all only second-rate, and inferior to other works; and to speak of humiliation in connection with the body was, to say the least of it, not the language which the spirit of the age affected or approved. And yet true; there it is at the best like some savage islander gracing the victor's triumph, uncouth yet conquered. To his eyes who had seen

---

[1] 1 Cor. ix. 27.   [2] Phil. iii. 21.

nobler things, not pure beauty, pure strength, a dress of gods and heroes, but a human nature lower than what is divine, higher than what is vile—" the body of humiliation." And this body is the same in the priest as in any one else; the character impressed upon us at ordination, "the active power for the exercise and ministry of Divine worship," does not spiritualize by one great act the body in which we move. It will not subside in sullen obedience simply because we are priests, or at the sound of the rushing wind of the descending Spirit. It has not relinquished so entirely the victories won in the past. There are detachments left still in those apparently abandoned quarters, there are sunken mines beneath that apparently smooth surface. The enemy has retired. But what is that fancy which we stop to consider, the luxury which we pause to enjoy? Is it the floating machine of a desperate subterfuge; a toy outside, but filled within with destruction, and big with death? It is but a passing imagination, a fancy, a passing weakness, which brushes by us; but the heart is on fire, our spiritual life cracking and rending, and death approaching. The priest, if any one, needs to curb the body; here is the weakest point in the line of defence, where so many acquiesce from very weakness, in the dismemberment of their empire, and in piecemeal disintegration. "Satan shall have this one part; it is unimportant, and does not touch the soul." Judas ropes off the delight and greed which he feels at the grip of silver. "It does not matter; silver does not touch the soul, and to handle silver does not mean to be covetous. The cravings of appetite can never be meant to be harshly judged. When they reach beyond a certain point they can be curbed." Satan humiliates the body by alienating it from the strong circle of moral obligation, by withdrawing it from the empire of the will. And it is not a little remarkable to notice how, in the early heresies which disturbed the Church, he attained his end through false doctrine; in two ways different to each other, yet coming from the same point. The Gnostics, especially in their contempt of the body, as being utterly worthless and beneath contempt, either quite neglected it, and trampled on it in every way, or else they reasoned that a part of our being so low and despicable could not come under the influence of morality or religion at all; so that the bodily passions might be indulged with impunity in every sort of excess, as being in a manner indifferent, and incapable of affecting moral conduct. Now in fasting we carry the war into the enemy's camp. If he has ever laid us low, or threatens to do so, by this we can show, that so far from being attracted or alarmed, we can take up or let alone, taste or not taste, touch or not touch, enjoy or not enjoy, in the absolute freedom of temperance; that so far from being tempted by what is unlawful, we can of our own free will lay aside what is lawful, at the bidding of the will. Fasting, moreover, is the cutting down of the strongholds of Satan; a city prepared for a siege is absolutely disencumbered of all that would harbour the enemy, or interfere with the fire of the guns from the forts. It is not unknown for an army to devastate the country before them, that the enemy may find no shelter or means of subsistence. So we cut down all those outer things which obscure our aim, or which give Satan an ambushment, or afford nourishment to his hosts. Men all around us are being laid low by appetite. The priest has laid low his appetites, lest they should lay low him; he has cut down the shelter for the enemy, and narrowed the circle of his attack, and made himself more able for the fight. Nor is this all. Fasting is not only a precaution; it is a sign of mourning, an expression of sorrow and penitence. And is there nothing to sorrow for in the priestly life? As the priest has lingered at the altar, and gazed up at the form of the Crucified, the one great Sacrifice for sins for ever, has he seen no signs of anguish which sin has caused? As he has gone out into the parish has he seen no golden calf of sin, and the people whom God has given to him as a charge, degrading themselves before it? Is there no duty which he owes to Nineveh threatened by God's curse? No avenging sword for whose withdrawal he can fast and weep? Fasting is a sign of sorrow, which we may believe is precious in God's sight. Just as when a man has heard bad news, he cannot eat, it turns him sick; so in fasting we try to reproduce the involuntary result of sorrow in a voluntary way, and endeavour to make ourselves feel that sensation which sorrow, if it were real, would tend to produce. The sight of a Saviour suffering, and of a world's sin, the remembrance of the sins of the parish committed to our care, even more the thought of our own sins, should all tend to give point to fasting, while we feel that in the presence of the great mysteries which gather round sin and the Atonement, fasting is at least an attitude of reverence.

And further yet, how often we find that there is some one especial sin in a parish which, like the dragon of the old country-side legends, sweeps away its annual batch of victims! A hopeless house, or a demoralizing trade, or even some recurring pest, such as a race-meeting, or a popular fair, or ill-conducted village feast, which settles down like a blight to sweep away all the tender growth of a year's holy aspirations. Or we are wrestling for some one soul; we are trying to drive out that dumb spirit, which will not pray, or worship or serve God. And as our Lord comes down from the mountain, He tells us the reason why our efforts hitherto have been so futile and disappointing. "You will not do it by this worldly life, or by human weapons, by neglected fast-days, and an undisciplined will. 'This kind goeth not out but by prayer and fasting.'"[1]

IV.

Fasting is a powerful engine, and one which a self-satisfied age like our own seems to shrink from using. The moralist, the physician, the counsellor, the priest, the law, are all invoked to stop the fearful ravages of

[1] It is right to notice that doubt is thrown on the genuineness of this reading both in S. Matt. xvii. 21, and where the same expression occurs in S. Mark ix. 29.

sin which a man's will, in some cases, seems powerless to dismiss. But what, or at all events how many advisers, recommend fasting? And yet those were not all old dreamers or mystic visionaries who carried it to such extremities, but men who had studied what their Lord meant when He told them to cut off the right foot, and pluck out the right eye, and get to heaven somehow, even with a lame foot and mutilated body. We are too apt to accept our blessed Lord's teaching with reservation, and to make selections from the Church's rules, and expurgate from her system all that jars upon our comfort. Fasting, did we but credit it, would make us like Christ. It comes to us charged with the blessing of the Church, and is full of discipline, holy sorrow, and power. While to us who are pledged to administer the Church's discipline it comes as no open question, but as a rule of obligation, imposed upon us by that loving care which hastens by a rule to ensure the fulfilment of the Bridegroom's prediction or command, "Then shall they fast in those days." Let us make it as much a part of our system as prayer and almsgiving; they all stand together. It will be to us, as it was to Moses,[1] the prelude to the ascent into the hill of the Lord before we celebrate the holy mysteries. For we, if any, shall feel the force of spiritual instinct, and the voice of the Church behind us, when we comply with that "custom of the Church of great antiquity, and proportionable regard, that every Christian that is in health should receive the Blessed

[1] Deut. ix. 9.

Sacrament fasting." So we shall find it ever the preparation for the heavenly food which is to carry Elijah in Divine strength to the mount of God.[1] It will be to us, as it was to Daniel,[2] the atmosphere in which we see visions of heaven and heavenly things; the earnest of future blessings, as it was to Cornelius.[3] While it is through self-abnegation and the life of the Cross that the truest happiness comes. The Roman empire in its decline is a sad witness to the weariness of a glut of pleasure, and of the satiety which follows sensual satisfaction. "I saw in the Pompeian frescoes the great characteristic of falling Rome, in her furious desire of pleasure, and her brutal incapacity for it. The walls of Pompeii are covered with paintings meant only to give pleasure, but nothing they represent is beautiful or delightful." So true it is here, as in everything else, "He that findeth his life shall lose it; and he that loseth his life for My sake shall find it."[4] We have something more to consider than mere robust health and well-regulated desire. It is not thus that the scientific explorer pushes his conquests, or the doctor benefits the human race; it is by self-forgetful campaigns within the domain of what is stern and forbidding, and even dangerous to life. The spiritual life also has its secrets, which lie in the gloomy corners of self-denial and the darkness of self-forgetfulness, to be reached by crucifying the flesh with its affections and lusts.

[1] 1 Kings xix. 7, 8.
[2] Dan. ix. 3.
[3] Acts x. 30.
[4] S. Matt. x. 39.

CHAPTER VI.

PURITY.

> "Then every evil word I had spoken once,
> And every evil thought I had thought of old,
> And every evil deed I ever did,
> Awoke and cried, 'This Quest is not for thee.'"

"Dealba me Domine et munda cor meum, ut in sanguine Agni dealbatus gaudiis perfruar sempiternis."

'Εν ἁγνότητι.
("By pureness.")

HERE is a point, surely, in which men must have been looking and longing for "the minister of God"—some authoritative voice to tell them that conscience was speaking true; that God made them for something better, and would help them to attain to it, while He put a barrier between them and their vices. The heathen world of this time is an awful picture, sated and wearied with sin, driven about by the body, towering over them, a monster of their own raising—merciless, insatiable, abhorrent. Whither were they to turn? Was it to their gods? Oh, the weariness of appealing to higher beings, whose lives were on a lower stage of morality than their own! Was it to the elevation of art? It was too often designed to inflame the passions, or at the best to portray a materialized beauty. Was it to poetry? Here, also, in too many cases the snake of sensuality lingered among the smoothly tuned verses and charming cadences. Was it to the theatre, the games, the recreations of the day? Was it to public opinion? Listen to those words breathed forth into the calm air of the hillside in a remote corner of the unheeding empire, "Blessed are the pure in *heart;*"[1] and then look out over the heathen world, and see not merely vice, but the consecration of it; not merely human nature beaten down by passion too strong for it, but passion lifted out of the region of conflict and placed on the platform of a deified dignity. There is plenty of vice now; London and Paris could ill afford to throw stones even at Rome under the Empire. But now it *is* vice—a man is vicious, and knows it; but then, a man could be vicious, and label his vices virtues, and his degradation religion. To many, and to an increasing number, it must have been a welcome thing to see the stern, vigorous personality of a man like S. Paul; it would seem to bring new life and new hope, opening the window, and letting in the fresh air of heaven on the poisoned atmosphere of heathendom. Many a slave to his passions must have gathered strength to throw off his fetters and be free. Many a one who felt there must be something higher must have welcomed his message as a voice from another

[1] S. Matt. v. 8.

world. It had been wafted out to mankind from the Mount of the Beatitudes, "Blessed are the pure in heart;" as a fragrant breath across the fetid marshes of the foulest sin. And now there is one who can point to himself as the minister of God, by patient endurance of trials within and without, but perhaps even more, in the midst of a world's corruption, by pureness.

And we shall find this estimate still remains unaltered. The minister of God still approves himself by pureness. It is a fact which forces itself upon us more and more; which makes us feel that something else is wanted than scathing denunciations of vice, and elaborated systems of morality,—the terrible unhappiness of sin, and the slavery it imposes on its victims. And more particularly is this so with the sin of sensuality. It is surrounded by degradation, riveted by despair, and bound down by habit. Men welcome still, as a message from a higher world, the gospel of freedom, of purity and holiness. They look for, and welcome the priest, who sympathizes with the sinner and shudders at the sin. They welcome the higher standard of morality, to which the sacraments lead, instead of the scolding which quickens despair; the morality which bids the hungry be fed and clothed, while it withholds the food, and supplies no clothing; and the endless preaching to a convinced but impotent soul. Here is something tangible, within the grasp of a true repentance; something which stands unshaken amidst the wreck of houses, and the uprooting of trees, and the *débris* of life, which is carried down on the flood-waters of sin. The possibility, the beauty, the happiness of a higher life, as set before them, keeps many a poor creature from sinking. Here is a flower of sanctity growing above the flood-mark of sin, within the reach of the most abject sinner, not too high for the most degraded to climb to.

I.

"By pureness." We are clearly in the region of the especial privilege which Christ vouchsafes to the priest. It is to the clear, unclouded vision that there is vouchsafed the sight of God. This is no dream of poetry, or creation of fancy. God promises the sight of Himself to those who have eyes to see it. And surely it should be to those who wait on His services and minister in His courts, who are day by day busied about the things of God, that the vision ought to appear. S. Paul was caught up into the third heaven; S. John was vouchsafed visions of the glory of God. What is to give us that peculiar gift, which is not cleverness, nor brilliancy, nor intellectual power, nor persuasiveness, nor eloquence, but that which is more powerful than all—spirituality? Is it not purity? What is to help us to see accurately and nicely that "path which no fowl knoweth, and which the vulture's eye hath not seen,"[1] deep down in the hidden things of God's Law? What is to help us to track the Presence, to trace His footsteps, and see

[1] Job xxviii. 7.

where the King has gone before us? Is it not purity?
There are few passages of Holy Scripture so humiliating in what they do not say, so significant in their silence, as that which shows to us the Priestly House, where the honour of God's Sanctuary tottered in the hands of a weak old man, whose sons were active hindrances and immoral pests. There they are, holding offices of spiritual trust, incumbents as it were of the family living, sleeping in the sacred precincts it may be. But no revelation comes to them. God's voice passes by His representatives, and appeals to the pure childlike spirit of the young Samuel. "Eli perceived that the Lord had called the child."[1] There are visions of God playing about our heads: what if we cannot see them? Voices of awe and dread revelation: what if we cannot hear them? There are many mysteries of God's Holy Word, many visions of His beauty, many glorious chalices of precious truth, waiting for us to discover them in the enterprise of our professional life, if only we can approve ourselves as the ministers of God by pureness.

II.

Even more than it speaks of a privilege in the priestly life, opening up regions of spiritual enterprise and Divine revelation, purity suggests a necessity in the delicate and difficult work to which we are called. We remember what we have to do, we remember where we have to stand, and we feel at once it is no unmeaning

[1] 1 Sam. iii. 8.

comment. "Be ye clean, that bear the vessels of the Lord."[1] If it were only a question of that highest and most characteristic duty which devolves upon us, the celebration of the Holy Eucharist, of which the author of the "Imitation" thus speaks: "O how great and honourable is the priestly office, to whom it is given to consecrate the Lord of Majesty, with sacred words to bless with the lips, to hold in the hands, to receive with his own mouth, to minister to others! O how clean should be the hands, how pure the mouth, how sacred the body, how stainless the heart of the priest, to whom comes so often the Author of purity!"[2] But there are other services as well, only less solemn; the Divine office, which is threaded with pearl-like psalms and golden prayers, beautiful and glistening if kept pure and clean, but more liable than things less delicate to catch the driving dust of dissipated thoughts, and the falling blacks of unhallowed imaginations. There are sacraments to be ministered, and prayers to be offered, and warning and help to be given. "Out of the abundance of the heart the mouth speaketh."[3]

There is a fire which comes out from God, which consumes the men that offer strange incense; an abyss which is open to swallow up those who tamper with Divine worship in a rebellious, unprepared heart.[4] While we stand in the fierce light which streams from the throne, amidst the glittering company of saints, where the body makes a shadow as we go;

[1] Isa. lii. 11.
[2] "Imitat. Christi," iv. 11. 6.
[3] S. Matt. xii. 34.
[4] Numb. xvi.

where in the court ceremonial, as it were, of heaven, a trifling defilement, which would pass unnoticed under other circumstances, becomes a sin in such surroundings. "Friend, how camest thou in hither not having a wedding garment?"[1] Is it this that chills our utterance, and deadens our devotion, and petrifies the living stream waiting to gush forth at our bidding? We are out of sympathy with heavenly things, the contrast chills and depresses us; in every dazzling service we see only the reflection of our own defilement, and we shrink from a presence of beauty which only shows us our own unworthiness. And this necessity is equally clear if we turn towards the side of our ministry which deals with men. There are painful cases which we have to deal with, as dangerous to our spiritual life as if we were handling explosives, which at any moment might work our ruin. Painful scenes in which we are compelled to intervene, in an atmosphere stifling and deadly. Added to this, there are fierce winds of temptation which assail those in high places. If we are to do any good at all, if our ministry is not to be a hollow sham, we must keep that deep inward purity of heart, across which will pass every action that we do, every word that we speak, every enterprise which we take in hand.

We cannot avoid the muddy stream of life as it flows beside us; there is no village so small, no ministerial path so hedged in, that it can escape it; but as the pure river of life whirls out of the still lake, with its vigorous rush, it must take good heed to

[1] S. Matt. xxii. 12.

run side by side, if need be, with the muddy stream, which carries in it the wreckage of storm and tempest, the foulness of corruption, and the accumulation of a turbid life, itself unpolluted, blue as the heaven, clear as the fountain, with the great lake behind. But contact with evil must ever be full of anxiety and danger; let the streams once mingle, the invisible barrier be broken down, then contamination becomes rapid, and defilement inevitable.

III.

But when we have gazed into the regions opened out by purity, and seen its necessity for the priestly life, we are better able to measure its extreme difficulty. Purity of *heart* is a demand which is far-reaching and difficult of attainment.

We have traced before now some beautiful stream from its source in the hills, where it gushes out so fresh and clear; the long ferns dip their fronds into it, and the little pebbles shine like precious stones in its pure bed. And now it has leaped down the hill, and is passing through the village, past houses under the bridge. Here and there a black stream from some cottage filters into it. A few yards lower down you notice nothing different; it still sparkles and bubbles, and plays around the stones which mark out its course; but its taste is bitter, it leaves a slime behind it on the tender leaves which it touches. There is death in it; men can only drink of it by straining out its pollution. But now it has got broader and stronger; its freshness and life are gone, with the froth and foam of its earlier course; the great town is emptying its sewers into it; it is brown and foul. The very ships it carries on its bosom add to its defilement; not even the full sea pouring into it, with its rushing tide, is able to carry off with it the daily foulness of its poisoned waters. Can it be cleansed? Can it be made at least healthy? Yes, it can be purified, but never again to be the same—purified water rather than fresh water; with the purity of the filtering-bed, not of the mountain-home. Is it so that the stream of our life bears in it sometimes the traces of a schoolboy sin, or the dregs of the big town, or the defilements of our activity, the refuse of our daily work? Is it cleansed, is it purified, or is it passing on, mingled with life's strong stream, to our parish work, taking the refreshment from our words, the life from our ministrations, the good influence from our daily conversation; steady and strong, but not healthy; sparkling, but not satisfying; bubbling and frothy, but not refreshing? We are all of us too apt to think that absolution goes by lapse of time, and that forgotten means forgiven. We have got used to the stream of life, and little dream how much we have done to mar it. But what can we expect, as we have been obliged to run so close to the beautiful yet poisoned rivers of antiquity; when the carelessness of companions, or the recklessness of fiction, or the heartlessness of society, or our own nature so easily deflected, so easily corrupted, have all added some pollution of their own? It is not without reason that every service is hedged round by penitence, and the Holy Communion especially by more than one barrier. Life is too delicate, too subtle a thing, to quite escape all the blackness which is being showered down upon it. And yet God is too awful, too holy, to be worshipped by any but one who is pure in heart.

Purity can only be ours by a constant and deliberate effort. There must be the resolute purpose that none of those black streams shall be allowed to filter through the protecting barriers of our life. There are three main sources of defilement of the heart—the body, or as it is called when it has become our enemy, the flesh; the world in which we live, with its smoking, flaming, vomiting defilements, scattering showers of sooty dust all around us; and Satan, ever at work deliberately to pollute with the refuse of literature, of imagination, of art, of human life, of past malignity. On each of these, he who would guard the heart with its issues of life, must keep an eye, and resolutely determine to exclude them. Have we reckoned sufficiently with the body? There it is, splendid in its humiliation, but ever waiting to flood the whole course of our life. Strong are the bands which we have girded round it to keep it in check. Baptism enclosed it, Confirmation banked it in, each Holy Communion purified it, Absolution drained off its malignity. But still as the flood-water of prosperity roars through it, or the vigour of health, or the joy of friendship, or the rush of imagination, or the tide of human weakness, it shakes and quivers and groans within its barrier. Already it has tainted our best virtues, turning ambition into pride, resentment into anger, emulation into envy, tenderness into voluptuousness, peace into sloth, the healthy hunger into gluttony. And now it would have its influence on the clerical character too, and make the ministrations of life to be ministrations of death; turn David the psalmist into David the sinner, wise Solomon into Solomon the sensualist, Balaam with his visions of beauty into the minister of foulness, Hophni and Phinehas into the hinderers of true religion. Watchfulness must be our remedy here; never to forget this stream fastened up within us. In the great engineering feat which drove a tunnel underneath the Severn, as the work lagged, and men became impatient, and money seemed swallowed up in a bottomless pit to no purpose, or with a scanty result, the engineer was grappling with a foe which at any time threatened to wreck his work. Not the Severn above with its tidal rush, not the material through which the tunnel must be pushed, but a land-spring from within was the enemy, fierce, impetuous, unintermittent. Even now should the pumping-engines cease for a short time, the tunnel becomes impassable. The land-spring imperfectly restrained has ruined not a few mighty enterprises of God, wrecked the sanctuary of the priestly life, and flooded with infamy the Church of God.

And then there is the world circling in and out of our life, ever trying to leap over the spiritual barriers and poison the springs, as strong in the very heart of the clerical profession as in any other. It comes in the form of a subtle temptation, that after all, knowledge of wickedness, if not exactly wisdom, is yet practical experience in dealing with sin. That to read the world's books, and study the world's ways, and not to be too prudish, is, after all, the best chance of flooding that turbid stream with a flush of pure water. But experience is against us, our better self is against us. Delicacy and refinement of tone are soon gone. The poor sinner, plunging and falling into the mire of sin, welcomes the higher nature which promises new help; not the hard experience which has been successful merely where he has failed, and can but recommend remedies which hitherto have proved to him useless. The priest enters on the difficult work of helping the fallen with this conviction, that Christianity is the only force which has been able adequately to grapple with sins of the flesh. And in his own life he feels that he must beware of the world. Purity, absolute purity of heart, is to win the sinner back, if anything will, unpolluted with maxims of worldly prudence, uncorrupted with worldly taint. But only a great effort will keep the taint out. It waits for us in the cynical conversation which sneers at purity; in the conventional truce which has been made with laxity, in the low estimate of Christian character. It jostles us in the streets; it flaunts itself in novels; it is branded on the newspapers; it is a foul stream in history. Sensuality, bound up so closely in human nature, has made friends with the world, and bade it lower the uncompromising attitude of overstrained hostility which the Church adopts towards the frailties of human nature. It preaches gentleness and forbearance, and a charitable remembrance of mortal weakness. It paints in unreal colours the forgiveness of the Magdalen, and would pit the tenderness of Christ's love against the sternness of His command. Our only chance here, again, is to be still uncompromising. One oozing trickle of worldly laxity will take the freshness out of life, the vigour out of sermons, the power out of influence. Men ought to be able to trust a priest's heart as much as they trust his outward conduct, and feel here at all events is a purity which will not deceive our longing for a higher life.

But a stronger enemy still awaits us in the devil, so malignant in his warfare, so unscrupulous in his methods, that he does not hesitate to poison the wells. "Out of the heart of men proceed evil thoughts,"[1] says our blessed Lord; and we know who puts them there. On the dancing tide of imagination, on the far-off murmurs of memory, on the sudden inrush of the moment, floats the poisonous germ. In a moment it is upon us, and all within reach of it dies as the deadly poison widens out. Happy the man who has such a check on his imagination, that no thought passes into his mind unchallenged; who has been accustomed to pass memories through the sieve of penitence, and to retain only a sinful past as a stimulus to penitence and humility, not as the poisoner of present bliss; who watches each thought

[1] S. Mark vii. 21.

as one who must give account, and strives to bring it into captivity to the obedience of Christ.

One thing stands out clear—we must be vigilant and bold, and above all things strengthen the will, and keep ourselves in constant communication with Heaven above us. Like divers who seek for hidden treasures beneath the storm-swept surface of the sea, who drink in life from above supplied to them through pipes and shafts; so we, as we grope for treasures amidst the wreckage of humanity, beneath the waves of sin, must keep our communication with Heaven unimpaired. "Send down Thine hand from above: deliver me, and take me out of the great waters."[1] And in a life evenly balanced, with faculties uncorrupted and entire, let us wait for our Lord. The body, soul, and spirit, each obedient to the will. The senses the useful servants, and never the ruthless masters. The mind clear and clean; above all things, the spirit in full communion through prayer and sacraments with above. This is what we look for and live for, and by God's grace shall achieve. But oh! what watchfulness it demands, what constant cleansing, what constant repairs of the banks of resolution which keep back the poisoned flood of sin, what constant draughts of the holy influence from on high, before we can rid ourselves of the treacheries of the flesh, shake off the tender seductions of the world, and beat back the menacing assaults of Satan, and so commend ourselves to the world, and to those among whom we work, as ministers of God—by pureness!

[1] Ps. cxliv. 7.

CHAPTER VII.

KNOWLEDGE.

"Credo ut intelligam."

'Εν γνώσει.
("By knowledge.")

THE prayer of Ajax, covered in the thick folds of mist, which hid alike from him friend and foe—

'Εν δὲ φάει καὶ ὄλεσσον—[1]

is the prayer of many a combatant in the uncertain conflict, and hidden dangers of life. "Give us light if it be but to destroy us; let us at least see what we are doing." It was some such petition as this that was going up to "the unknown God"[2] when S. Paul commended himself as the messenger of God; when he came with news from another world, not as one who guesses, or has views, but as one who knows. We may well imagine the joy that it must have been to know anything for certain, in that grim game of chess with an unknown antagonist, in which a false move was followed by a blow without a word. What was the meaning of pain? Was the Stoic right in

[1] Hom., "Il.," xvii. 647.   [2] Acts xvii. 23.

ignoring it, with senses so disciplined that they dare not utter a cry, or quiver beneath the lash? Was the Epicurean right in his dexterous efforts always to sail on a smooth sea, beneath an unruffled sky, while he resolutely banished all that tended towards discomfort? What of the other world, the world beyond the grave?

> "Esse aliquos manes, et subterranea regna.
> . . . . . .
> Nec pueri credunt, nisi qui nondum aere lavantur."[1]

Was natural timidity to be hushed into philosophical curiosity, and imagination to do duty for faith, and the other world to be entered on as a *pis-aller* for this which crumbled under the feet? What of the gods themselves? Were they the sensual voluptuaries which the poets feigned them to be, quaffing nectar while men hungered and were faint, careless of human suffering, untouched by mortal anguish? Were they a passionless first cause, dressed up in anthropomorphic dolls' clothes; or an inexorable fate, whose deadly and stealthy machinery was decently covered up by fable and poetic softness? Any one who claimed to know, to speak with the authority of a revelation, would be welcomed as a messenger from another world. The serious and the anxious and the bewildered would eagerly cling to him—

> "Lest, sunk in sin and whelmed in strife,
> They lose the way to endless life;
> While thinking but the thoughts of time,
> They weave new chains of woe and crime."

---

[1] Juv., "Sat.," ii. 149.

I.

There is one derivation, at all events, of the word "king" which would bid us see in it the man who "kens," or knows; and so is the natural leader of his people—as much as, or even more than, he who "can;" who can wield material force and disperse enemies. Knowledge, after all, is, in more senses than one, power. And if the doctor in the parish is supposed to represent the medical skill, the lawyer the legal knowledge, the different professional men different degrees of professional eminence, is it too much to ask that the priest should be the one who most intimately knows all that has to do with a man's soul; the highest, the best, the noblest part of man? He might be, in very many cases he is, the *persona* of the parish; his lips do, as they ought to do, keep knowledge, and men do inquire of the Lord at his mouth.[1]

But what knowledge? What department of that vast field in which men know, and seek to know more, and would enlarge and correct, and improve their information? We, at all events, believe that God has spoken; that He has revealed Himself to the world; that He has told us all that it is necessary for us to know on all points which concern our salvation. And round the interpretation of this revelation circles the controversy of the day; with difficulties which vary with each generation—perplexities born of wilfulness, or nourished by despair, or fostered by neglect. The priest is placed in his position of

[1] Mal. ii. 7.

authority with a formulated interpretation gathered up into the Creeds. He is ever refreshing, increasing, extending, verifying this knowledge by a constant and systematic study of God's holy Word. Men ought to be able to come to us and say, "I am upset as to the authenticity, scope, and objects of the Old Testament. What course am I to adopt in the face of the persistent calls to me to readjust my ideas, and believe in the infallibility of criticism?" or, "I am perplexed about the Sacraments; what is the position which they hold in the Christian economy?" or, "I am told that Episcopacy is unessential to the constitution of the Church; what does the Church herself say?" or, "I am told that the Church of England is not part of the Catholic Church; what do you bid me believe on that point?" The priest is placed in a parish as one who professionally is called upon to know about all these things. And he will not approve himself as the minister of God if he lets his people drift off to reviews, which take every side and believe in none; to religious novels, where heroes and heroines walk through their three-volumed existence like sandwich men in the streets, to advertise some new quackery; or to newspapers, which first and foremost have an eye to their circulation. If a man does not study, he does not seek to know. It is true he is not worried with eager parishioners, who neither regard time nor convenience, but it does not mean that they have no doubts.

II.

"In knowledge." That was a glad message which the Samaritan woman brought to her friends. "Come, see a Man, Which told me all things that ever I did: is not this the Christ?"[1] The minister of God is not a mere repository of speculative knowledge on theological subjects; he must also show who he is, and whence he comes by a knowledge of human character, human nature, human suffering and human pleasure. Sympathy is an easy thing in theory, but terribly difficult in practice. It is no mere surface-feeling, on which the reflected image of another's lot shivers in rugged expression of grief, as the storms break upon it, or smiles in faithful reproduction of its sunnier moods; it is, as its name tells us, a real feeling with another in the alternations of his pleasures and pains, sunshine and storm. How long, for instance, it seems to take to get to the bottom of that strange, hard manner, so unimpressionable by outward influences, so cold to all earnest advances! We only find out, after a quiet talk, when the man had come in shyly to ask for a subscription to a local institution, or to petition for some ordinary professional assistance, that there is a deep sorrow somewhere lurking within, a fox tearing at his vitals, and eating out his life, and he too proud to cry out, or let any one even suspect it. We only find out, in the course of a parochial visitation, as we thought quite uneventful, if not absolutely thrown away, that the flippant man, with whom we

[1] S. John iv. 29.

seemed to have no points in common, is fond of his children, or fond of his garden, or addicted to some pet study. We only find out, in talking to the man at his home, how utterly and completely he misunderstood all that we had said in that fine sermon, whose sentences had been so carefully weighed, and whose cadences had rolled off our tongue, with such proud self-consciousness of a charming effect of convincing eloquence. We did not know that " the Incarnation," "the Atonement," "the Holy Eucharist," were names to him and nothing more; that practically we had been preaching in an unknown tongue, because we did not know the language of the people.

And, alas! is there not another region of knowledge, another source of experience of human character, and a deep fount of sympathy—the knowledge of the plague of our own heart? We know something of the shame and sorrow of humanity, where it has touched the issues of life within. We know what that young man wants, from our own sad experiences in the past. We know just the phase he is going through; in our sermons, like Eugene Aram, when we seem to be describing an imaginary dream, with much vividness of detail and force of expression, we are describing an experience which is no dream, an action intimately known to our own heart, in which it has been the principal actor. We know something of the deceitfulness of sin; and in dealing with others we look at the record within, of symptoms and of cure, of sinfulness and of grace.

And, in speaking of experimental knowledge, we

recognize at once that a priest must have a practical knowledge of the instruments which he is habitually called upon to use in his professional life. Prayer must be an engine carefully gauged, thoughtfully and earnestly directed to effect its purpose. Its difficulty will have been appreciated and measured; each constituent faculty will have been studied and approved —the understanding, the affections, and the will, each in their full force and subservient power. He will know what he means when he is explaining the Catechism to his children, or expounding the Sacraments to his people; the sacramental life will be a reality to him, and the inward part of the Eucharist be as familiar to his spiritual life as the bread and wine are to the ordinary perception. He will know how to wield the knife of absolution with a steady hand and discriminating eye. Do we really know how to prepare a boy for Confirmation, or a man to die? It is a piteous thing to be set down in a parish to administer the Church system, without having gained any experimental knowledge except that which our own mistakes have taught us, without having made an effort to master the principles of our craft, or to understand the true pharmacopœia of the ministry, and the diagnosis of spiritual disease. It is easy enough to trust to an inspired common sense, or to justify our unpreparedness by a general dislike to casuistry. But the soul as well as the body needs careful study and scientific handling; and something more than the light of nature in one who claims to be a physician of the soul. In the Crimean War, the practical common sense of the country was shocked to find that although stores were sent out from home, in many cases those responsible for their application, and those needing their help, either did not know where they were to be found, or else found them inadequate to the purpose for which they were intended; and so men died of want, of wounds, and of pestilence, for lack of knowledge and from absence of method. And what good can a priest be to suffering humanity, who is set down in a parish with a Prayer-book which he does not know how to use, and with a Bible whose principles he has not mastered? We must be ever learning, not only how to deal with human nature in its manifold twists and turns, but how to use the spiritual stores which God has put into our hands. In this once more commending ourselves as the ministers of God, by the knowledge of one who knows, not only the joys and sorrows which his people feel, but also how to sympathize with happiness, how to heal sorrow.

III.

"In knowledge." Above all, the priest must commend himself by a wider range of experience and a more elevated view. He is higher than others, busied about higher subjects, raised above the ordinary things of the world, and therefore he must see more. He must be in closer touch with heaven and heavenly things; he has more leisure to mount the watch-tower and scan the sky. He can linger longer round those channel-courses down which sacramental grace is pouring into the Church. It is his to stand by the death-bed at those solemn moments when the door is opening into Paradise, where the light flashes out from its uncreated source, as the gate opens and shuts to receive a soul. He must see more than others, when in the ministrations of Divine worship he stands just outside the veil, and hears faint murmurs of the voices of the angelic choir, and catches dim shadows thrown across from the brilliant company within. It is he whose privilege it is to catch the first signs of the approach of the King to His altar-throne in the sacramental mysteries. Men ought to feel, as he recites the Psalter, that the Psalms vibrate with a meaning which dawns upon him as one to whom every word is a reality; to whom the Lessons, as he reads them, are a message first received at the mouth of God; who preaches the Word which the Lord has put into his mouth with a solemn sense of responsibility, and as in the sight of God. There are few things more painful to witness than a perfunctory, irreverent, careless priest, because his actions proclaim with melancholy eloquence that he neither sees God nor knows Him, and that he has no practical realization of the great verities in which he is engaged. It should be the same when he passes into society. We are painfully conscious of the utter forgetfulness which men display to the great mysteries among which they habitually move. The *Benedicite* of nature, which is constantly mounting up to God in the countless sounds and myriad activities and marvellous excellences around us, commands but few listeners and few fellow-worshippers. We seldom pause to think of the great cloud of witnesses which surrounds the amphitheatre of our struggling life—tier upon tier of bright angels or grave-faced saints, who have fought and overcome. The majesty of God is not a felt Presence to us—about our path, about our bed, and spying out all our ways: although a sudden death will often serve to remind people how very near they are to the other world; or a sudden reversal of fortune, or breaking of cherished hopes, or tragic and striking retribution following on sin, will bring before men the truth that God has not abdicated His power, that He is where He was before. How great, how helpful it would be, if we could remind people without being obtrusive, and lift them up without being ostentatious, and put them quietly in mind of the importance of life! There is a seriousness about any great surgeon, or, at least, not far absent from him, which makes us think irresistibly of the tremendous scenes in which he sometimes moves. We can trace the same in many scientific men—"that indefinable expression which tells you that a man is still in the shadow of a scene which he has just passed through." We priests move amidst the very highest things. We consecrate the awful mysteries, wherein Christ comes to us and through us. The ordinary dress of everyday life has passed, we are told, into the Eucharistic vestment; would that the vestments of our ministry would, by an act of reciprocity, shed a halo of serious recollectedness over the outward clothing of our daily life! We concentrate the rays of Christ's love on the world; would that our own hearts were warmer! We have to listen to and alleviate the sorrows of the penitent; and, firstborn as we are, we are tempted to cry out with an exceeding bitter cry, "Hast Thou but one blessing, my Father? bless me, even me also, O my Father."[1] We who are so often in the courts of heaven, must surely be gaining a growing familiarity with its glorious life. Its radiance must be playing round our heads, its beauty making itself felt. Here is a power which seizes on little things and elevates them into sacraments of life. "By blessing visible elements it maketh them invisible grace."[2] So our Lord and Master passes through a cornfield, and it becomes instinct with teaching for the Church. He watches fishermen at their nets, and He prophesies of the salvation of souls. The mustard tree speaks to Him of the extensive power of the Church; the leaven in the bread put into the oven, of its intensive efficacy. He looks through the outward circumstances of men and women to the internal interests and concerns of the soul. He marks the character and labels it with a name, at once a prophecy and a tradition; He attends a marriage feast, and God's glory is manifested and disciples believe. He sits at meat, and a sinner departs into peace. He reads the lesson in the synagogue; a new meaning is imparted to the familiar words. "Never man spake like this Man,"[3] is the

[1] Gen. xxvii. 38. [2] Hooker, "Ecclesiastical Polity," v. 77. 2.
[3] S. John vii. 46.

testimony of those sent to take Him. "That the Scripture might be fulfilled,"[1] is the motto of His life. He lived in a setting, as it were, of Divine truth. Everything that He did furthered a Divine purpose. We can see it in His life as the prevailing dominant characteristic. Whether He ate or drank, or whatsoever He did, He did all to the glory of God. It would be something if we set ourselves more deliberately to look out for the higher aims and motives in life. In parochial visiting, at least, to watch for our opportunity of touching on sacred things, and have courage to seize the favourable crisis, which may land conversation on a higher level; in little things not to be ashamed to let the inner life shine forth before men. The quiet grace before meat bearing witness to the sense of a higher Power present at the table, and instinct with gratitude to Him Who feeds His people; the quiet reverence paid to God's altar-throne in the church empty of worshippers; the reverent manner, which feels God's presence as something to be respected, even more than the presence of the clergy, the singing of the choir, or the convenience and comfort of a congregation. How often we may see in one of those scenes of hurry and confusion, a death-bed in a poor cottage, when the distraction of those who are being left mingles with concern for him who is going away; when the idea of preparation for the end, or of comfort in the struggle, seems absorbed in a desire to receive a sign of peace, or some unreal sentiment, from the lips of the dying man;—

[1] S. John xix. 28.

how often in scenes like this the coming of the priest seems to give calm and peace! It is the coming of *one who knows*. So might it be in all the manifold difficulties and joys of life. Even more than in sympathy, he could come as the expert who knows the treachery of the smiling morning, or the silver edge to the storm-cloud. All through the ups and downs of life, to him, again, knowledge is power.

How impossible to affect a knowledge like this, if it is not born of experience! How hollow, how misleading, how distasteful! But if the priest habitually lives in the higher atmosphere of certainties, then the different events which seize upon his sympathy, or detain his pity, would be only so many hands which grasp at the supple elastic bough: loosed, it flies back again; free, it shoots up towards life and heaven. More and more our hearts should become filled with the higher knowledge, which belongs to them who are always within sight of God; whose words and whose actions, whose life and conversation, inspire confidence in those who grope in the darkness and are blinded by the fog. For they see us moving with certainty and precision, as men who know they are right, because, above the mists of doubt, they can see.

CHAPTER VIII.

LONG-SUFFERING.

Πάντας βάσταζε ὡς καὶ σὲ, ὁ Κύριος.

Ἐν μακροθυμίᾳ.
("By long-suffering.")

HERE is another note of commendation which S. Paul can point to, as one of the credentials of his Divine ministry—"Long-suffering." And the thought arises, as we read a word of such profound connotation, the label of so grand a virtue, what it must have cost the Apostle before he could write this in among the other virtues with a good conscience and without suspicion of any irony. How he used to hate those Christians, so provokingly obstinate, so ignorantly prejudiced, so hopelessly illogical in their wrong-headed opposition to the traditional piety of the best minds! He would ride them down; he would go anywhere—along the northern roads, under the burning sun of the scorching midday. He would hunt them out like vermin. How unflinchingly he stood there and saw S. Stephen die beneath the stones as they showered upon him! "Serve him right; he had spoken 'blasphemous words against Moses, and against God.'"[1] How it marked his character with a line furrowed and deep, the impatience of all insult or affront! "God shall smite thee, thou whited wall: for sittest thou to judge me after the law, and commandest me to be smitten contrary to the law?"[2] High priest or not, he forgot it at the moment (οὐκ ᾔδειν). He is a Roman citizen, and he will maintain to the utmost the privileges allowed him by the *Lex Porcia*. "Is it lawful for you to scourge a man that is a Roman, and uncondemned?"[3] "I appeal unto Cæsar."[4] He will insist on justice being done to him, and will not bow before prejudice. Still, in spite of all this, he is not afraid to write down now, among the very characteristics of his high service and the badges of his Master's authority, μακροθυμία ("long-suffering")—the power to bear on.

I.

How long it takes to form character! Sometimes it seems all to depend on our power of bearing. We recognize the constant call to us in Holy Scripture—"Be strong," "be strong." And we see characters snapping off on all sides of us, giving way beneath the strain. One lies before us, a hopeless and disabled drunkard; he turned to intoxication to drown his sorrow, and he woke up to find himself crippled and in chains. Another, worn out and weary beneath the load of sorrow, with his own hands snaps off the

[1] Acts vi. 11.   [2] Acts xxiii. 3.
[3] Acts xxii. 25.   [4] Acts xxv. 11.

life which he had grown to regard as intolerable, and hastens to accomplish that irreparable error—

"Propter vitam, vivendi perdere causas."

Both the one and the other being deficient in the strength which might help them to sustain God. And if we look back in our own case, we are startled to find how near we have been ourselves to falling away. Confirmation was only just in time to turn upwards, into a useful fruit-bearing direction, those branches which were trailing along the ground at the mercy of the first foe, and running hopelessly to waste. "My feet were almost gone; my treadings had well-nigh slipt."[1] That great disappointment which upset all my calculations and disturbed my views of life was really to me the parting of the ways; I had almost determined to throw over a vocation, in impatience of a rebuff. That long illness seemed so unnecessary, so absolutely paralyzing to work, I almost gave up any further hope of usefulness again. The site on which our character has grown up is terribly uneven, with its hills and depressions and made ground; we are conscious that some great virtue, as it seems to the outer world, is built on an arch of stern resolution, turned over a bed of shifting sand, on which nothing could be raised but ruin. But God, with His master-hand, has seized upon all; the very defects and unevenness of the ground have been turned into fresh developments of character. It all fits into one harmonious whole. It is I myself; my character

[1] Ps. lxxiii. 2.

is upon it all. Its abruptness and unevenness, its weaknesses, its dangers, have been moulded into one design of consecutive art. Can we bear what God has yet to do? There are settlements still to be made good, weak places to be underpinned, bad work to be cut out, faulty places to be strengthened. The perilous elevation presses down into ruin many a homely grace on each side of it; there is a thrusting outwards from the roofing in of the settled life which threatens the old simplicity. Life is like an ancient building which needs constant repair and constant watching, lest disregard of proportion or a too carelessly imposed weight should wreck the whole design. And this is known to the Master-builder, God. It is always present to Him, we may reverently believe, how much we can bear, the initial virtue of long-suffering. For it is not only in the formation of our character, but in the carrying out of His own work in the world, that He has to lay a burden upon us. Think of the old prophets, and the burden which God put upon them. One has to see the desire of his eyes taken away with a stroke,[1] without a sigh or a tear, that he may be a sign. Or another has to go naked and barefoot,[2] that he may be a sign. While at another time the prophet has to remove all his household furniture into another place[3] that he may be a sign. Those were stern orders given to the German cavalry at Mars-la-Tour: "The regiment is not expected to succeed; but if it hold the enemy in check only ten minutes, and fall to the last man, it has fulfilled its task." Just

[1] Ezek. xxiv. 16.   [2] Isa. xx. 2.   [3] Ezek. xii. 3.

to labour and to die without joy and without success. God asks us to go sometimes and be what the world calls a failure.

II.

Μακροθυμία. This is the long lesson of our parochial life. We must labour on until this character be formed in us; until we be like the candlestick in the tabernacle, whose work was of wrought gold, hammered into shape, with ornaments beaten out by patient and minute care. The controversy of the day, the controversial attitude and temper of the time, is a hammer of the patient virtues. We are all of us a little apt to feel, firm as we are in our convictions, and confident in our grasp of truth, that we only need to put the truth before people in its strong beauty, and they must needs give in; that we have only to beat the controversialist in argument, and he must be convinced; that demonstration means conviction, and conviction victory. But a very slight experience corrects this estimate. There are deeper barriers than those of misapprehension. There are moral barriers, and spiritual barriers, such as our blessed Lord spoke of, when He referred to those who could not believe: as if they were morally and spiritually incapable of the effort. It seems so tempting, as one stands outside the living ant-heap of human unrest, just to step in, and put it right, by a simple direction of energy. Human life seems like a novel of which we know the secret: one word of explanation would settle differences, and smooth over obstacles; but the misunderstanding goes on from volume to volume, just for the want of the spoken word. It is then that one has to resist the temptation to lower the standard of truth, to refuse to buy off the Danes, or to toss a Creed or a Sacrament to the ravenous wolves to satisfy their gathering onslaught. The battle of the faith has to be fought somewhere, and we cannot always choose our ground. The Creeds themselves were not given to us without controversy and struggle. God Himself appeals to us as the patient One—God Who is "provoked every day."[1] Those who are on the side of truth can certainly afford to wait. We need this in every department of our work. How much friction there is now too often between the fellow-workers in the same parish; between the incumbent and the curate, or the different members of the clergy house! Jealousy of each other's powers, a dislike to play the second part, a dislike to obey orders, or forward the success of things not originated by ourselves; a grudging concession of the minimum which duty requires, rather than the absolute *abandon* which a loving work ensures. How little recognition there too often is of the important duties which devolve on the school-teachers and the organist, finding its expression in want of sympathy, want of help, and final abandonment of all personal interest in two of the most important parochial agencies! How tired we get of the petty local jealousies and their narrow feuds! How indignant we are—ourselves but just free from a huge debt

[1] Ps. vii. 12.

of wasted school-life, and misused opportunities at the University, now forgiven to us by the patient God—with the man who owes us a hundred pence, in neglected teaching, despised help, wasted time, or flagrant ingratitude! It requires a strong character to go on fishing day after day in the apparently barren waters; to let down our nets once more at the voice of Christ, with promptness and enthusiasm, when last Lent, the last Mission, the last Confirmation, the daily patient round of unheroic visiting, have apparently produced no result. To explain the parable again and again, to warn without result, to encourage without response, to proclaim mysteries to a dwindling band, to find the chosen three asleep in the blaze of glory or the gloom of sorrow, to see the apostle a devil, the foundation-rock shattered into dust, the faithful incredulous. The cure of souls requires many virtues, but none more continuously than long-suffering. It is but a strain, or a jerk, or a straw's-weight too much, and all the labour is undone, and the work of a parish thrown back for years. It is a question which a man must ask himself again and again as he seeks to revive Church life in a stagnant parish. Is this wilfulness? Is this self-pleasing on my part? Is it obedience to an unspoken party order, or an unuttered party cry? Is it a mere deference to a passing fashion; a desire to attain to that dangerous adjective known as "correct"? Or am I making this alteration, introducing this custom, stopping this old use, simply because I believe it to be for the good of the Church, and the well-being of the souls committed to me? In a well-known fairy story told us in the collection called the "Arabian Nights," the master and owner of the marvellous palace reared| by magical art, surpassing anything of the kind that had been seen before, is persuaded by his enemy that only one thing is wanting to complete its magnificence—a roc's egg suspended from the roof of the vestibule. At once he proceeds to ask the genie who supplied his every need, for this *plus quam perfectum* of decoration, when he discovers to his dismay that he is asking really for the death and disgrace of his supernatural benefactor, and that to request a thing of that kind was to merit to be torn to pieces. How many of us risk a united parish, and the beauty of devotion, and the comfort of our own lives, simply for the roc's egg whose need we had not experienced, whose absence we had not lamented, which could add nothing to the utility, and little to the beauty of what was there before, and which threatens to bring down everything that we had done in a common ruin, a holocaust on the altar of a passing fashion![1]

III.

And we must not grudge some of this μακροθυμία, for the instrument, for ourselves. Satan pulls down many by vulgar pride, which turns them giddy on

---

[1] I owe this illustration, as I do many other things, to my early training at Wantage. The addition of the perilous roc's egg was a constant warning against Ritual developments in perilous times, earnestly insisted on.

an eminence to which they were not accustomed. He also prevents many from climbing, from a settled conviction of their own impotence; and contrives by the scars and bruises of past falls to hinder them from aiming at higher things. It is a great spiritual help to entertain the certainty of success at some future date as the reward of unintermitted effort, and the constant grace of God. Never to lose sight of that projecting ridge, now over our heads, where once for a moment we stood, and saw the path clear before us to the very top; and then the earth crumbled, the foot slipped, and gradually clutching at bushes, and slowly sliding down, we reached our old level, beyond which few care to climb. Still, to have done it once, to have stood once on the higher ridge, is the reason why we should stand there again, with greater deliberation, and more prudent foresight, as one who knows the danger and counts the cost, and does not despair of his own powers, nor frustrate the grace of God. And this not only in the region of the spiritual or moral life, but in the aiming at intellectual excellency as well. The ordinary derivation of "silly," or rather the history of the deterioration of the word, is not a thing to be proud of, or to fortify by examples. If we renounce intellectual triumphs for ourselves, at least we shall feel bound to place every excellency within our reach, and every faculty in its highest stage of development at the service of our Master. To take only one instance, how many fail conspicuously and utterly in that extremely valuable work of the ministry, preaching, simply because, from a fixed sense of their utter incapacity either for composition or rhetorical effort, they think they can at least escape ridicule or unfavourable criticism, by neglecting even to try. Men forget that the sermon differs from the ordinary speech, and that even some of the most convincing and celebrated speakers have achieved success, and obtained a hearing, in spite of serious defects of voice and delivery. If a man feels himself deficient here, that is just the reason why he should not acquiesce in his own deprivation; just as he never should allow himself to embarrass the finance of the parish by careless accounts or heedless expenditure, resting on the comfortable generalization that clergy are not good men of business; or neglect his parishioners in parochial visitation because he believes himself to be constitutionally shy. It is only too easy for a man who possesses but one talent to go and bury it; whereas it only needed a little enterprise and a little trading, and the one talent would yield its increase. Here, too, we must be patient with our failures, and humble under our disappointments, until the word comes to us with greater power, and we are able to speak boldly as we ought to speak. So will it be all through our ministerial life. How patient we must be with ourselves! How difficult it is to pray, how difficult to realize Christ's Presence, how difficult to carry out the precepts of the Sermon on the Mount! How easy it is to turn disappointment into rebellion, and difficulty into despair! We thought that the ministry would be an enchanted life, where temptations would seldom penetrate, and worldliness would be unknown. We longed for the time when devotion would be something more than a πάρεργον in a busy life, and the Holy Scriptures be a study full of interest, and religion be an ever-expanding, ever-widening joy. But a feeling of weariness has crept over us. We remember the old days of freedom, the long hours in the open air, the boating, the cricket, the hunting, the congenial companions; and the cottages seem more and more monotonous in their narrow gardens, where the changes of the weather, the vicissitudes of the crops, and the welfare of the domestic animals seem to be the only topics of interest. The hot, dusty streets of the town, the baking pavements, the stifling courts, seem more and more oppressive. The voice of the Church in its recurring services seems dull and mechanical, removed from present-day interests, unresponsive to the weary heart. The books on the shelf in our one room hardly look inviting. We listlessly take down the commentary; we commence to make up our tale of bricks—the hour's reading which we had set ourselves to perform. Never did Holy Scripture seem so leaden and lifeless; the last review looks down mockingly upon us from the table, telling us that Holy Scripture is no doubt inspired, only that the sparks of Divinity must be caught as best they may from the friction or diverse aims and contending parties which contributed to its composition, and bidding us, when we have separated the several constituent threads which make up the narrative, gauged the direction of the prophetic mind, allowed due weight to the love of the supernatural, and the exaggeration of affection, to enjoy whatever remains as a precipitate of inspiration. And we feel that we must turn to something else, whose words can be received with less caution, and whose statements can be accepted with less suspicion. And the thought will intrude itself: "Is the message which I bring of a supernatural religion, the thing which the people really want? They do not understand it, they resent it; the pendulum seems to sway between superstition and scepticism, or between hypocrisy and blank rejection. And in these things I am to spend my time, stagnating in a parochial ditch, armed with discredited weapons, hopeless myself, to rouse others from despair; incredulous myself, to teach faith; discontented with my own lot, to elevate the life of a parish." Over and over again, on dark days, we need μακροθυμία in dealing with our own faint-heartedness and disappointment. The remedy is surely to be found in recalling ourselves to the reality of our own profession. Spiritual things are spiritually discerned. We do not expect to understand Holy Scripture from the pages of a magazine article, any more than we should expect to understand anatomy from the discussions of an art *critique*. We must not expect the parish life to be outwardly attractive, or the interests which concern the immortal soul to be reflected necessarily on the garden, or to illuminate with obvious beauty the street traffic. The approach to a gold-mine is not strewed with gold, neither has the observatory the attractiveness of the drawing-room, nor the hospital ward the refinement of a beautifully illustrated book on the human frame. The joy of the expert begins when he has got beneath the surface; when he finds in the scantily furnished cottage and the simple home, cases which try his skill to the uttermost, and waken up his whole soul into professional interest; when he finds in the streets and alleys of the town the souls for whom Christ died, which it taxes his utmost powers to save and protect. It is when he has passed the penitential barrier which hedges in the service of God, and has learned the language of heaven, that he finds that which was before at the best only a melodious sound, is articulate with the needs of the world and the blessing of Heaven. It is as he studies Holy Scripture with the eye of faith, to get God's message out of it, rather than read ingenious puzzles into it, that underneath its plain surface he finds the deep things of God. Μακροθυμία will do many things for the priest. It will keep him quiet; it will teach him truly the old lesson—

"Cœlum non animum mutant, qui trans mare currunt;"[1]

—that happiness is in self, not in places, or books, or change of work. It will teach him to keep his eye more closely on the spiritual faculty, and will bid him see whether that is truly developed within him. The great naturalist has told us how, by some extraordinary process, the higher æsthetic tastes left him, and that he hated, after the age of thirty, to read poetry, and disliked pictures or music. In a well-known work

[1] Hor., Ep. i. 11-27.

of fiction there is a wonderful description of the gradual development, in a man hardened by self-introspection into moroseness and sorrow, of a better and hitherto unknown self, under the magic influence of a little child, which chance seemed to have thrown in his way. It is possible that all this time we had accepted the ministry, the Church, Holy Scripture, simply on outside testimony. Told that it was a grand profession, we acquiesced; told that the Church was ablaze with supernatural glow, we seemed to see it; told that Holy Scripture was inspired, like a child mistaking the roar of the air in the convolutions of a shell for the moan of the sea, we fancied that we heard in the simple words a voice from off the ocean of God's eternity. It is possible that all this time we have intellectually acquiesced at the best, and nothing more; that we have never actually made these things our own; and that, after all, this dryness and despair are merciful pains which warn us that all is not right within, and that some vital organ of heavenly influence is choked, or severed by accident, or maimed by disease. Above all things, never let us despair; it is in the dull uneventful routine of the ministry that the temptation most often comes; when there are no more Red Seas to be crossed, no Amalek to be fought, no immediate prospect of Canaan; when life has settled into its long, slow tramp. But we may well believe, in a hurrying and impatient age, that not a few are led to thank God for the marks of a higher life, and for a message from another world, when they see one who has learned to possess his soul in patience, who cheerfully accepts God's will concerning him, as the very best that could befall him; who in his most eager marches, and within sight of some cherished goal, does not forget to accommodate his pace to the weak and lagging; who, above all, shows that he has taken an estimate of himself, his powers, and his shortcomings, and has learned, wherever he may be, and whatever he has to do, to pray earnestly for himself and others. "The Lord direct your hearts into the love of God, and into the patient waiting for Christ."[1]

[1] 2 Thess. iii. 5.

CHAPTER IX.

THE GENTLE LIFE.

"Si non potes te talem facere qualem vis, quomodo poteris alium ad tuum habere bene placitum?"

> "More skilful in self-knowledge, even more pure
> As tempted more; more able to endure
> As more exposed to suffering and distress,
> Thence also more alive to tenderness."

Ἐν χρηστότητι.
("By kindness.")

As the portrait grows under the master's hand, we wonder at the expression subtly developing itself, beneath the tiny strokes which add to its completion. These have been sketched in with a strong outline, all the different sufferings which are imposed from without. Self-discipline is there with its sharply defined characteristics. A breadth of supernatural life is shed over the features by such virtues as pureness, knowledge, and long-suffering. And now it would seem to be only a very little which he adds —a mere dash or dot of the pencil. How could that great scholar and vigorous missionary; the stern champion of truth, attacked now on this side, now on that; at one time denouncing Elymas, at another in conflict with the Roman authorities, undeterred by claims of friendship, or even Apostolical authority, where a principle was at stake;—how could he find time to think of such a little thing as this? Had he really a care for such a spiritual decoration as χρηστότης? Yes, there it is, side by side with "pureness," and next to "the Holy Ghost." While, if we pause to consider, we find that it is the very same virtue which appears elsewhere as a "fruit of the Spirit," and is there called in our English Bible "gentleness," having the same neighbour also in the other list, "long-suffering."[1]

And what is gentleness but the bearing of the true character of the gens or race, affinity to the spirit of the race? And what is kindness but the same affinity to the kind, namely, the whole human family? A meaning of the term which Hamlet plays on, when he says, in speaking of his uncle—

"A little more than kin, and less than kind."[2]

And if we seek to turn this into modern phraseology, if we think of the needs of the present day, we should perhaps not be wrong in saying that S. Paul is here writing in, as a mark of the minister of God, that description which we know so well, and are so little able either to define or describe, that he commends himself as a gentleman. It is surprising to find how often this comes up, apart from all testimonials of merit and records of success. "Is

[1] Gal. v. 22.   [2] *Hamlet*, Act i. sc. 2.

he a gentleman?" seems to gather up into one a multitude of scattered excellences, and by no means dispensable trifles. "You see, he is not a gentleman," carries with it at once a recognized ἀτιμία, which sinks the sphere of a man's usefulness, and seems to bar the way to a particular form of excellence. Over and over again we find, that people who would scorn and hate any upstart exclusiveness or foolish pride of race, or the vulgarity of a boasted extraction, yet still express the same thing in other words, and look for the same excellence under another name. Yes, it is well to face it; what is really meant by "being a gentleman," is a fruit of the Spirit. It is an atmosphere of a superior nature, which stamps off at once the fact that he who possesses it, and is possessed by it, has access to the noblest development of life, and is in himself, and commends himself as being, the minister of God.

I.

Now let us look at this a little closer, this kindness, this spirit of a gentleman, this "fineness of nature," as it has been called. How does it show itself? First of all, it reaches right back into the region of the heart. It extends to the way in which we look at things; the estimate we form of daily life, its calls and duties. It is not too much to say that this estimate makes all the difference in our professional life. Our blessed Lord has, with His own hand, drawn the distinction between the true shepherd and the hireling.[1] In the same sort of way, the true priest has a refinement of spiritual nature which supplies the right motive for the ministry. We can ask a gentleman to do things which a man would resent doing who had not the same fineness of nature; and in like manner the true priest shows himself in his readiness, his simplicity, and self-forgetfulness.

> "Cur igitur non amem Te,
> O Jesu Amantissime?
> Non ut in cœlo salves me,
> Aut ne æternum damnes me
> Nec præmii ullius spe,
> Sed sicut Tu amasti me,
> Sic amo et amabo Te,
> Solum quia Deus es
> Et solum quia Rex meus es."

And therefore it is a cause for sadness if at any time in the Church there is developed a craving for posts of honour, independence, emolument, or definite recognition of work. It is a cause for anxiety if work in country parishes is despised, because there is no life, no society, no foeman worthy of a warrior's steel. If sentiments like these become prominent, they indicate something wrong underneath. Holy Orders is not a profession which we enter expecting an advance, or some sort of recognition as a right after so many years of work. But it is rather the giving up of self into the hands of God, without stint and without reserve, and letting Him set the work. It is the recognition of the fact that God has many kinds of work to be done, and that the best paid

---

[1] S. John x. 12.

are not always the most honourable. The Holy Spirit chooses a desert road for the work of an Evangelist, or He bars the way to a region of useful preaching; or He points out the presence of many adversaries almost as an inducement to the taking up of an important post. Neither do we read that S. Paul, at the end of his ministry, complains that he is rewarded only with a prison. There had passed over him the feeling of kindness, the losing himself in others, the forgetfulness of self, in which perhaps, more than in anything else, he displayed the spirit of the true gentleman. Tender, refined, endowed with all the best qualities which human nature is able to bear; such qualities as reached their highest possible excellence in Him of Whom we read, "God giveth not the Spirit by measure unto Him."[1] The priest, then, if he is to commend himself as coming from God, must have a heart full of the finest qualities of the human race, on whose behalf and for whose salvation he is ready to devote all that he is, and all that appertains to him.

II.

Being a gentleman at heart and in his motives, the priest will next show the dignity of his extraction and the fineness of his nature by kindness in action. He is a man who will do all he can to try and understand his parish. It is sad to see how, without this, the square man gets squarer and more angular—a

[1] S. John iii. 34.

man whom you may break, but cannot bend; and the hole, which he is conscious that he does not fit, gets rounder instead of squarer. Priest and people both irritated; both wishing, in the last resort, the same thing; both hopelessly antagonistic as to their way of reaching it. Their thoughts, their words, their ways, their wishes, keep up a constant jar of friction, and progress is only possible with heated wheels and a smothered tendency to conflagration. To understand a parish, is a matter that takes time and patience. To work a parish without understanding it, is to fish in troubled waters, and where every bait is viewed with suspicion, and well-meant actions are thought only to conceal a barb. On the other hand, it is a thing well worth the effort to try to understand that little portion of corporate life known as a parish or district.

When we are paralyzed by the very vastness of the social problems of the day; when an increasing population treads on the heels of an almost stationary ministry; when ideas, colossal in their size and quixotic in their character, are being prepared as to "the submerged tenth;" when the fact of the millions who go nowhere to church, and care for nothing religious, weights the footsteps and deadens enthusiasm; when heathendom rises up in its black masses, and the ranks of our fellow-countrymen in the colonies appeal to our sympathies in tones which cannot be ignored;—what a comfort it is to feel that in the parish, circumscribed in its area and limited in its extent, there is a definite piece of God's vineyard on which to concentrate work, and which diligent effort and unremitting toil may reduce to an organized whole. It is here, where work can be properly aimed and systematized, that he who has this kindness of heart, this love for his fellow-men, sets to work to understand those who have an immediate claim upon his sympathies. He will begin by studying the children at school: whether he has had experience or not, whether he has educational powers or not, he feels that he must ever be *in loco parentis* as regards the children of the parish. He will be found in school every day, at least to see to the religious instruction, and to open the day with prayer. He will be there not so much in the character of a scriptural instructor, certainly not to teach the children mere Bible history and geography, or to cram them with the necessary materials for getting a place or a prize; but he will be there to teach them religious truth in a religious way, and to set a religious tone to religious teaching. He will endeavour that the children shall draw in their first impressions of the great fundamental truths of life in a serious, gentle, and reverent manner; and to this end he will go through the school, from the bottom to the top, varying his class from day to day, so that the youngest child may get to know him as a friend, and have memories of his teaching and confidence in his love, when the parents and god-parents once more entrust their charge into his hands to be prepared for Confirmation.

If the parish priest does nothing else, he will never regret the knowledge of his future parishioners which he gains at the school. Unconsciously he will set a good tone, and cheer with sympathy the teacher's monotonous task, and show him that education is something more than cram relieved by examinations; that, in the eye of the parish priest, at all events, it is one of the most solemn duties of his parochial day. If the minister of God had this more clearly before him, we should hear less of surrendering our children to what is at best the uncertainty of a Board School, or of thinking a child to be educated who is instructed in useful knowledge, decorated with a powdering of religious facts, instead of being trained in the principles of life which are embedded in religion.

Next in importance to studying the children at the school, will be the knowledge which he gets of his people at their own homes. It is here that he has to see what can be done with the rich as well as with the poor—with the farmer, the tradesman, with those who do not at first welcome him or care for his ministrations. Here, among many revelations disappointing and startling, some of which have been touched on in other chapters, almost certainly he will find the reasons why so many break away, and why it is that the hold on truth is so loose. Oftentimes it will be found that the anchor of faith which has dragged through creeds and dogmatic definitions, and lost all hold of sacramental life, is fast caught up and stayed by some firmly embedded belief, it may be prejudice—a sabbatarian view of Sunday, a superstitious view of the Bible, an inordinate belief in sermons—which the parish priest, who does not know his people, would loosen and pull up in the exigencies of a remorseless logic, or intense love of symmetry, or even from sheer inadvertence, little knowing how much lay embedded in those unshapely prejudices, which time alone could remove without a disaster.

We seldom find in a well-visited parish a congregation alienated from Church on account of some foolish trifle; and yet, when we remember that the Indian Mutiny blazed out over a greased cartridge, we cannot afford to despise prejudice altogether. Most certainly a contribution to a good understanding will be an intimate knowledge of the people's thoughts and feelings; it will help to a solution of the difficult problem as to what is to be dismissed as a foolish prejudice, what to be respected as a cherished sentiment.

Kindness will lead him further. It will help him in the exercise of discipline so much needed, and yet so difficult. As a follower of a Master Who cursed the barren fig tree, and cleansed the temple-courts, he will not allow himself to put up with failure. It is said that the African, whenever a tree falls across his path never removes it; he goes round it. So with a stone: he never takes it out of his path; he goes round it. So we, all of us, are terribly tempted to go round our obstacles instead of removing them; to put up with a disorderly choir; to acquiesce in the selfish indifference of parishioners who neglect their share in almsgiving; to tolerate scandals, or to carry on bad work for lack of correcting it.

And then a special kindness will lead him towards those whom the world regards as the unfortunate, the disagreeable, the unprepossessing. It will lead him to be watchful over the weak, to rescue the fallen. Kindness to him will mean minute care; the same affinity to the race which God Himself displays, when He, while giving His gifts to all, yet discriminates in those to whom He gives them, having regard to their characters, their powers, and their surroundings, and the use which they will make of them. A rough-and-ready man will treat his people in the lump, and deal with them in the mass. The kind priest will rather treat them individually, according to his knowledge of their several needs, bearing long with them, studying them, forming them, travailing until Christ be formed in them.

III.

Besides kindness of heart and kindness of action, we may be sure that the Apostle would not have refused to include in this mark of the ministers of God, kindness of manner. When people talk with displeasure of sacerdotal pretensions on the part of the clergy, they very often mean that they have encountered some who are not quite gentlemen; who have not, that is to say, cultivated this distinctive kindness, at once a badge of the true servant of God, and a fruit of the Spirit, which penetrates through to the outward manner. We need to remember the necessity for this in our everyday dealing with people, more especially with those whom we call our inferiors. This is most particularly to be observed in cottage-visiting, where a true spirit of kindness could never allow us to forget the courtesy of knocking at the door, of waiting to be invited in, of avoiding meal-times, or occasions when a visit is obviously inconvenient and unwelcome. In like manner, a kind priest would not be disposed to lay great stress on little points which magnify his own importance, while all the time he believes himself to be upholding the dignity of the Church. It may well be doubted whether we should have heard of many of the so-called "burial scandals," manufactured in the interests of party, if some silly want of "kindness" on the part of the incumbent had not contributed the very occasion which sectarianism was looking for, while at the same time it safe-guarded no principle.

And so the priest, all through his dealings with others, must be careful to avoid anything like condescension and patronizing airs on the one hand, or roughness and rudeness on the other. More especially in controversy he will be on the watch to curb a combativeness which leaves a sense of soreness when it is most successful, and coerces without convincing, and leaves behind it a sense of a defeat hereafter to be redressed. It is startling to see the power of a little virtue, as it seems, such as this. Some men seem to be able to do anything with their parishioners, others alienate them for trifles. S. Paul himself, in that exquisite letter (if we may so style it with reverence) addressed to Philemon, has given us a wonderful example how to deal with kindness and courtesy in a delicate matter.

Onesimus, after all, was Philemon's slave. Onesimus had run away from his master, and S. Paul had become cognizant of the fact. We cannot imagine him as a man, apart from his inspired Apostleship, to be in sympathy with slavery; yet property had its rights, and mastership must be respected, while at the same time to a Christian there must be the opening up of a better relationship, preparatory to a nobler state. So we see in the letter the kindness and the skill of one who has a difficult task. The good, kind actions of Philemon are gratefully recognized; the Apostle's claims on his generosity are suggested only to be withdrawn. The personal sufferings of the Apostle are put forward as a pretext for a bold request, which has to do with Onesimus, whose name is withheld until nearly half-way down the Epistle, then to be introduced in company with S. Paul's, as his son. We see how higher thoughts, and higher aims, and suggestions of the good Providence of God, even in a runaway slave's affairs, are woven in with gentle appeal and veiled injunction and tender courtesy. Whatever else we may say of the Epistle to Philemon, we say at once it is the letter of a perfect gentleman. It shows us that S. Paul was not exaggerating when he said that he recommended himself as the minister of God by χρηστότης, or kindness.

And how much there is which really lies at the bottom of all this! Kindness, or the true spirit of the race, is a virtue implanted by Him, Who communicates Himself to us in the closest sacramental union possible. The gentleman, the kind man, is the man of pure race and heavenly extraction, in whom is ever working the constant purging away of ill by the abiding presence of Christ, the constant inpouring of good from the power of the indwelling Saviour. It is just what we thought of it in the first chapter; here is one of those virtues in which men see a visitant from another world. "The gods are come down to us in the likeness of men."[1] It is a tribute, albeit a mistaken one, to the supernatural power of S. Paul and S. Barnabas. Fineness of nature, purity of race, all this comes to us through the sacramental life, with its constant driving out of what is lower and base. It is true, if we take up with a lower line, we may rise in our profession; we may be known as great, clever, and successful priests. But there is a refined character which the Greeks marked as κάλος κἀγαθός, which the Holy Spirit designated as χρηστότης, which we in our day develop into the idea of a perfect gentleman, which means a great deal more than mere purity of birth, as the world accounts it. That may be diluted into the veriest selfishness, meanness, and vulgarity. But it does mean purity of birth from above, a constant influx of His Spirit, Who would wish His ministers to be distinguished for their kindness as well as for their work. A true line of beauty running through to the inmost fibres of character, developing itself more perfectly as the years roll on. "The beauty of Greece depended on the laws of Lycurgus; the beauty of Rome on those of Numa. Our own on

[1] Acts xiv. 11.

the laws of Christ. On all the beautiful features of men and women throughout the ages, are written the solemnities and majesty of the law they knew, with the charity and meekness of their obedience; on all unbeautiful features are written either ignorance of the law, or the malice and evidence of disobedience." Here is a characteristic gentle and slight, a very bloom of ripe saintliness, but unmistakable where we see it, beautiful and good, beautiful *because* good.

CHAPTER X.

SPIRITUALITY.

"Swiftly and straight each tongue of flame
　Through cloud and breeze unwavering came
　And darted to its place of rest,
On some meek brow of Jesus blest.
Nor fades it yet, that living gleam,
And still those lambent lightnings stream;
Where'er the Lord is, there are they;
　In every heart that gives them room,
They light His altar every day,
　Zeal to inflame and vice consume."

'Εν Πνεύματι Ἁγίῳ.
(" By the Holy Ghost.")

THIS is more than a mark of " the minister of God." It is to the life what expression is to the face. The coming to the surface of an inner life, to be seen clearest when the outer veil is worn thin in suffering, or laid aside in devotion, or at times when no eye is consciously directed upon it.

And to be told to commend one's self as the minister of God by the Holy Ghost is a tremendous thing; it is as if one were told to appear as, and display the characteristics of, a leader of men or a genius, or to pose as the possessor of some unique gift. Can the priest—can any man—command the presence of the Holy Ghost, that it should appear as one of the marks of his ministry? Is it a presence and a power appreciable by the outside world at all? Will not the claim to it be regarded as a piece of transcendental ecclesiasticism and unmeaning cant—a part of the usual mysticism which clings to religious enthusiasm, leading off into sudden flights and unmeasured abstractions? "By the Holy Ghost!" And yet it is a mark which stands out when suffering, discipline, purity, and self-forgetfulness have worn away crust after crust of outer selfishness; when there is laid bare no asceticism, nor stoicism, nor barren contempt of the world; but within it all, as the sun pouring through the scudding cloud-drift, the living presence of the Holy Ghost.

Spirituality,—here is a central mark of the Θεοῦ διάκονος. We are face to face with the very life and inspiration of the priestly character, the light and spring of every worthy action which claims our recognition. It dawns upon us with more and more conviction, that here is a power of the very first importance to the priest, for the absence of which nothing else can compensate—spirituality. And yet we know that the world has its ordinations as well as the Church. At one time the very charter of its social salvation is knowledge. Education is to do everything, and the warning of superior intelligence will gradually obliterate the empire of evil. So having theorized and talked, "we give you the authority which belongs to a minister of the Established Church. Go forth and teach." At another time the love of humanity and the religion of benevolence is gradually to elevate human nature from the bestial regions of appetite to the celestial state of progress. Here, again, "having organized and subscribed, we send you forth as relieving officers." Or, once more, culture in art, poetry, and music is to raise man out of himself. We are entering on a golden age. The patience of investigation and the triumph of discovery will redeem the earth.

"Magnus ab integro sæclorum nascitur ordo
Jam redit et Virgo, redeunt Saturnia regna."[1]

"Having crammed and coached you, we send you forth as teachers and improvers." But the Church goes on still, in her quiet out-of-the-way cathedrals as well as in large centres of life, with a supernatural creed and supernatural sacraments, in obedience to a never-changing command. Now as of old, now in the nineteenth century as in the first, she lays hands on the priesthood and they receive the Holy Ghost.

And what a power it is which then, breaking through the barrier, leaps in!—a power which the world little dreams of or understands; and yet, if Christianity be true, the greatest power in the world in the formation of character, in the shaping of history, in the ordering of the universe. To ignore it in education is to put the clock back; to neglect it in morals is to be retrogressive; to supersede it is to put a bar in the way of progress. Ignored it may

[1] Virg., "Eclog.," iv. 5.

be; forgotten, unknown, it is still there. So the lightning-flash toppled down towers, crashed trees and killed life, before men bound down electricity to be their penman. So steam displayed its power in every house in the land before men harnessed it to their carriages. Now and then a brilliant life starts up, out of an inexplicable environment, and in contradiction of all heredity. Now and then we can see flashing out a virtue unknown to any treatise on ethics; we see an enthusiasm which we cannot explain, a light as from another world, which we cannot copy; but few think of the great power encircling our lives with its unknown force—the power of the Holy Ghost. There it is, close to our parched lives, a perfect reservoir of grace and goodness, actually touching our crying and clamouring needs, if only the connection were open between them! Let the obstacle once be removed, and in flows wisdom, the power of knowing the highest things; the knowledge of God, of things as they are, of man, of the end of man, of the plan and design of God. Understanding trickles in; the intelligence, which is the expression of wisdom, making us clear and able, capable of instructing others. Counsel pushes its way through opposing barriers—" the light . . . shining in the heart of a just man whereby he is able to choose the right path." Ghostly strength rises with a steady stream over the crumbling ground in face of the enterprise and burden of life. Knowledge bursts in through manifold cracks and chinks. While godliness ever freshens with a new accession of grace quick from its source the gathering stream of religious life, and holy fear helps us to realize the strength and power of the weight of grace within. So in sevenfold gifts, through sevenfold channels, the grace of God waits to come into our life. And it is by a full heart, a heart full of the Holy Ghost, with all this accumulated treasure informing the life, the words, the look, the very face, that the priest will commend himself as the minister of God.

> " And *he* shall lean *his* ear
> In many a secret place
> Where rivulets dance their wayward round,
> And beauty born of murmuring sound
> Shall pass into *his* face."

II.

There comes a time when every serious person looks back upon his life, and sees the turning-points which he has had, and how much he owes to influences which have come across his path. Many an artist has owed it to the discernment, patience, and generosity of a friend that he has been able to bring out his artistic life into any expression. Many feel that they have owed it to some strong influence and cheering voice that they have been able to recognize their vocation and realize it in life's work; but the greatest of all influences is the Holy Ghost. Here is the Maker of heroism, of saintliness, of greatness, of usefulness. Here is the influence under which, if we were true to it, we could become really ourselves, and give that message to the world for which we were sent here—the message which none but we can give; the individual contribution, the life's work which we are kept alive to accomplish. For if we are ever to get out our message, if ever we are to do our work in the world outside, the Holy Spirit must help us to do it. For first of all we are conscious that here is the only Force which has ever been able successfully to grapple with the power of the passions. It is one of the most awful sights which can be seen, a man who has had the best education, who has climbed to a high position, who has even taken Holy Orders, beaten, crushed, and degraded by the lingering taint of passion, never fully eradicated. The world pleads for its low standard and comfortable respectability; the flesh clamours to get the supremacy; we hear the plea of nature set up, and the subtle suggestion of worldly compromise. But the Holy Ghost closes round us firmly with an unyielding power. No, this may not be. If it be the right foot, it must come away; if it be the right eye, it must be plucked out. "Knowledge of wickedness is not wisdom."[1] Nature is not animalism unrelieved by instinct; but the strong passions curbed and guided by reason, and illumined by the Holy Ghost. Happy the man who has early passed into that service which is perfect freedom; who, under the strong guiding of the Holy Spirit, scarce feels the hedge of the law, as he walks evenly between its bristling barriers, held in now by no bit and bridle, but guided with the eye; who has won that most difficult of all victories, the victory over self.

[1] Ecclus. xix. 22.

And even more does the Holy Spirit become to us the inspiring Power of our lives. He shows us the dignity of achievement, and helps us to get rid of that dread selfishness, and the impotence of effort, which is such a terrible characteristic of the times in which we live. A day of blurred enthusiasms, where "there is a blight on every flower, a canker in every fruit, and a baldness on the head of every prophet." There is a sad waste of energy, a sad withdrawal of useful strength from the world, from the lack of self-denying enterprise. Young men who have had large sums of money spent on their education, who have been brought up at the feet of our greatest teachers, and have enjoyed the fullest privileges; when our big towns are clamouring for workers, and our villages need constant help; when the mission-field is white to harvest, and the imminence of adversaries challenges the chivalry of arduous strife—simply fall away into nothing, without delivering their message, without realizing the end of their existence, because they cower before the threatening storm, or fear the humiliation of failure, or shrink from the initial sacrifice which bars the way to professional life. It is a well-known scene in the picture-gallery of history, which shows us the Roman emperor surrounded by his legions, on the seashore of Northern Gaul. He had fired his veterans by hopes of plunder, and the glory of an expedition in remote Britain; and now, when all was in readiness, and martial spirit was running high, he sets his soldiers to gather the spoil of the ocean-wave, picking up shells on the seashore, and then sends them home again. Caligula was mad. But are they less mad who, when all life has been shaped towards a great end, and everything is ready and prepared, forego its conquests, that they may pick up its shells, abandon enterprise and part with seriousness?

It will be a terrible thing if the curse fall on us. "Therefore the Lord shall have no joy in their young men,"[1] because we withhold from Him ourselves in the consecration of our strength, and the surrender of our powers to His service. Many a strong life has been withheld from the ministry, because under the guise of having no vocation has been hid the shrinking from a higher life, and the cowardly fear of renouncing easy pleasures. Once to have faced life in all its greatness and importance, once to have faced such a vocation as that which ends in the ministry, leaves a man altogether in a different position. Then only at the peril of his own salvation can he shrink; or take up a profession of lesser obligation with any other view than this, "Here is the place in which I can serve God best," not "Here is the place in which I can give God least, or feel the smallest amount of sacrifice, and the *minimum* of religious restraint." And hence it is that at ordination the life is especially endowed with a fresh gift of the Holy Spirit. It could not be otherwise in view of the work which is then enterprised and undertaken. It has been admirably pointed out, "What claims do the most brilliant mathematical faculties or the keenest scholarly in-

[1] Isa. ix. 17.

stincts give to a man to speak with authority on things of the Spirit? Are we not told, on authority before which we bow, that a special faculty is needed for this special knowledge; that eye hath not seen, and ear hath not heard; that only the Spirit of God—the Spirit which He vouchsafes to His sons—knoweth the things of God? And does not all analogy enforce the truth of this lesson? One man has a keen, sensitive musical ear, but he is colour-blind. Another has a quick eye for the faintest gradations of colour, but he cannot distinguish one note of music from another. . . . Here is a mathematician, who sees in a sublime creation of imaginative genius only a tissue of unproven hypotheses; and here is a poet, to whom the plainest processes of algebra and the simplest problems in geometry are mere barbarian gabble, conveying no distinct impression to the brain, and leaving no intelligible idea on the mind. . . . Believe it, this spiritual faculty is an infinitely subtle and delicate mechanism. . . . Nothing—not the highest intellectual gains—can compensate you for its injury or its loss."[1] And so, as life goes on, we learn more and more to value this sacred gift, as the message to be delivered in sermons becomes more vivid, and we realize how not only the heart of the preacher, but also the heart of the hearer, has to be prepared by a holy influence; as we have to breathe longer in the rarefied atmosphere of devotion, where only with difficulty and with gasping effort we can sustain the spiritual strain. On the mount of intercession, when

[1] Bishop Lightfoot, "Cambridge Sermons," p. 305 (1890)

our hands sink weary with effort, and we feel doubtful of our powers; when failure again and again has followed our most earnest efforts; when the temple, cleansed once, has to be cleansed again, amidst the same or even greater difficulties; when parables are still misunderstood, and the closest band of discipleship is unable to exclude the machinations of evil; —in all these the abiding power of the Holy Ghost is a presence of joy and strength, and whether in success or failure we can point to the same result, God's holy Name is glorified.

III.

"By the Holy Ghost." There is a special part of our composite being, a special organ as it were of God-consciousness, by which we have fellowship with the Holy Ghost, called the spirit. This faculty, implanted in our first parents, it is quite possible was impaired at the Fall. It existed in the heathen world, and does exist now in the ordinary man as conscience, and in Christian men is the special faculty which is developed in the new birth at Baptism; which is indwelt by the Holy Spirit at Confirmation; is the subject of all religious aspirations, the object of all religious grace, until it becomes the supreme guiding power in a Christian's life. An ordinary man will be conscientious, guided by conscience, whereas a true Christian will be spiritually minded. He will be held in, not so much by bit and bridle, as by the look of an everpresent God. This organ of God-consciousness, this spirit-faculty, must be more and more increasingly developed in the priest, if he is to commend himself as the minister of God by the Holy Ghost. And at once we become aware that a faculty like this, so delicate, so subtle, which is almost a refinement on nature, which the ordinary man can even dispense with, must be singularly liable to injury and defect. And so accordingly we find that the spirit even in professing Christians may be absolutely dormant. What has been found to be true in its reference to the æsthetic faculties of the mind, is equally true of the spirit; and it is no uncommon phenomenon to find it dormant, practically inoperative. And yet the priest, at all events if he is conscious to himself of any spiritual deadness, any dulness of spiritual vision, feels that he does not acquiesce in it. Just as it is possible to cultivate a taste, or to arouse a hidden faculty, so it is possible to quicken the spirit. There was a time when men shrunk back from the bare snow-clad outline of the Alps as from a cold and chilly horror, to be hurried by as quickly as possible by the traveller who was unfortunate enough to be intercepted by them; and now men and women travel from all parts of the world, if only for once in their lives to drink in a vision of pure beauty of mountain glory and mountain gloom. And in speaking of a dormant faculty, we may well remember the extraordinary and wonderful career of the great missionary Henry Martyn, the senior wrangler of his year, of whom we are told that he had actually started to leave Cambridge in despair at the end of his first term, because he could neither master nor appreciate the first proposition of the first book of Euclid.[1]

If the spirit, which is not quickened, may lie dormant, it is also possible that it may be a ruin. How sad it is to wander through the roofless aisles of some magnificent abbey-church, where once the praises of God used to ring out—

> "Linger and wander on, as loath to die,
> Like thoughts whose very sweetness yieldeth proof
> That they were born for immortality"—

and to see them now, at the best a picturesque adjunct to a landscape, or a place for a picnic! So it may be with the spirit. The place where we used to have contact with God may lie waste, existing only as a monument of spent enthusiasm, and almost forgotten fire. Past enthusiasms, past religious impressions, how terribly hard it is to rekindle them in a ruined spirit! Is this the secret why formalism, the bane of priests, crops up where we should least expect it? Is this the reason why a hard mechanical devotion is made to do duty for the fresh vitality of true religion? The spirit is a delicate, tender thing, soon crushed, soon obliterated; but he who has once felt its power and beauty cannot acquiesce in its destruction altogether. He still keeps up the temple, while he pollutes the courts; he still performs the duties, but it is a tithing of mint, anise, and cummin, which requires no spirituality. He still condemns sin, but he holds the stone in a hand which his conscience convicts of

---

[1] "Life of Henry Martyn," by Dr. Smith, pp. 19, 20, note.

hypocritical injustice, and it falls at last by his side. Goodness must always be a difficult thing; spiritual-mindedness can only be attained by a constant effort. As well might we mistake a ceiling painted with blue and gilded with spangles for the boundless heaven above us, as to think formalism a substitute for holiness, the memory of the past for the living force of the spiritual present. Alas for a spiritual life which exists only as a ruin, which has ceased to be a living force; only a picturesque ornament of a worldly life!

And there is another peril yet, which yawns for the spirit in the priest. It may be in itself actively perverted. Every child, when he is baptized, promises through his god-parents "to renounce the devil and all his works." Perhaps we should be wrong to consider these "works" as a tautological expression for all sins, some of which are specially renounced afterwards. It seems rather to point to a region of sin in which the devil is paramount; more particularly, so to speak, at home—spiritual sin. We are familiar with that vast region of the sins of the spirit, starting from a distorted spirituality; proceeding onward, through superstition, pride, envy, falsehood, and other sins, right up to the blasphemy against the Holy Ghost. A petty jealousy is the spiritual disturbance which leads to the first murder. Pride and ambition strew the road of history with the prostrate forms of fallen angels and ruined men; while Satan tempts our blessed Lord Himself with a spiritual sin, when he urges Him to cast Himself down in obedience to a perverted precept of garbled Scripture. A misguided spirit is a form of spiritual disease which hangs about religious people. Sometimes a man is so spiritual that he despises his body altogether, and thinks that because God is a Spirit, and is spiritually worshipped, we should best approach Him by divesting ourselves of all helps which the body can give to Divine worship; forgetting the living sacrifice which God demands of him in it, and looking upon it only as an active enemy, a votary of formalism, a minister of superstition, to be sternly repressed by the spiritual man. Or sometimes a man is so spiritual that he despises his intellect; he refuses all mental exercise, he declines to reason and to argue, and becomes a fanatic. Or sometimes he is so spiritual that he quarrels even with the methods of Almighty God. "His gentleness," it has been said, "His condescension, stagger human nature. Man rebels against it. It hurts his pride. . . . Man has a greater quarrel with God's condescension than with all His other attributes put together. He would be a Christian without the sacraments, a Christian without the Church, a Christian without the Incarnation, a Christian without a revelation."[1]

So, if we would show forth in our lives the evidence of the indwelling power and presence of the Holy Ghost, we should do well to see that all the pathways are open which lead to God; to cleanse away the cobwebs of formalism, and anything which hinders the inrush of devotion into our lives. To see whether the light shines through the pages of God's Word, so

[1] See "From Advent to Advent," Rev. Aubrey Moore, p. 55.

that it be a lantern unto our feet, and a light unto our path, in something more than name. To see that the royal road of our communions is ready for the King, and the way of the Lord prepared. By the spirit we have access to the spiritual world, and are made partakers of the Divine nature. How sad, if when God's mercy passes by, there is no point of contact; the spirit dormant, without response, ruined, without full co-operation, even perverted in opposition to His love! Spiritual things are spiritually discerned. Here is the region where the phantom-mists which haunt our path melt away; here is the region of absolute serenity, where, looking out from the bosom of God across the treachery of friends, the gathering of mysteries, the agony of self-mistrust, we

> ". . . hear at times a sentinel
> Who moves about from place to place,
> And whispers to the worlds of space,
> In the deep night, that all is well."

CHAPTER XI.

LOVE.

"The widest love is personal, not a vague undefined sentiment, but a practical recognition of a real claim."

> "O hidden fire, your heat pervades
> All nature, like the generous sun,
> That blesses all he looks upon
> With influence fadeless, though he fades."

'Ἐν ἀγάπῃ ἀνυποκρίτῳ.
("By love unfeigned.")

THE word "unfeigned" here, appended to love, might seem to suggest that in the ministerial life there is a certain display of love. That love in its outward expression is the attitude, so to speak, of the minister; only, in "the minister of God," it will be "love unfeigned." For if love means a giving out of self to God, to man, and to nature, the ministerial profession is full of it. The minister is, theoretically, the slave of God; he is the servant no less of his fellow-men; he is in every parish, in every sphere of work, expected to be foremost in all that promotes progress and tends to the amelioration of the world. Only we feel that here is an echo of a warning which comes to us more than once in the pages of the Bible, "Let love be without dissimulation."[1] Let the minister of God approve himself not only in the outward display of professional kindliness, but in the inward unfeigned love of the heart.

I.

And, first of all, the minister of God will love the Church. This love and devotion has been set forth in these glowing words: "She will appear in their eyes not only venerable as a mother, but beautiful as a bride; she will command at their hands not merely the reverence and gratitude and service of dutiful children, but that more tender and soul-absorbing passion which a young man gives to the mistress of his heart. 'As a young man marrieth a virgin, so shall thy sons marry thee.'"[2] And certainly the Church has a powerful claim to the deepest love of those who minister within her charmed precinct. Ransack the records of experience, and see what it is which has inspired love. Is it the personal love, of which holy matrimony is the most complete example? This very sacrament does but symbolize the mystical union which is betwixt Christ and His Church. Is it the love of friend for friend — the $\varepsilon\nu\nu o\iota a$ $\dot{\varepsilon}\nu$ $\dot{a}\nu\tau\iota\pi\varepsilon\pi\acute{o}\nu\theta o\sigma\iota$ $\mu\acute{\eta}$ $\lambda a\nu\theta a\nu\acute{o}\nu\sigma a$?[3]

Here is the reciprocity of mind and service which

---

[1] Rom. xii. 9.

[2] Dr. Liddon, "Devotion to the Church of Christ," p. 9. (Rivingtons.)

[3] See Ar., "Eth.," viii. 2, 3.

envelops us in the "Communion of Saints." Tier beyond tier they stretch away into the far distance, till the eye loses itself in the dizzy undistinguishable throng, fading at length into a faint haze, a quivering gleam of sentient life. So that we cannot but say, out of a full heart, "The lot is fallen unto me in a fair ground; yea, I have a goodly heritage." [1] Or if we have regard to a well-tried constitution, stable laws, and perfect personal liberty, such as we feel conscious of, with a glow of thankful admiration, when, after a sojourn in a foreign land, we step out on English soil once more; or whether we picture to ourselves the almost love which an artist feels for the perfectly adjusted instrument, which has enabled him to express himself, outside the circle of his own consciousness, or triumph over the difficulties which thwarted his efforts;—in these ways, also, it is possible to feel the unfeigned love which the Apostle speaks of as a sign of the minister of God, with respect to the Church, in her beauty and fitness. Here the sacramental union is carried to such an exquisite perfection, that it is not blasphemy to say, "Not I, but Christ liveth in me." [2] Here the Communion of Saints is so perfect, that their presence becomes an inspiration, their example our strength. Here they call from the land to us struggling on the tossing sea, linked together, if we could but feel it, in the common bond of the Church's Eucharistic feast. Here, as he views the Church's system so complete and strong, with its well-tried laws

[1] Ps. xvi. 7.   [2] Gal. ii. 20.

and Divine constitution, the minister of God feels how true it is, "My citizenship is in heaven. I am a citizen of no mean city."[1] Here is an instrument ready and fitted to his hand, by which he can grapple with the ugliness of sin, or work out on the other hand the perfection of spiritual beauty. And it is striking to note the poverty of resource which breathes through the discourses and the advice of these who have an imperfect hold on the Church system. How meagre, how blunt, are the weapons which they display! Men are to be advised into self-control, or scolded into obedience. "Give up your sin;" "Come to God;" "Be firm;" "Be temperate;" "Be pure;" "Be honest;" "Be true." But how? And here there is no answer. No grasp of that exquisite system which He Who knew what was in man left behind Him as best for man. And so the minister of God can never treat the Church as an open question, or as the most venerable among contending sects. He does not feel at liberty to alter her constitution, or pursue an eclectic course amid her doctrines; or spread out her sharply defined dogmas into a shallow residuum of truth, " to which no one has any particular objection," called our common Christianity : not deep enough to float a ship, not strong enough to turn a wheel—bare, scanty, stagnant, lifeless, with patches of brown earth protruding here and there, which not even the diffused flood can preserve from aggressive worldliness. There is a sad absence of true professional pride or of love unfeigned for the Church

[1] See Phil. iii. 20; Acts xxi. 39.

of our Baptism, if we are tempted to give away its distinctive truths, or tamper with its deep sacramental life, in order to extend its boundary or reconcile opposition. We may gain in extension, but we shall lose in intensity. We may widen the expansive ripple of its bright surface, but it will be only at the cost of a sacrifice which changes depth into shallowness, and force into stagnation.

II.

The unfeigned love, which is a distinguishing badge of the minister of God, will flow out over a district of life distinct from, yet allied to, the preceding. He will not only love the Church in the abstract, but he will love that particular department in which he is most interested—the ministry. He will be an example of one who has a love for his profession. And having this love, he will never be ashamed of it, or dress as if he were an officer in the army, or hasten, as he says, to get off duty, or try to get into the world as much as possible, while he magnificently murmurs that he objects to a priestly caste. He will rather allow his whole life, and the aspect which he takes of things, to be tinged by it. The ministry is a profession in which there is leisure and special opportunities for studying the things of God. "The clerical mind" should not be a reproach, or allowed to suggest narrowness and intolerance. But men should be able to feel that here, at all events, is one who has made the things of God his special study, and who is able to view everything on its religious side and speak to them of God. The Church, whose minister he is, certainly presupposes that he will love it, inasmuch as by the terms of his ordination vow, and the obligations put upon him, he is compelled to devote to religious service and spiritual work and study a large portion of his time. What a blessing these obligations become, if only the love is unfeigned! It would be impossible to imagine a happier profession for those who enter fully into its spirit and obligations, or one more irksome, on the other hand, to those who have to assume the love professionally which they do not feel inwardly. We call some professions essentially healthy, because, as we say, they force a man to be much in the open air, where he can drink in the breath of heaven, and exercise his limbs and develop his powers uncramped and unconfined. How healthy it is, then, for the minister of God that his workshop or office should be God's house, whose prayer is no income-tax deducted grudgingly from the overflowing exuberance of a worldly life, but rather the very work of his existence, which brings him constantly within sight and sound of God, and teaches him the manners of heaven, and breathes around him the atmosphere of the Royal Court! What a joy to feel that here he is busied about the very highest department of human work, and dealing in questions which touch men's greatest needs; a student of the queen of sciences—theology! Surely the priest aims more and more at gaining this love—deep, unfeigned, pure. He aims at getting beyond the mere ritual of the service; that is like marrying for beauty; the impression soon fades, the glory grows dim, the attraction dies away. He gets beyond the mere love of music; that is like marrying for brightness of wit, or smartness of conversation. He gets beyond thoughts of a professional advance, or the position of an officer in the Established Church; that is like marrying for money. He tries rather to get into the very heart of the Church's life, the inner sacramental strength, the deep voice of the Spirit, the fount and spring of the stately services, the true dignity of his position as given him by God, in a character which man did not bestow and man cannot take away. Thus he finds that inward peace which is superior to change, and is able to resist the spirit of restlessness, which drives men from religion to religion, seeking rest and finding none, with a heart disturbed because it has not gained its peace with God. The ministry of the Church is a profession which may well inspire love, and love unfeigned; while we remember that love is not admiration, nor feeling, nor mere fondness, but the profound affection of an earnest heart.

III.

But the minister of God further commends himself as such by an unfeigned love for souls. His is the hunger and thirst after righteousness which the mouth of the Lord proclaimed blessed. This is the end of his own sanctification, this is the work of his life, to win souls to God. A great French preacher said, in writing to a friend, "I am of your opinion about mountains, the sea, and forests; they are the three great things in nature, and have many analogies, especially the sea and forests. I am as fond as yourself of them; but as old age creeps on, nature takes less hold upon us than souls, and we feel the beauty of the saying of Vauvenargues, 'Sooner or later we enjoy only souls.' This is why we can always love and be loved. Old age, which withers the body, gives the soul a second youth, if she be not corrupted and forgetful of herself. And the moment of death is that of the blossoming of our mind."[1] Our people expect this of us; they send for us in cases of illness, distress, death, spiritual anguish. It is ours to make the expectations which they have of us a reality. Our blessed Lord has portrayed the seeking and the welcoming work of the Church in three parables—the lost sheep, the lost piece of money, and the Prodigal Son. In each of these there are notes of sacrifice and self-abnegation. "Until he find it." Here is no mere touching of a sinner with the finger-tips of a parochial organization; or a speaking to him once; or a lavish expenditure of the cheap commodity known as good advice. We have another search-party at our side; and there, there are bleeding hands, and weary feet, and broken hearts, and tender patience, and ears deaf to insult, and eyes blind to imperfection, and a will which refuses to give up. It means, perhaps, that the search is a long one. You have been track-

[1] Père Lacordaire, "Letters to Young Men," p. 128. (Richardson and Son.)

ing him ever since his school-days, when his bright answers promised so well, and your hopes of him were high; you missed him in the Confirmation class —he was irregular; you missed him after his first Communion—you doubted his sincerity; you missed him as strength returned to him after that severe illness; and now at last you have found him, hard but frightened, anxious but forgetful. The world is in his heart, and the devil clutches at his prey. But the old grace begins to work, the words of prayer begin to tell upon the mist; first here, and then there, an object stands out of the dense gloom like a spire, or a tree, or a smooth surface of water; memories open up, and the old religious aspect comes back to him, pieced together out of the gloom, and he begins to feel out for God. It may be another voice, and not ours, which falls upon his ear, and brings back the soul to God. But the soul is found. And love for our people means going after them until one can go no further, hoping right up to the end. More than this, love for souls means sweeping diligently in the long-neglected house, not afraid of the dust, if the lost coin can at last be found. It means sweeping away the cobwebs and dirt from long-forgotten ordinances, setting up the Altar, offering Absolution, elevating Church worship. And the dust is tremendous. People call out, annoyed and distressed, as it flies in volumes, and the blacks settle down on respectability. It disturbs their comfort—they oppose, they threaten; but there appears as the result many a coin stamped with the Master's image. And the priest knows that

God gives to humanity οὐδεν ἀκόνιτι—nothing without the dust of toil.

And the unfeigned love for souls means, further, putting away all the touchiness and fussiness and self-love which impedes the penitent. It means forgetting all the roughness, the rudeness, and the shame, while we make it easy for the sinner to return. We all of us must feel, that when the blame is adjusted by an unerring Judge, a large share will fall on those who were placed in positions of authority, responsibility, and trust. The story of S. John is well known—how he reclaimed the robber-youth who had fallen from his first faith, and how he rebuked the bishop to whose charge he had confided him, saying, "Where is the pledge which I gave to thy keeping?" Full of disappointments this seeking for souls must ever be, even if it is full of joys; but we must not shrink from it. It means labour, it means self-devotion, it means sacrifice, it means sticking to our work; it means making a little piece of work as perfect as possible, and labouring at our own especial department as if the whole success or failure depended on our own efforts.

IV.

To attain this love, then, we must endeavour in each case to make full proof of that which we profess to love. The Church must be no bare abstraction, but a living reality to us; its Word and sacraments our hope and stay. Our profession, not a grudging service taken up because there was no more congenial path in life open to us, but a real joy and happiness. Our love for souls accentuated and increased because we have learned the value of our own. The life of unfeigned love diffuses its influence all around it, if once itself has become possessed of supernatural power. The greater interest which spreads over life makes itself felt as higher joys and capacities open out all around. Under the guidance of a higher love, life becomes transformed. We are like travellers who visit some familiar scene in the company of one who knows its history, and can unlock its true meaning. He unfolds before us the interests hitherto unnoticed, which lie buried in its walls, or stamped on its fields, or enshrined in the configurations of the landscape. It was so when two men walked along the Emmaus road, and a third joined them, Who made their hearts burn within them as a new light flashed out of familiar history.[1] So it is now in a profession where prayers and sacraments habitually put us in His path; we see things around us and within with some of the love which He bestows upon them. No! the prayers are not too frequent, nor too high-strung; they supply us with words which bring us near to the abounding love of God. No! the mysteries of religion are no unreal, empty things, no waste of time. They shine with a celestial glow; they are full of power. They produce, where there is no rebellion of the passions, no perversion of the will, no treachery of the mind, no trickery of the imagination, the peace of God, which keeps as with a garrison our heart and

[1] S. Luke xxiv. 13, etc.

mind through Christ Jesus. While in the power of religion, in the light of the face of Jesus Christ, life assumes a more steady *equilibrium*. There is less of the selfishness of apprehension, which stifles love; less of the fear of surprises, which keeps our foot back on firmer ground while reaching out after the sinner sinking in the mire. Living with God, living in His presence, we feel the perfect love which casteth out fear; the confidence in Him which can take away the absorbing care for ourselves which so cripples our energies. With Him we feel that death may be only one step onwards. With Him already we have met sorrow. We have bowed our back to the Cross, and lo! the Cross has lifted us. With Him we have borne disappointment, and now we can trust Him even to death itself. The love of God gives us a joy and peace in believing, which sets us the more free practically to love our fellow-men, while the glory of the work more and more opens up before us. To have been of use in the world; to have got out our message; to have kept back the tide of sin only from some one soul; to have lightened the weight for another; to have lit up one more beacon-light that travellers towards heaven might feel less lonely,—this alone would be an exceeding great reward; but how much greater to have been allowed consciously to work with Him, Who has bid us believe that God is Love!

There is, of course, a fearful alternative, in which the Church becomes repugnant, our professional duty a most wearisome and much-grudged tax, and the dealing with souls an unfamiliar, irksome, and repulsive occupation. There is a significant passage in a modern historian in which he complains of the inevitable lowering of religious sentiment, which he thinks follows from the use of liturgical forms in public prayer, of a kind which can at most be appropriate to a very small fraction of those who use them. "The selfish," he says, "the frivolous, the sceptical, the worldly, the indifferent, or at least men whose convictions are but half formed, whose zeal is very languid, and whose religious thoughts are very few, form the bulk of every congregation, and they are taught to employ language expressing the very ecstasy of devotion. The words that pass mechanically from their lips convey in turn the fervour of a martyr, the self-abasement or the rapture of a saint, a passionate confidence in the reality of unseen things, a passionate longing to pass within the veil; and the effect of this contrast between habitual language and habitual disposition is disastrous —the sense of truth is dulled."[1] It is a service like this that the minister of God has to use at least twice a day. If he does not love it he must hate it, or at least cover its deep-toned pleadings with the metallic ring of formalism, which only prevents the words becoming his condemnation, because he takes from them their value and deadens their interests. To minister at the altar of love with an unloving heart; to belong to a profession of self-sacrificing love, while at the same time seeking only selfish interests ; to

[1] Lecky, "History of England in the Eighteenth Century," vol i. p. 817.

offer words of love to suffering souls, which are hollow and common;—this, alas! brings with it its own punishment. If the minister of God does not know how to commend himself by unfeigned love, he will at least, we must fear, be an example of unfeigned disappointment.

CHAPTER XII.

TRUTH.

"Ut veritas pateat, placeat, moveat."

'Ἐν λόγῳ ἀληθείας.
("By the Word of truth.")

It is almost startling to think of the immense number of sermons which are poured forth week by week from the pulpits of the Church. And it is startling also to find the immense importance attached, by English people at all events, to preaching; while at the same time, as we have already seen, signs are not wanting of a growing rebellion against sermons which are purely perfunctory, without love, without learning, and without life—the unwilling utterances of a paid official. And yet it would be a strange blindness which refused to recognize in preaching a great power. And before long we shall lament the folly which has driven away a ready audience, untaught, untouched, and unconverted, simply because we wished to show that worship was higher than sermons, or because we had not courage enough to master our own coldness of sympathy, shyness of expression, or want of rhetorical power. Surely this is some part at least of what S. Paul means here, when he speaks of another mark of the minister of God, as being that he commends himself by the Word of truth; that he has realized that he has a message to deliver to the world, and cannot rest until he has learned to express himself.

I.

"By the Word of truth." There seems to be some danger of forgetting the absolute and intrinsic value of truth in itself; beauty, refinement, delicacy, are no adequate substitutes for truth. It has been said, "Only truth can be polished." And it is the possession of truth which is one great secret of ministerial power. To be powerfully convinced one's self, is a considerable step onwards towards convincing others. "*Ardeat orator qui vult accendere plebem.*" If men see that we have never committed ourselves to the truth of the statements which we wish them to believe; if they see us shifting here and shifting there, and refusing to put our foot down on any definite statement, lest the ground should sink crumbling beneath us, can we blame them for adopting an air of intelligent criticism, which does not easily settle into conviction, when perhaps all that we had put before them was, that there was no one way particularly right, and no one way particularly wrong, only that the balance of truth on the whole seemed to lean in one direction? Men look for truth where it can be had, not probability, in those who professionally study a revelation from another world.

And when they ask for bread, they will not put up with a stone. There are interesting speculations of all sorts and kinds in the books and magazines which flood our libraries. There are beautiful dreams of fiction, and exquisite creations of poetry, and fanciful combinations woven with extraordinary skill, which give an outlet to the passionate heart, in mourning over the sorrows of a dramatic hero, or following the complications of a life's romance. But from the minister of God men want to hear the rugged voice of truth, to see the unadorned outlines of real combinations of human lives. To hear what God really did say, not what men imagine He might or ought to have said. To hear that clear and definite ring of precise truth, which the saints of old heard, and laid hold of, and said, " Here at least is something to go by, something to live for; not death itself shall rob me of this little bit of pure truth." They look for from him a clear direction amidst the Babel of conflicting cries. We have never accurately studied human nature, or gauged the wants of our congregation, if we have not noticed, and provided for this craving for truth, and the absolute homage which it commands when once it is recognized. As an example, perhaps we are familiar with that genuine homage paid to a fine impersonation of a villain on the stage, where the audience, instead of applauding the successful actor, are carried out of themselves by the truthfulness of the representation, and hiss the villain. The minister of God must deal in truth, not in views, and preach the truth, not opinion, and not be ashamed to be known as the minister of a Church which does not hesitate to say, not "I think," but "I know."

And is this the cause of halting sermons, and cold utterances, and half-hearted platitudes—which irritate where they do not plunge into a deep sleep—that we ourselves are not convinced? That we see the sneering philosophers surrounding us on the Areopagus, and we wince as we think what they will say of our Easter sermon; how some will mock, and some will say, "We will hear thee again of this matter."[1] And not being intensely convinced, we preach of a moral resurrection which is a poetical name for a conversion, or talk loosely about churchyards and cornfields, where indeed no one disputes our statements, but no one is moved to believe the truth. Or we are terrified as we see that the one part of the congregation are Sadducees, and the other Pharisees, and we fear to excite clamour, and so avoid burning questions, and talk platitudes on our common beliefs. But men who are disputing and wrestling with doubts within, and questions without, want to know what we think on vital topics—whether God really has spoken, or whether everything is wrapped up in a flimsy wreath of sentiment and evenly balanced speculations; and whether truth in each age is only a name for the theory which on the whole is the least incredible. Think of the deep tones of truth which swayed through every movement of the great Apostle, whose

[1] Acts xvii. 32.

portrait is growing before us in these words of his Epistle. How the truth of the man seems to stand out like a bit of rock in the seething sea, and blinding storm of fury, which sent the Eastern mob howling across the sacred pavement of the temple to tear his very life out. "I beseech thee, suffer me to speak unto the people."[1] This was his first thought, when the storm was at its full height. Look at his stern and rugged sincerity, again, before Felix,[2] setting off the tinsel and the dross which was gathering upon Roman justice, which had begun to sell verdicts, and make a man's liberty dependent on his powers of purchase. If Felix hoped for a bribe, at least he should hear some stern truths about life. How strong and massive it stands out against "the great pomp"[3] of Agrippa and Bernice, who just know enough of the mighty controversy which was whirling the Apostle towards Rome and Western civilization, to give a smattering of consequent justice to the furthering of an appeal case to the emperor, which ought to have been long since dismissed with an honourable acquittal! S. Paul's course may be traced through history, by the storm-path which follows after it, by angry mobs, and excited crowds, and heated words, and the shrivelling up of shame, and the falling off of masks, and the unravelling of cant terms, and the fury which waits on the uncompromising announcement of unwelcome truth.

[1] Acts xxi. 30.   [2] Acts xxiv.   [3] Acts xxv. 23, etc.

II.

Certainly he who would commend himself as the minister of God must feel this also—that he must not only appeal to men by the Word of truth, but that he must appeal to them by the whole truth. We are too apt to think that some doctrines are unimportant, and some parts of the Bible as meriting but scant respect and slight attention. It is possible that we should hardly have given a thought to the unmuzzled mouth of the ox[1] as he trode out the corn, or have looked for Calvary in obscure passages of Zechariah,[2] or have dwelt on the Queen of Sheba,[3] or have lingered over the difficult history of Jonah.[4] Baptismal regeneration seems remote from modern difficulties, and Confirmation a needless stumbling-block to ingrained Puritanism. One age obliterates the text of a manuscript of the Gospel, and writes over it the works of a Syrian Father as being of more importance; while another age deplores their folly, and tries to undo their mistake. The history of the Codex Ephraem is but a parable of what is constantly going on around us, and of the treatment which truth receives at our hands. Human opinions, human words, are written over the Word of God; or parts of it are cut out, despised, and neglected; or some doctrines are dwarfed and the commandments of men put in their places. But the minister of God commends himself by preaching the whole Word of Truth. There are two texts

---

[1] 1 Tim. v. 18.   [2] Zech. xiii. 6.
[3] S. Matt. xii. 42.   [4] S. Matt. xii. 40.

which we might with great advantage keep clearly before us; the one, "I have not shunned to declare unto you all the counsel of God;"[1] and the other, if we may so interpret its meaning, "Whether prophecy, let us prophesy according to the proportion of faith."[2] At first sight nothing seems easier—a clearly defined cycle of doctrine, a well-proportioned faith, enunciated without fear or favour; but a little experience shows us that it is no easy matter to preach the whole truth; it requires courage. There are some doctrines which are very unpopular; there are some people to whom certain doctrines seem a personal insult, as, for instance, the Eucharistic doctrine of the Church, the doctrine of the priesthood, and of sacraments in general, or the awful possibility of eternal punishment, or the paramount importance of a right faith; or at another time the stern morality and discipline of the Church becomes a barrier and an obstacle.

There are many S. John Baptists now who are socially imprisoned by adulterous parishioners, or the devotees of some Act of Parliament infringement of the marriage law. Fasting is never a popular subject, nor a popular practice; almsgiving may be pushed out of the limits of good taste, and be resented as a system of perpetual begging. Thank God, we may search through all ages, and not search in vain, for examples of men who have not shrunk from speaking the whole truth. See S. Ambrose shutting the doors of Milan Cathedral against the blood-stained Theodosius, until he acknowledged the truth of God's

[1] Acts xx. 27.   [2] Rom. xii. 6.

awful law by a true and heartfelt repentance; or, rapidly glancing across the pages of time, see Bishop Ken manfully resisting three kings in succession, in no way deterred by the fear of princes, so as to lower the integrity of morality, or the integrity of faith, or the supremacy of conscience.

And to speak the whole truth needs not only courage, but also *knowledge*. It is astonishing to find how, among other injuries which it has contrived to inflict on the truth, modern controversy has been the cause of this also, that it has succeeded in labelling large tracts of doctrine as dangerous; and we scud along our way, dexterously avoiding them, afraid of controversy, afraid of party spirit, afraid of extremes, forgetting that we are allowing ourselves to miss a great deal out of the roundness and fulness of the faith. Romanism has much to answer for in this connection; it has contrived to leave a series of labels which men can easily clap over Church doctrines, and refuse further to look at them. So transubstantiation has obscured the Eucharistic doctrine of the Real Presence; the confessional has raised repentance into a scare; purgatory has driven people from the contemplation of the intermediate state; sacerdotalism has involved the priesthood. And yet the minister of God cannot acquiesce in this large alienation of fertile tracts of Christian doctrine, or accept on hearsay the traveller's tales of danger, which he has never verified. We ought, before we pronounce an opinion, or resign a region covered by a doctrine believed in by thousands of our fellow-Christians, at least carefully to explore the ground, and to try to realize the systematic proportion in which the Church exhibits her matchless symmetry. Undogmatic may mean inaccurate; undenominational may mean spiritually poor. The Church, with her doctrine, seeks to cover the whole area of Christian life. She has a doctrine of grace, a doctrine of sin, and a doctrine of salvation. We must take off the labels which fear has placed over many rich mines of wealth, and not be frightened by error, nor held back by a fancied moderation. The minister of God, who is pushing on towards truth, does not feel daunted at the splashing storms of controversy which have washed away familiar landmarks, and loosened the ground, and made progress dangerous. He will, if necessary, make it his business "to seek for light even at the expense of warmth;" for, alas! it is quite possible that he finds within him another feeling fatal to honest investigation, and a wide outlook into the realms of truth which takes the form of partiality. Some doctrines commend themselves to him; some he dislikes; some he would be very much grieved to find with even a substratum of truth, or any obligation of practice. Why, for instance, has it fared so badly with fasting and almsgiving—two practical outcomes of Christian truth? They stand on the same level with prayer in the Sermon on the Mount; and yet people who would shrink from giving up prayer, bring themselves to believe that fasting is hypocritical, and practically neglect almsgiving. Or take repentance, again. Why is there so much angry feeling always available to distort the patient investigation of Absolution? There are some things we do not wish to be true, and with many people these are some of them. Instead of throwing themselves into the fulness of the faith with an utter and complete surrender, they ask instead, What will do? What is the smallest possible stake which a Christian can make as to the truth of his profession? Is there any danger of going back in this respect? Men who remember old days look back with something more than the customary laudation of past time to the older Tractarians, with their intense reverence, which seemed to shed around it a halo of worship which the most ornate service, with every ceremonial adjunct, seems unable to achieve; or they point us to their dogmatic precision, which showed itself in such solid contributions to Church literature, as "Eucharistic Adoration," "The Library of the Fathers," and the determination to reach to the bottom of an ideal Church life.. Is there any danger now of skimming over the surface, instead of being rooted and grounded in truth?

Here, in personal likes and dislikes, in favourite doctrines and pet heresies, we have a fertile cause of doctrinal disturbance. Are we settling down into æsthetic churches, choral services, short sermons (short, that is, because we have no interest in our subject), invertebrate theology, formal fasting, or blank neglect of it altogether, meaningless terms, and a general eclecticism? Let us take care. "What I like" can never be either the $\mu\acute{\epsilon}\tau\rho o\nu$ or the $\mathrm{\mathring{a}}\nu a\lambda o\gamma\acute{\iota}a\ \tau\tilde{\eta}\varsigma\ \pi\iota\sigma\tau\acute{\epsilon}\omega\varsigma$.

III.

"By the Word of truth." Apart from all question of ourselves, our courage, our knowledge, our receptivity, it is abundantly clear that the minister of God must ever be on the look-out to see that the truth be kept in its true proportion. If one side of the faith is pressed out of all harmonious unity, error seems to settle down at once. This has been the history of the principal sectarian divisions which have rent and do rend the Church. An undue pressing of the individual responsibility in Holy Baptism, or of the value of subjective piety, or of the rights of the congregation, have each in turn made great rents in our Church of England. And it is a thing which the minister of God at all events must be constantly watching, in the Church, and in his own life—the undue bulging out of disproportioned truth, or the pressure of favourite doctrine, or the neglect of safeguards. The Church is always in danger, more especially from one foe—which is never far absent—that is, formalism; a spirit which develops the externals of religion without a corresponding dogmatic substructure, or growth of spiritual life. Can we regard, for instance, without apprehension the rapid growth of the practice of frequent communion among all sorts of people? Of course, if this be accompanied with earnest preparation, it is a source of deep thankfulness; but are we sufficiently faithful in pressing the necessary preparation, while we urge our people to the privilege of communion? The exigencies of a Sunday morning already well filled, or a dislike to the strong terms employed, or even to the doctrines therein advocated, have combined to bring about a disuse of the warning invitations which the Church puts before her people. And how very seldom do we hear of anything which serves to take their place! How many of our people know the stress which is laid by the Church on self-examination, confession, and repentance, "*in the mean time;*" which cannot be satisfied by a mere general expression of sinfulness in picturesque language, or a running under the forms of absolution without any general knowledge of the heart's sinfulness, or a confession of its sins, or of sorrow for its sinning? How little method we see in the communions of our people! How little approach to the truth enshrined in what may be an exaggerated statement, but which yet contains a measure of truth, "It is impossible to estimate the effect of one communion less in the life of a Christian"! Our unfenced altars, our unprepared communicants, our overpressed privileges, may, if we are not careful to adjust the proportion, lead to a reaction, in which sacraments will be cast aside in favour of a subjective piety, and the great objective service of worship which unites heaven and earth be cast away once more and neglected; because the uninstructed communicant, injured instead of fed, can turn round and say, "I do not feel that it does me any good." This same want of proportion will take out of the armoury of the minister of God another weapon of truth, if he is not careful—God's Holy Word, the Bible. At one time it is set up, above sacraments; at another, it is neglected and despised, looked upon as a *corpus vile* for every youthful critic to try his hand upon. Are we giving this, again, its proper place in the proportion of the Church's teaching and life? Are we using it as a help to devotion and spiritual life, not as a polemical weapon, with which to beat an adversary; or as a mere volume of history, in which it is useful to study the science of comparative religions; or a simple volume of ancient literature, curious from its antiquity and attractive from its beauty? Surely, if the Holy Bible is to retain its place among us, it must be applied to its right purpose, and be worked into our lives by diligent, systematic, and reverent meditation. So it is, again, with what is known as Church work. Mere Church activity is bound to run itself dry, like a torrent, if it is not regulated by a rightly proportioned faith. In vain do we run up a towering fabric of organized activities without Christ. "Except the Lord build the house, their labour is but lost that build it."[1] Of little use is it to pile up a flimsy erection of wood, hay, stubble, under the sacred name of Church work, and upon the solid foundation laid for us in the ages of faith, if it is unable to withstand the fire, which sooner or later must try every man's work of what sort it is. It is a thing which needs constant watching, the tendency to secularize the efforts wherewith we are striving to reach men, to content ourselves with improving their

---

[1] Ps. cxxvii. 1.

position, or enlightening their understanding, or disarming their hostility, or even shaping their political bias, while we forget that first and foremost the minister of God has to reach a man's soul. It would be something, surely, if we attained to a more measured proportion in our own characters—those characters which contribute so powerful a setting to the Word of truth; if we tried to cultivate the points in which we are deficient; to make what is deplorable in ourselves less an object of regret, to make what we in our pride think to be admirable less obtrusively aggressive in its crudeness and disproportion; if we aimed at being less one-sided, and more careful of those aspects of truth to which by nature we seem less disposed. We talk of the evidences of Christianity, and how it may best be commended, whole and unimpaired, as the Divine system of salvation for the race. Such evidences have their value; they may satisfy historical inquirers, and meet intellectual difficulties; but they will never make men Christians. Nothing will effect this short of the recognition by those without, that there is in those within the sacred influence of the Church, a brighter and a higher life than they have yet been able to attain to.[1] This is how the minister of God must commend himself by the Word of truth, in setting forth a life fashioned and framed in true proportion, on a right basis gradually to be attained to, by pulling down what is faulty, and building up what is good; by

[1] See "The Ascension and Heavenly Priesthood of our Lord," Professor Milligan, pp. 275, 276.

sacrifice, by the study of the highest ideal, and the unsparing use of every possible help which the truth has put at our disposal. It means capacity for believing, capacity for doing, capacity for suffering. It means surrounding with the measuring-line of truth every part and portion of our life, and bringing every thought into captivity to the obedience of Christ.

CHAPTER XIII.

POWER.

"There is a bitter epigram—bitter but seemingly true—that more evil is done in the world by weak men than by wicked men."

Ἐν δυνάμει Θεοῦ.
("By the power of God.")

WHY was it that, according to S. Cyprian, the Emperor Decius "would with much more patience and endurance hear that a rival prince was raised against himself, than a bishop of God established at Rome"? What was it that brought Constantine in all his pomp to preside over the assembled bishops at Nicæa? What is it which causes men to writhe and shift uneasily, and mutter, "Priestcraft"? Is it not this—that the Church, however much oppressed and ill treated, asserts itself again and again as a power which cannot be ignored, and must be very carefully taken into consideration in political calculations? And power is put before us here as one of the marks of the ministers of God; not, perhaps, power in the abstract, but the power which comes from and belongs to God. It would be well for us clergy sometimes to remember that we are called upon to fulfil a position of power—a position which public history and private biography both show us it is only too easy to abuse; while we must not forget that, if some have abused their power by arrogant pretensions, others have fatally degraded it by criminal weakness. It is the fashion, in certain states of political opinion, to fasten on the clergy the stigma of intolerant bigotry and lordly arrogance; to decry the priesthood as degrading to men's sense of freedom, and the dogmatic faith which they profess as the grave of enlightened inquiry. But we must not forget, on the other side, that it is more damaging for an army of defence to be despised than to be defeated. It is better to be accused of intolerance than to be ignored; to be denounced as a tyrant, if need be, than simply to be put on one side in the battle for truth. A frivolous, invertebrate clergy, dealing in views, and dexterously keeping their footing amidst the convergent rush of opposing principles, committing themselves to none, are not opposed, it is true, but they soon drop out of reckoning. The furious letter to the county paper, headed "Priestly Intolerance," seems at the time to be damaging and irritating, even where its facts are more than usually untrue; but it may well be questioned if it does so much harm to the Church as the contemptuous scorn of expression, in which the man of the world wonders how the clergy can find so much time to spend in social gatherings, or why, at a tea-party, the only professional man who seems able to be present is a clergyman. Unjust and exaggerated such statements generally are; but we do well to recognize this side to our clerical responsibility. The very claims which we make, and the position which we occupy, make men more than usually captious, and eager to detect inconsistencies.

If power can be pressed unduly into arrogance, the absence of power, where men are entitled to expect it, becomes a damaging weakness.

How, then, can the minister of God show the greatness of his commission by the power of God?

I.

First of all, we ought to be very careful so to live that the power of God may come out and be displayed in us. There must be no quarrelling with our part in the work, nor desire to assert self, mistaking prominence for greatness, and fame for faithfulness. Few higher commendations can be given to a man's conduct, than to say he is quite natural; because it means that he is carrying out the part which God gave him to do. The popular proverbial use of the prophet's mantle as a symbol of transmitted power shows the impression which the history of Elisha has made on the world. And it is not a little instructive to us in this connection. When his master was about to leave him, and had made him an offer of a parting gift, wide-reaching in its scope and munificence; when he had asked for the portion of the elder son— for a double portion of that spirit which had made

Elijah what he was; when the condition attached to the gift had caused him to strain every nerve to be found worthy of it; when he had resolutely turned his back on the seething glory of heaven which covered the departing prophet; when he turned to face Jordan, and what lay on the other side, with a cloak instead of a companion, a memory instead of a presence, to be a teacher instead of a servant, it was not another Elijah, a bad imitation which stopped with his cloak, that started forth on the prophetic path, just stripped of its brightest ornament; Elisha and Elijah were two different men, with different natures, diversely endowed. It is one thing to imitate, another to copy. And we should do well to notice the different kinds of power which God employs in carrying out His work, each adapted to the needs of the moment. When a child gazes at a piece of sculpture, he thinks that a hammer and a chisel are all that is required for its production. He knows nothing of the different kinds of tools that are requisite for the different gradations of the work. Paint, canvas, and a paint-brush represent to him the requirements for a work of art in painting. He knows nothing of the minute differences and nicely adjusted instruments necessary for the perfection of the artist's conception. So there is always a danger in life of under-estimating the value of second-rate men. A supreme moment has arrived. The monarchy of Israel has to be hammered out, and there appears a Samuel to shape it and to form it; and rocks fly, and fortunes are made or marred, and there is shaped out the rough features of a monarchy; while no one pauses to look at the smaller prophets, who smooth its outlines, and round off its edges, and clear out the grit, and follow up the features. Or a temple has to be built, and a Solomon is raised up in all his magnificence; and one is found who can make good use of the accumulated stores, strike in at the right moment and build; while no one thinks of the hewers and drawers, the cutters in Lebanon, and the masons in the far-off workshops, who are all helping to raise the temple. Or Israel is in the throes of a crisis, and an Elijah is raised up. He hews out the features of a true theocracy, where, without sin and error, God shall reign unchallenged by a rival. But there is also room for an Elisha, who dwells in cities, who lives in intercourse with his fellow-men, constructive and conciliatory. He follows, as it were, to smooth, and do simpler work on the great outline; an imitator, it may be, a servile producer of the same design, but not a copyist.

It is of all-importance that we should recognize the value of second-rate power, and, as we cannot all be Elijahs, to be natural, and remember that we may be Elishas, and, as such, can have even a double portion of the prophet's spirit in our own line. How many a servant of God, fixing his eyes on some great example, is straining his efforts, forcing his powers, losing his simplicity in aiming at some work, which requires a man in possession of ten talents, the need for whom, it may be, has passed with the crisis! God asks for some quiet detail to be finished in a country parish; His servant spends all his time and energy elsewhere, or refuses to work at all, because he is not in a town. Or he thinks it servile to take up work which he found, and thinks that originality must be displayed in starting everything from a fresh basis. Whatever Elijahs may have crossed our path, and dowered our activity, while Elijah's mantle makes Elisha a rich man, he still remains Elisha. His power is in being natural. God has a work for each single instrument to do, and His power is displayed in the doing of it. It is not without significance that our Divine Lord and Master, when He represents in a parable the use which His creatures make of His talents, shows us the man who misuses His gifts, and neglects to trade, as the man who had received one talent. First-rate men make their way; with whatever shipwreck, with whatever accident, they deliver their message and leave their mark. But the second-rate, who have to do simpler work, who fall on times when God needs simple workmen—cutters instead of carvers, workmen and not designers, men who can carry out instruction, not strike out a new design—fail from mistaking their work, and in thinking it to be all cast in one groove, to be chiselled by the same men. Here, then, is one way in which the minister of God displays himself in his true colours. By putting his natural powers at the disposal of God and quietly carrying out the work which He has set him to do, he manifests the wisdom of God, which, whether it comes feasting or comes mourning, is justified of all its children.

II.

"By the power of God." Many circumstances combine to put a great deal of the material of power into the priest's hands. Here in England there are few positions of such unlimited authority as that in which he finds himself who has the cure of souls; at least in matters which concern the Church and services. But, apart from this, the enemies of our Established Church are never weary of pointing out the social power which they imagine come to him from State patronage. Or there is the intellectual power which belongs to one who is drawn in most cases from the ranks of those who have had the inestimable privilege of a liberal education; or there are special powers which he may develop which find an immediate and useful field for their exercise, such as the power of organization, or of transacting business, or of literary aptitude; or he has had committed to him certain natural powers which bring him prominently to the front. But, beyond all these, the generous trust of the people committed to his charge invest him with opportunities of influence and usefulness such as are vouchsafed to few. He is with them at all times, in their joys and in their sorrows, on the bed of sickness, in their days of happiness; he teaches the young at the school, prepares them for Confirmation at the most impressionable moment of their lives; is looked up to as a recognized teacher of morals, to reprove, rebuke, exhort. It is almost a source of fear to a conscientious man, with a sense of responsibility upon him, to see how his opinion is appealed to and his word followed. The temptation to him will be constant to forget that it is the power of God which must come out; that to retain a percentage of reputation for personal aggrandizement is to divert what really belongs to Him. There must be a firm repression of the spirit which would lead him to be the aristocratic superior, the fussy superintendent, the unbending schoolmaster, the uncompromising autocrat, the excellent commercial genius. All these qualities may too easily mount up like black vapours thrown off from the very intensity of earnest life, and obscure the power of God, just where rays from Him are most needed to lighten up the idolatry of education, to spiritualize the hard mechanism of organization, and to soften the rough distinctions of class. Wherever power comes into our hands, there comes with it the danger of officialism and the fear of pride. We need more and more to put everything we have at the disposal of religion; to let our religion be the illuminating force, behind a life bare and gaunt without it, throwing a spiritual light upon our ordinary powers. But it is in the simple affairs of life such as these that the power of God makes itself so wonderfully felt. It is in the touch with which the minister of God is able to relieve the common ills of life that he shows himself the agent of no human scheme of empiric philanthropy. Where philosophers soar away into magnificent Utopias, he is able to bring the little remedy which sets free the imprisoned life, which, so far from flying, can cleave only to the dust in the cruel snare of sin. Where other schemes of power and intellectual magnificence open out their great promises, he recognizes that the starving scholar must be first fed and then taught. Where the calls to activity are so many and so various, he recognizes that he must first be able to satisfy the perplexity of the soul, which needs an answer to these two all-important questions, "Where am I?" and "Whither am I going?" It is right that a man should have influence over a soul which he has saved from death, or turned into the right path where the crossing of the roads was most perplexing, or which he has fed amidst the weariness of the way, or welcomed on its return from the exile of sin. The faithful use of the remedies and stores of the Church will always bring power to him who dispenses them, only he must see to it that he steps back and makes way for God. Just as his Master passed through infancy, boyhood, manhood, and left each and all of them bathed in a heavenly light and aglow with new beauty, in the same way the minister of God was meant to commend himself by the power of God, as a power which runs along the salient features of his character, turning shyness into modesty, boldness into confidence, fierce passion into vigour, anger into discipline, softness into gentleness, slothfulness into peaceful work. By the transformation of character, as well as by the repression of an evil self, the power of God displays itself in the human agent of a superhuman work. And once more it comes true, as with S. Paul, so with more humble agents, when they heard "that he which persecuted us in times past now preacheth the faith which once he destroyed ... they glorified God in me."[1]

III.

"By the power of God." Our real powers, however, lie deeper than this. They can be traced back to ordination, and to the grace which came to us through the imposition of hands. Without this commission, we feel it would be the merest impertinence on our part to attempt to interfere in the heart-troubles of suffering humanity, which concern them and their God. But, at the same time, the priest is not a machine, the last link in a chain of automatically working causes. He has tested the instruments which he uses; he has systematically studied the wants and diseases of the soul. He knows something of the labour and research of those who have worked in this field; of those who have set out more clearly the will of God as contained in Holy Scripture; who have traced out the mystery of sacraments, and of man's co-operation with God's grace; who have studied the inroads of sin, and the subtle approaches of temptation; who have mapped out the outlines of a holy life, and the safeguards of piety. He is powerful as the holder of supernatural gifts, but he is also powerful in the strength of a tradition; a tradition which has been brought down into his own life, and some

[1] Gal. i. 23, 24.

of the chapters written as it were yesterday. When
David went into the battle to fight with the Philistine, he did not merely rest on the tradition of the
invincible God of Israel, strong as that was and
powerful to help him; he rested on the memory of
a boyish victory over a lion and a bear, whom he
had repulsed from his father's flock; and confident
in the victory of God, as shown to him in the circle
of his own experience, he goes to meet greater difficulties, and to overthrow the champion giant which
menaced God's people Israel. It is in vain to talk
about supernatural gifts, and to rest on a mechanical
preparation for dealing with souls, and on an official
power which, after all, is not sufficient to make people
forget Hophni and Phinehas in the guise of the priesthood, or to accept professional sanctity in the place of
personal piety. If our ordination power is so great,
it only brings out into stronger relief the need of
personal fitness in those who aspire to wield those
powers. There streams in the living fountain, but
the basin is broken which ought to receive it and
transmit it, or it is foul with neglect, or choked up
with rubbish, and the land is parched with drought,
while the fountain splashes in mockery of its thirst.
Innocence or penitence, one or the other, must have
occupied the heart which is to be the recipient of
God's power. What an inestimable treasure do they
carry, who bring to the priesthood a life of innocence,
undisturbed by passion, unscarred by the throes of
some awful conversion; where no trembling joint, or
halting limb, or dimmed eye, or feeble heart show

the traces of a fight whose issue seemed at one time doubtful, whose scars can never be quite effaced! This power of innocence has been thus described. "Whatever else . . . is lost by the absence of experience of evil, by the calm and even life which needs no repentance, this is gained. The especial work of guiding, moderating, softening the jarring counsels of men is for the most part the especial privilege of those who have grown up into matured strength from early beginnings of purity and goodness; of those who can humbly and thankfully look back through middle age and youth and childhood with no sudden rent or breach in their pure and peaceful recollections."[1] Happy indeed is he who can thus offer a life to God at his ordination in which no disturbing break dissipates the power of God which comes to him. But where this is absent, penitence must do the work, and restore what it may of the grace of innocence. Without it, power insensibly melts away. We wonder why our influence is so poor, our congregations so scanty, our results so feeble; it may often be that the power of God is being weakened by contact with an unworthy life. How many a man has gone, and does go, to his parish in debt—in the debt of sin! He has allowed to go on accumulating the great mass of gathering sin; the access of grace at Confirmation was to have paid it off, and made him free. Each Communion was to do it, or the new start at the University,—certainly his ordination was to see the last of it; but sin is still

[1] Stanley's "Jewish Church," i. 409.

there, and he stands before his people with a want
of spring and elasticity; he feels, and they know, that
he has no power about him. Bears and lions attacked
his flock when he was a boy, and he never beat them
off; and how can he beard the giant now, so much
more terrible and difficult to deal with? He can
look back on few victories won, that he should hope
to win now. He has always been beaten by sin himself; how, then, can he reprove or encourage others?
What is a tradition to him, if he knows nothing of
its virtue in his own life? What are the powers of
the Church, if they exist side by side with his own
unvanquished sin and unremedied weakness? Self
is the obstacle all along, which puts a barrier in the
way of God, and prevents the unfolding of His power
and the display of His omnipotence. Where men
hoped to see the glory of God, they only see self-
importance fattening itself on the assumption of
supernatural power; and not unnaturally they talk of
priestcraft. Or they think they detect the servile
imitation of a popular favourite; and they conclude
that the priesthood is, after all, only another profession
in which men seek to catch the vulgar ear, and mount
to eminence by means of popular applause. Or they
note the startling discrepancy between a man's words
and his practice, or the absence of any effort to commend the doctrine which he preaches, by the sincerity
of a holy life; and again they abhor the offering
of the Lord. Religion is a deep and solemn thing;
too sacred to be made a mere lay figure for ceremonial
display; too absorbing to be relegated into one de-

partment of life only; too exacting to be confined to books and phrases. Day by day, as he prays for the incoming of the Holy Spirit, let the priest ask, with all earnestness and deep penitence, for the spirit of power, that he may be able so to approve himself as the minister of God, Who "hath not given us the spirit of fear, but of power, and love, and soberness." [1]

[1] See "The Form of Ordaining or Consecrating of an Archbishop or Bishop."

CHAPTER XIV.

CONTROVERSY.

*" Who overcomes by force, hath overcome
But half his foe."*

Διὰ τῶν ὅπλων τῆς δικαιοσύνης τῶν δεξιῶν καὶ ἀριστερῶν.
(" By the armour of righteousness on the right hand and on the left.")

THE preposition here changes from ἐν to διὰ in speaking of instruments which belong to the ministerial life, viz. the weapons of righteousness, "weapons of integrity which smite with perfect impartiality, undirected and unhindered by fear or favour, or any regard for self." Weapons have an ominous sound in this connection. It is as if we saw some one taking up a weapon and girding it to him before going his rounds; it suggests at once a dangerous task in a hostile and menacing country.

The precise form of expression here used has been made the subject of some comment. Does the Apostle merely mean situations and opportunities of life, whether prosperous or adverse? Or does he mean weapons which are perfect in their adjustment? Or does he mean defensive weapons like the shield on the left, and offensive like the sword on the right? We cannot be wrong in thinking that S. Paul is urging on the minister of God preparedness, readiness, to assail if need be, to defend when called upon to do so. It will perhaps be more convenient to narrow it down still further, and regard him as reminding the priest of God that he must be ready in a combative age for controversy, and to defend, if need be, the faith once for all delivered to the saints.

Controversy is so congenial to our fallen nature, it runs up into regions so swept with passion, and so perilous to Christian love, that we may well be thankful to have it put as it were on a right footing, and recognized as a part, painful but necessary, under certain conditions, of the ministerial life. And, in a matter so difficult, it might be well to fall back on the very highest Example; to see how the perfect Man, the Truth, the meek and lowly in heart, the Author of Love, the Prince of Peace, met the assaults of an adverse world, and drove back His enemies with the sword of Truth. To see, when we are asked to gird our armour on, how we must conduct ourselves in the fray; without fear, without passion, without self-assertion—"looking unto Jesus the Author and Finisher of our faith."[1] And we remember at once how almost every step of His earthly ministry was challenged, His statements disputed, His very sanity called in question, His sanctity denied, His miracles attributed to Satanic agency. But, for our purpose now, we shall best consider Him meeting the assaults

[1] Heb. xii. 2.

of controversy, and instructing us in the use of our weapons, by calling to memory the events of the Tuesday in Holy Week, when the opposition seemed to culminate as the end drew near; when He Himself met His enemies with the most uncompromising severity and unveiled rebuke. Look at the excited throngs gathered together in the temple at Jerusalem, awaiting the arrival of our blessed Lord, as He comes from Bethany. They are smarting under the open rebuke of the cleansed temple; they have been goaded to fury by the Messianic cries of the children. Legalism, Formalism, Sectarianism, Cæsarism, are there with envenomed subtleties and angry protest. "Master ... what sayest Thou?"[1] That is the type of their attitude. You curse fig trees, you cleanse temples, you preach a higher morality. What is your authority for what you have done? What is your decision in a difficult case which we have to deal with? "By what authority doest Thou these things?"[2] "What sayest Thou?" We are in the nineteenth century again; we are at a vestry meeting, at an indignation meeting; a question is being asked about us in the House of Commons; we are the object of a paragraph in the local newspaper. Whether we like it or not, we must put on our chain-armour under our ecclesiastical vestments; we must have a shield on our arm, and a sword in our right hand; for we shall have to play our part in many a weary contest, and rescue souls for Christ only with some conflict, and after, it may be, a sharp struggle. We must not shrink

[1] S. John viii. 5.   [2] S. Mark xi. 28.

from it. It is quite true that there are the heathen, whose sad conditions are sufficient to tax our strongest energies; there is the great work which needs attention in our towns and villages—sick and needy to be rescued and fed; still there are theological, intellectual, and moral difficulties on which the Church has spoken out, and on which we must speak out too. Barren fig trees which must be cursed, temple-courts which must be cleansed, Pharisees who must be silenced, doctrinal questions which must be settled. One great and important office of the Church is to teach; and to teach the truth carries with it, if only by implication, the condemnation of error. It may seem hard and unnecessary to stop the work in order to combat some provoking controversialist, and grapple with a vexatious opponent; to build and fight at the same time; to be dragged against our will into politics, or lashed with the scourge of anonymous journalism. It may seem hard, when we are wrestling with some soul, to be told that " our fathers worshipped in this mountain; and ye say, that in Jerusalem is the place where men ought to worship."[1] Controversy is a weary thing—blighting, vexing, crippling; would we could be quit of it! But the Apostle, with his eye on our blessed Lord, can only bid us take up the armour and be ready; look at Him, armed and equipped at every point, not with the weapon of a shallow controversialist, but with the armour of righteousness. He is moving in a higher circle altogether, undeflected by policy or fear, or any trace

[1] S. John iv. 20.

of sin with its blindness and uncertainty. To meet Him was to encounter a shock, as it were, of Divinity; to hear Him speak was to be brought into contact with conceptions not of this world. The sinner shrunk back ashamed, little children looked up with confidence, the brave gathered strength. And so the minister of God finds out that he is entrusted with a treasure which he will have to defend in many a combat, and with many a blow. Satan himself tests our most cherished beliefs; we must know why we believe. The hundred-tongued inquirers of the day, ever ready to label and ticket off the adherents of its various sects, challenge us. There are people who have a right to ask from us, to whom they look for guidance and support, "What sayest thou?" and we must not shrink. It may be that we are frightening back intelligent and enlightened people by hard dogmas; if so, we must risk it. It may be that we are out of touch with the spirit of the age; if so, we dare not follow it further over the broken ground of speculation. It may be that we are sticking out for principles which Parliament will never consent to recognize; that the strong stream of the democracy is against us; that we are bringing about Disestablishment, or alienating the Nonconformists, or coquetting with error. The murmurs are loud, the cries conflicting. "What sayest thou?" It is hard to be obliged to defend truth against the numerous assaults which are brought to bear upon it; to maintain it against timid policies of surrender, or threatening menaces of spoliation. The world which cannot understand, that floating neutrality which hangs round the fringes of controversy, can always be counted on to oppose earnestness. Satan is always at hand to hurl a mob into the theatre, to shout, "Great is Diana of the Ephesians!" Whatever may be the precise nature of the controversy, noise and opposition are all he wants to silence an Apostle. The flesh is always content to sit down and fold its hands, and say, "A lion is in the streets."[1] But the closer we look the more we see; why armour on the left hand to defend, and armour on the right hand to strike, is one of the marks of the minister of God. It shows that he, at all events, is always ready, always prepared, not to win a victory, or defeat an opponent—God forbid—but to gain His cause for God.

I.

And so there are certain marks which distinguish the warfare which is waged by the priest, certain principles which regulate his use of the weapons of defence and attack which he carries in his hands. And, in the first place, there is that which we have considered already, and which will come before us again—a firm hold of the truth; this lifts him at once out of the ordinary field of controversy. He is not fighting for a party; he is fighting for the truth. We have to remember again and again that "there are many people who wish to have truth on their side, but very few who wish to be on the

[1] Prov. xxvi. 13.

side of truth." It is a fact which we are slow to recognize, that over and over again it is put before us, by precept and example in Holy Scripture, that a right faith is necessary to salvation; and it is also a fact of everyday experience. Many a strong man is lost, either because his friends do not know the right thing to do, or omit some minute detail in a case of emergency or accident. And the more highly developed and delicate the object matter, the greater the need for accuracy. The monument in S. Paul's erected to the memory of those who went down in the Captain, enumerates this among the causes of the accident, a slight infraction of the original design on the part of the contractors, increasing her draught of water about two feet, and a diminution of her freeboard to about the same extent. The electric coil which gives light, will kill if it is imperfectly protected and thoughtlessly handled. The powerful drugs in the surgery must be nicely measured, the delicate operation accurately performed. And yet men plunge about anyhow in matters which concern the welfare of the soul, and mutilate Sacraments, and dilute Creeds, and doctor diseased souls with powerful poisons, and think there is no risk. "This is the Catholic Faith, which except a man believe faithfully, he cannot be saved," is written over the dispensary of the Church, and the laboratory of her methods. Here, at all events, we can least bear an empiric. So that we are face to face with the main equipment of the minister of God amidst the attacks of controversy. He is wrapped round with conviction; he knows little of views and opinions; he cares little for dialectical excitement. He does not argue for arguing's sake. Truth is something before which sometimes we must be silent. But truth it is which raises up the right hand to strike a loyal blow. Truth it is which on the left covers over the body with a shield, which turns the edge of controversial flippancy. Let us guard with all our might against lapsing into mere controversialists, unless God has given us special talents in that way, which we can use with fear and trembling as given us for the special defence of truth and of the Church. As we follow Him after the day of disputation up the slope of the Mount of Olives, and watch there, in the blood-red glow of sunset, and the purple of the deepening gloom, and the blackness of approaching night, Jerusalem with its individual history and palpitating heart of religious frenzy, melting into the judgment of a world, and the crash of falling kingdoms, and the winding up of final doom, how little all the controversy has become, in the face of a world's sin and a world's judgment! Jesus Christ was the Truth; and as the Truth, He met and laid low controversy.

II.

Another mark of the priest's warfare will be spirituality. Jesus Christ was God. His Godhead penetrated through to His words and actions. And this is essential. Repartee and smartness are all very well, but when men have heard, however faintly, the sound of the great "I am,"[1] they go backward and fall to the ground in involuntary homage. Philistinism does not care for a whole army of controversialists; it cares exceedingly for one David. And we cannot hear without a feeling of anxiety the statement which is not unfrequently made, that we of this generation have failed to retain some things which the old leaders of the great Church revival displayed in their lives. With all our magnificence of building, and pomp of worship, like the Jews who wept over the old temple when they saw the new, because they missed the Ark, and the Urim and the Thummim, and the Sacred Fire, the Shechinah and the Spirit of prophecy, so men say there is something wanting now; beautiful and splendid it may be, but there is something wanting. Is it that abiding sense of the Presence of God, with its intense feeling of reverence, where every action and every word said, "Thou God seest me"? With simple or no ritual the ministrations of those men were eloquent of God. They were able to express by the sheer force of their holiness the sense of the great visit which God pays to His Church in the Holy Sacrament. When they spoke about Holy Scripture, they spoke from within it, with their hand on the pulse of its vitality, with an eye quick to notice the flow of its life and the continuity of its inspiration. Who could imagine Mr. Keble, for instance, a formalist? So strict in his fasting that sometimes for a whole week together he would hardly taste food until

[1] S. John xviii. 6.

middle day, and yet so tender, so deep, so unsparing of work, so heedful of the great end in view, a man of such simple reverence that he seemed to see God. Whether he walked beneath the overhanging majesty of His presence in nature, and brought out of the inner treasure the best words in their best order, clothed in the Sunday dress of poetry; whether he listened in Holy Scripture for the going of the Spirit, and would see even in the duplicity of Jacob a mystery, which would vanish, if irreverently handled, like the features of a body in some hastily opened tomb, and leave only a shapeless dust behind it; whether he tried to discover the best in man in all his waywardness and weakness, and make allowances for him, so that he would write, "I think it desirable to go as far as one can with the world (in the matter of dress) where one has so often to go against it;"—it is always the same; there plays about him a deep-seated reverence which is more than anything else needed in one who has to handle, under the exigencies of controversy, the sacred things of God. Something of this Pentecostal gift of holy fear would stay our flippancy, stop our criticism, crush our cynicism, elevate our tendencies, deepen our appreciation, and make the fretful spirit of controversy calm under the restraining influence of a higher power, and enable us to speak for God, as before God.

III.

A third mark of the spiritual armour used by the minister of God will be love. Love which comes from a life hid with Christ in God; love which is no weak sentiment, but such as became the characteristic of him who was also known as Boanerges. We must not seek to triumph over a crushed foe, and drag him writhing at our chariot-wheel to grace a victory —a soul for whom Christ died. We ought to try and see beneath the surface in the weary controversialist, the fussy opponent, the bigoted antagonist. Harshness is a serious fault in a priest; harshness in controversy, harshness in discipline, harshness in dealing with sin. Let us beware of harsh judgments. There is a beautiful legend which may serve to illustrate this which runs as follows. Late one evening a careworn, haggard man came to a priest, and begged to receive absolution for the sins of a life of which he was weary, a life which had become to him a living death. The priest listened with attention to his confession. Crime after crime—a long tale of woe was poured into his ear. At length he interfered. "My son," he said, "God's Spirit will not always strive with man; your sins are too fearful. I dare not pronounce absolution upon such an one as you." The poor man rose up and went away, bent low with grief and remorse in the agony of unforgiven sin. That night the priest on his bed was visited with a strange vision. He seemed to be present at the judgment of a soul, which was to be arraigned before the presence of God. A large balance was placed firmly in the ground. A man whose face he recognized, whose crime he had pronounced unpardonable, was brought trembling before the Judge;

in one scale of the balance the devil was busily engaged in placing all the sins of a misspent life, and they were very many and very heavy. Doom was certain, condemnation inevitable, when a faint flutter of wings was heard, and an angel appeared, bearing in his hands a handkerchief all wet and heavy with tears. He cast it into the other scale; the sins were outweighted, the balance altered. The soul was saved. The priest awoke in fear and compunction. He hastened to seek out and inquire for the care-worn sinner who had sought his help. After some time he found him lying under a tree quite dead—dead of a broken heart—but under his head was a handkerchief still wet with tears; and then he remembered how it is written, "The sacrifice of God is a troubled spirit: a broken and contrite heart, O God, shalt Thou not despise."[1]

Love should be ours such as he possessed who leaned upon his Lord's bosom, and saw things as He saw them; such love as will ever temper the bitterness of conflict, while it refuses to part with any portion of the sacred treasure which has been committed to our charge.

Do not let us flinch in taking up our weapons; do not let us flinch in using them. We cannot buy off our enemies. Satisfied with a Creed to-day, they want a Sacrament to-morrow, and then the supernatural altogether, and finally, as a necessary consequence, the Incarnation. Neither can we make a solitude, and call it peace, by a dogmatic contempt or imperious

[1] Ps. li. 17.

scorn of a would-be antagonist; or by a cowardly retreat from conflict altogether, from the heights of an unapproachable fortress into which we have withdrawn ourselves. We must not refuse the contest, even if we take no pugnacious pleasure in the encounter, and shrink from its dangers, and dread the diversion of force and the waste of energy better bestowed elsewhere. Only the Apostle pleads for the armour of righteousness; men will yield to goodness when they will not yield to a clever argument.

Anger, resentment, discipline, are all difficult weapons to use. Along the south coast of England there is a line of Martello towers, part of a scheme of defence against a foreign invasion; but their battlements are empty, no guns appear in the embrasures; they are useless for the original purpose for which they were intended; for a shot fired from them by one of the heavy guns of modern warfare would bring the masonry crumbling to the ground. Resentment, judicial anger, are heavy weapons; they often injure those who use them more than those against whom they are directed. Many a parish has been ruined by temper and self-will; the minister of God took up his armour, but it was not the armour of righteousness; he struck, but it was not for truth; he defended, but not with the Spirit; he strove, but not with love; he took the sword, and then affected to be surprised at the inevitable result—that he perished with the sword. It may be that, after all, for most men a good life is the best weapon of offence and defence. Our life is apt to get blunted, and suggests a contrast between our profession and our practice; or inconsistencies only too painfully apparent challenge criticism; or we become sensitive to public opinion because we have lost sight of the presence and approbation of God. It is a great power which God has given to some of His servants to go peacefully on their way, undisturbed by the blows aimed at them, unterrified by opposition, often refusing to argue where clearly an argument is the one thing sought for, conscious that there is a certain class of error which simply lives by controversy, and feeds itself with the exposure of the faults of others, and mistakes denunciation for doctrine.

But still, if need be, the armour is there. S. Paul has thought it all out when afterwards, in the weariness of his confinement at Rome, he noted the equipment of the soldier that kept him, and wrote to the Ephesians to arm themselves as completely as the Roman soldier for the fight. With truth girding round their activity, and righteousness covering the heart, and the feet ready to run wherever God calls, being shod with the readiness of the gospel of peace, with faith like a shield over all, and salvation as a helmet, and the Word of God a very sword of the Spirit,[1] certainly the Christian priest, armed as the Apostle would wish him to be armed, will be able to give a good account of any enemy that assails him. He longs for peace, he labours for peace; he hates controversy—if possible, he avoids it; still, this may not always be. As the way to peace, he prepares for war.

[1] Eph. vi. 14-17.

CHAPTER XV.

SUCCESS.

"They are most to be envied who soonest learn to expect nothing for which they have not worked hard, and who never acquire the habit . . . of pitying themselves overmuch if ever in after-life they happen to work in vain."

$$\Delta\iota\grave{\alpha}\ \delta\acute{o}\xi\eta\varsigma\ \kappa\alpha\grave{\iota}\ \grave{\alpha}\tau\iota\mu\acute{\iota}\alpha\varsigma.$$
("By honour and dishonour.")

HERE is another medium of display in which the minister of God can manifest his true nature—the alternations of honour and dishonour. 'Ατιμία has an ominous sound; it seems to suggest almost loss of privilege, social or political ostracism. And there is a remarkable interpretation of a somewhat obscure passage in the Epistle of S. James,[1] which represents the writer as speaking of these ups and downs of life as the object-matter of temptation, in which the Christian must rejoice to be tried. To find himself as a brother of low degree suddenly exalted, or as a rich man suddenly brought low, is in either case a trial to be delighted in, as testing a man's real strength. The ups and downs of life are full of difficulty, as they

[1] S. James i. 9.

cause it to contract and expand, like an iron bridge under the vicissitudes of weather. So the elation of prosperity and the depression of adversity are trials in which the minister of God displays himself; able to bear, able to adapt himself, as one who has been heard according to the fulness of that petition so often on his lips, "In all time of our tribulation; in all time of our wealth, good Lord, deliver us."

I.

"By honour and dishonour." It is perhaps the first chill which nips the enthusiasm of the minister of God, who has just entered on his ministry. He has come fresh from the power of ordination, with all the consciousness of a call upon him—earnest, devoted, eager; with a new title of respect before his name, accredited with an official integrity, or even holiness; placed at once in a position of responsibility, with authority over children, with a *status* in the parish; called upon to teach even old, grey-headed people; with a consciousness, it may be, of seeing ancient truths in a new light; confident in his grasp of truth; feeling that people only need to be taught, and that he can teach them; with visions of valleys already filled up, and of hills already made low, of rough places made plain, and the crooked made straight; he is living in an enchanted atmosphere—and then to be confronted by all that is commonly connoted now by "the parson," or "the curate," or even "the young gentleman"! It is the first trial of the opening clerical life, the sudden expansion of official rank, with its adventitious exaltation, and then the sudden contraction due to his own personality; and yet the true man will welcome this, as helping him to test his real self, as helping him to get rid of self-importance, touchiness, and that troublesome dignity which is always snapping beneath the weight of life, and ruining its fairest promise. It will be a call to him to put a human life into the official dignity, and to gain an official dignity upon the old merely human life. Some will regard him as a mere machine wound up to say prayers, and preach a sermon, and teach at the schools, and visit the sick, and distribute the alms. It is for the minister of God to show how he throws himself into the honour of his position, not as an impersonal official, an ἐμψύχον ὄργανον of the Established Church, but as one who knows how to lay all his powers at the disposal of truth; who comes as a courtier from heaven to conduct the services, as an ambassador from God with a message to deliver, as a true disciple of Jesus Christ "Who went about doing good." While, on the other hand, he is always careful to show that he is something more than the young man fresh from the world, the good companion, the easy-going friend; that there is put upon him the gentle restraint and the easy yoke of Christ; that he has learned what it means to cast down imaginations and every high thing that exalteth itself against the knowledge of God, and bring into captivity every thought to the obedience of Christ.[1] "Through honour:" he shows himself as

[1] 2 Cor. x. 5.

something more than an official. "Through dishonour:" he claims respect, however young in years, or unfledged in equipment, or feeble in speech, or deficient in authority, as the ambassador of Jesus Christ, Who "hath chosen the foolish things of the world to confound the wise; and ... the weak things of the world, to confound the things which are mighty ... that no flesh should glory in His presence."[1]

II.

"Through honour and dishonour." This is almost the daily record of the ministerial life. He will find it as he goes his rounds, some will accept him, some will reject him. It is a temptation which he is obliged to resist, to linger over the pleasant visits, and go frequently where he is welcome, to waste time in frivolous talk, and light parties, without any attempt at elevating or raising the tone; while, on the other hand, it will be a temptation to slur over altogether, to neglect and not to visit the disagreeable houses, where the inhabitants are uncourteous, or begging, or dirty, or unprepossessing; where the roads are muddy, the distance long; where the rooms are close and stifling; where he knows that he must convey the unwelcome reproof. It is in these contrasts that the Θεοῦ διάκονος comes out. Surely, where we are conscious to ourselves of so much dependence on feeling, of our sudden liability to expand or contract in our sympathies under the

[1] 1 Cor. i. 27, 29.

influence of sun or frost, we ought to keep ourselves steady, by a fixed aim and a definite object, before we enter on the minute visitation of our district. We shall be conscious that in most districts there are at least four grades of souls to which we must minister. First, there will be the communicants, those who at fixed or irregular intervals draw near to receive the Holy Sacrament, and are conscious more or less of the demands which such a profession of religion makes on outward conduct; these must be deepened in their spiritual life; be led to see that the Holy Communion is their privilege, not merely their duty, to be prepared for earnestly, and received with thanksgiving, and the devotion of an earnest life. Then there will be the second class, of those who are regular church-goers, but who are either not yet confirmed, or, if confirmed, have not made use of their privilege to be communicants; these, again, have to be gently raised into a condition in which they can realize their full blessings as Churchmen, and understand the poverty of a life which, while nominally Christian, is a stranger to the Holy Sacrament of the Altar. A third class will be the indifferent, who seldom enter church, who "make no professions," to whom religion is an unwelcome subject; these, again, have to be brought to church, to be brought within sound of religion, to be brought to see the hopelessness of a life "without God in the world." While, outside them all, there lies the mass of practical heathens, godless, dissolute, profane, who have to be elevated and civilized, and made ready to receive the good seed of the gospel. Each visit would then have a bearing proximate or remote on an end in view, of rousing the careless, elevating the thoughtless, quickening the sluggish, deepening the spiritually minded. And the visiting of the parish would not be guided by questions of honour and dishonour, but by a well-laid plan, and an earnest desire to seek and to save all.

As it is with the daily routine of his life, so is it with certain great crises and certain aspects of life: δόξη and ἀτιμία press closely on each other, and strangely intermingle. At times the minister of God will meet with great success; at times he will have to break up, as it seems, the very framework of his organization in dealing with some flagrant abuse. In the one case the true Θεοῦ διάκονος will not write off to the newspaper to announce what a successful parish priest he is, but he will fear. In the other, he will not regard the slavery of statistics, but go on, if need be, with a diminished choir, fewer communicants, with a half-empty church, with no bell-ringers, with a thin Sunday school, with sullen looks around him, alienated supporters; in dishonour, διὰ ἀτιμίας, ostracized, suspected, a failure. How wretched the once bushy life looks, now cut down to the roots, all through the long months or years, until the new shoots burst up from the bottom! Statistics have a good deal to answer for in many ways. But God's minister can still go on apparently inactive, fighting a losing battle. A Fabian policy is always unpopular, and yet *cunctando restituit rem.*

We trace the same distinction, again, in the duties which the minister of God owes to the different classes in his parish ; if it is difficult to visit the poor to their edification, it is much more difficult so to visit the rich. We may equally make a mistake in refusing the hospitality offered us in honour in the house of a rich parishioner, as we do in despising the cottage home in dishonour. Just as mixed congregations are a difficulty to the preacher, so the variety in station and rank of his parishioners tries the capacities of the conscientious visitor. But it is here that the grace of ordination helps the true servant of God, who has yielded himself up to the grace which comes from above.

Tact, courtesy, knowledge of the world, are all excellent things; they may prevent a man from committing himself, and guard him from unpopularity, but they do not always succeed in winning souls. S. Paul must have made many converts $\delta\iota\grave{a}\ \dot{a}\tau\iota\mu\iota\alpha\varsigma$, by appeals out of season as well as $\delta\iota\grave{a}\ \delta\acute{o}\xi\eta\varsigma$, in season ; just as he startled an Agrippa out of his insolent complaisance by an unseemly appeal, while he won Philemon by a letter in exquisite taste. The ministerial life must ever be full of these strange vicissitudes, of honour and dishonour; the true man is neither elevated by the one nor depressed by the other, but through it all remains the simple minister of God.

III

"By honour and dishonour." It is impossible to read of honour in connection with the ministry without being reminded of the vexed question of preferment. It comes up again and again. "Behold, we have forsaken all, and followed Thee; what shall we have therefore?"[1] "We have spent long years on a liberal education; we have made ourselves efficient by a theological training; we have laboured devotedly amidst overwhelming difficulties; we have grown grey-headed in the ministry; younger men have been preferred before us; no honours come our way; I am labouring where my efforts are quite thrown away; the climate is bad, or there is no society, no episcopal recognition of honest work, no appreciation of long and faithful service;" from time to time this sharp and bitter wail finds its way into the papers. And, indeed, no one can deny that, viewed as a profession, there are few if any so poorly endowed, and with such wretched earthly prospects. Only are we quite sure that we are on the right track when we so complain? Are we quite sure that we have put before ourselves the right aim, the true professional object, for which we entered on the service of God, for which He accepts and will reward us? Surely it is the service which we have to do with, the entire offering of ourselves up to God; the kind of work, whether it be $\delta\iota\grave{a}$ $\delta\acute{o}\xi\eta\varsigma$ or $\delta\iota\grave{a}$ $\grave{a}\tau\iota\mu\acute{\iota}a\varsigma$, as the world counts honour, must be left to Him. It is He Who must judge whether this parish suits us or not, for He sends us there. The world might have judged Mr. Keble to be thrown away in a small country village, but he changed the whole aspect of the Church of England.

[1] S. Matt. xix. 27.

If we of the clergy would only set ourselves to do spiritually what the author of "The Natural History of Selborne" did as a naturalist, and what others do as archæologists and historians, to find out all the rich secrets of spiritual power which lie around us in our immediate neighbourhood, the difficult knots which wait for solution, the many and varied problems which lie about our path, the interesting cases, the moral beauties, the victories of faith and patience, the history of individual lives, we should find little time for dulness and discontent. At our ordination we professed to give ourselves to God for His service. We offered ourselves to Him as His soldiers, to go anywhere and do anything, where and what we were ordered; and God sets the work, through honour and dishonour. Some He calls higher, to places of trust and honour as the world counts honour; but, after all, the great actions of life may not be there. He Himself was born at Bethlehem, not at Jerusalem; and lived at Nazareth, not in Rome. There are, moreover, two passages of Holy Scripture which seem to show how very absent true greatness may be from great places and great men; how the humblest work may be linked on to the greatest forces, and bound up with the noblest inspirations.

The first is this: "Now in the fifteenth year of the reign of Tiberius Cæsar, Pontius Pilate being governor of Judæa, and Herod being tetrarch of Galilee, and his brother Philip tetrarch of Ituræa and of the region of Trachonitis, and Lysanias the tetrarch of Abilene, Annas and Caiaphas being the high priests, the Word of God came unto John the son of Zacharias *in the wilderness*."[1] The kings of the earth stand up, and the rulers take counsel together, while the destinies of the world are being swayed from the wilderness. With God on our side, we can do more from the desert than from the courts of kings where God is not. The other passage is as follows: "Now before the feast of the Passover, when Jesus knew that His hour was come that He should depart out of this world unto the Father, having loved His own which were in the world, He loved them unto the end. And supper being ended ... Jesus knowing that the Father had given all things into His hands, and that He was come from God, and went to God; He riseth from supper, and laid aside His garments; and took a towel, and girded Himself. After that He poureth water into a bason, and began to wash the disciples' feet, and to wipe them with the towel wherewith He was girded;"[2] where all Heaven seems bowed down to perform an action of the utmost lowliness, and the pre-existence of the Eternal Son is linked with the Atonement, round the simple bason, and the peasants' feet.

How impossible it is, therefore, in every way, to choose! If it were only a question of a true estimate, what mistakes we should make! In old days men shrank from the onerous responsibility of high posts of ecclesiastical honour. *Nolo episcopari* was a real expression of genuine dislike to take upon themselves so weighty an office. And now, to one who has

[1] S. Luke iii. 1, 2.   [2] S. John xiii. 1–5.

learned his lesson and made the great surrender, it matters little whether it takes him in the direction of honour or towards apparent dishonour, still he goes where he is ordered. One thing at least stands out clear—the minister of God can never be one who seeks out for himself posts of honour and distinction. It is impossible for him to besiege patrons with letters, or make advances towards posts of trust and high emolument. To do so is tantamount to saying that, after weighing well the responsibility and considering the duties, he is equal to the work, and thinks himself to be worthy of the reward. It is equivalent to saying, "This work is God's, and requires careful handling; having considered the needs and requirements of the case, I feel able to undertake it. I can do it better than any one else; appoint me." And then, if difficulties arise, and God's work languishes, and truth seems to fail, how inevitable is the self-reproach, "I asked for it, I sought for it; I miscalculated my strength, the fault is mine"! Whereas, if God sends failure in a work which he had neither sought nor asked for, how full of comfort is the assurance, "I was put here by a Power outside me, by a Will not my own, Who knew my weakness, and yet judged me worthy of trust"! Bishop Ken's favourite text is well known: "Seekest thou great things for thyself? seek them not."[1] Must he not have felt, as he found himself the antagonist of kings, and stern resistance thrust upon him, first to the vice of Charles II., then to the folly of James II., and

[1] Jer. xlv. 5.

finally to the Erastianism of William III., "At least I did not seek this; God has put me here, and I must meet the difficulty"? "I will speak of Thy testimonies also, even before kings, and will not be ashamed."[1] Even if it means the humble grave in the churchyard at Frome, and the stigma of "deprived" written after the record of his death in the parish register, still the danger was not self-sought, nor the combat invited. God put him into the post of danger to defend it up to deprivation and disgrace; it was not the hopeless loss of a fine position for which he had pleaded and intrigued, and which he had regarded as the crown and emolument of hard work and service done to Church and king.

The thought of our commission from God will also guard us equally from fickle change and constant unsettlement. It is maintained in some quarters, with a great show of reason, that the parish priest, like the Wesleyan minister, should not stay long in one place, but be moved on to other work, thereby giving himself and his people the benefit of a change. But it is well that we should also look at the other side. There is a power and a subtle charm in the presence of one who has been with his people through many years of their life's history; the father, the grandfather of his people, who has taken the children in his arms at the font, taught them their first knowledge of God at school, prepared them for Confirmation, watched them in life's opening troubles and temptations, helped them to prepare for their Communions, and fed them

[1] Ps. cxix. 46.

with the Bread of life. He has lived with them through many years; he seeks for nothing more than to die with them; stagnating in an unruffled pool, it may be, but, according to a juster and truer criticism, blessed with peculiar advantages by God in a work difficult from its very monotony, and wearisome from its uneventful repetition, but where he feels that he is exceptionally placed to perfect as far as may be one little portion of God's vineyard. At least, he will know nothing of that hopeless feeling which comes to a man who feels himself a stranger to his people, and standing outside their needs. He waits until he is moved; it may be he will have to wait until his death, or until God shows him that his work is done, when he must seek as best he may to make room for another.

"Honour and dishonour," going hand-in-hand for the most part, singly at times,—these in some measure await us all. It is not really of so much consequence that we should ask ourselves, "*Where* shall I be" in God's field, or "What shall I *do*," as "What shall I *be?*" It is the wonder of some great steam-hammer that it is so beautifully adjusted in its delicate mechanism that it can crack the slightest shell, or hammer out the huge slab of iron which is to protect a ship of war. It requires an equal force within, held in check by the restraint of God, to live the life of dishonour, unknown, unregarded, with the pent-up energy still fresh and ready to do God's service, as it does to lead the life of power, supported by the praise of men, and the approving plaudits of the world, to be the honour of the parish, the noted man in the diocese, the ornament of the Church, to be that most difficult thing, to play that most arduous part, the minister of God in honour.

Holy Scripture is full of warnings addressed to those who carry a commission from God. There are few pictures so sad as that of wise Solomon, whose judgment was so famous, whose proverbs were so terse, whose wisdom was so notorious—temple-builder, honoured by visions of God, consulted by kings, and loaded with riches and splendour—setting in the gloom of a moral night, which hides from us all the glory which characterized the opening of his prosperous reign. He is a type of the dangers which beset the minister of God in honour; while, on the other hand, the man of God out of Judah,[1] suddenly called upon to do a work of valour, and speak a word from God, who successfully resisted the wrath of the king, and refused his hollow hospitality, who was on his way home, having done a difficult work well, is shown to us torn by a lion, laid in a grave unnoticed and nameless, with an epitaph as pitiable as the "miserrimus" grave in the cloisters at Worcester—"The man of God, who was disobedient unto the Word of the Lord." He is a type to us of the man of God in dishonour, who forgot under the shelter of the old prophet's roof, in the humble hospitality which refreshed him weary with his difficult task, the uncompromising obedience which God requires to His most minute orders in those who attempt to serve

[1] 1 Kings xiii.

Him. There he lies, an example to us of the dangers which beset a man of God when he thinks himself to be off duty; a man who was faithful in much, but faithless in what was least. Ah! how many single talents which were meant to find their way to the bank are buried by those who do not know their value in the sight of God! Honour and dishonour! God's will must be done in both; both act as a touchstone of worth and a criterion of merit; in both there are opportunities for the minister of God to show his real nature.

CHAPTER XVI.

REPUTATION.

"Moral advancement, as a natural consequence, destroys the sense of merit, and produces that of sin."

Διὰ δυσφημίας καὶ εὐφημίας.
("By evil report and good report.")

IT is not a little astonishing that we should depend so much for our comfort, and even success, on the praise or blame of others. With many this seems to be the first thought before some momentous step is taken, "What will people say?" It is often the last bitter drop in a cup of degradation, when contrition and reparation have been faithfully gone through, "What will people say?" Just as in former days we have been told how a criminal, who had nerved himself to face death, would sometimes shrink back from the prospect of the living sea of hatred and execration surging round the scaffold. It is a real power over us, this public opinion—that mysterious, vapour-like influence which is thrown off from the lives that are being lived, the words that are being said, the actions that are being done around us. It hangs about the age in which our life is thrown; we call it the spirit of the age. It hangs about the place where we live; we call it popular feeling. It hangs about human conduct; we call it fashion. When it is bad, we recognize it as belonging to our old foe, the world; when it is good, we recognize it as tradition, an inspiring principle of emulation, in which all that is good out of the past lives on. This is the standard by which the minister of God finds himself judged before the tribunal of his fellow-men. How far must he yield to it? How far must he welcome it? Is there a reputation which may be cherished without pride? Is there an approbation which he may appropriate without a blow to humility? Or is it a never-failing criterion to recall him to neglected duty —" Woe unto you when all men shall speak well of you!"?[1] Is it a sign of weakness even to listen to the world's praise, a declaration of indecision to be influenced by its blame?

The minister of God should have learned to appraise at its right value the popular voice, and have settled with himself what attitude he intends to adopt towards public opinion—now ready to choke him with flattery, now hastening to crush him with abuse. S. Paul, if any man, had known the force of the popular mind, now hot, now cold, veering from quarter to quarter, stifling or chilling, soft or tempestuous, in turns. The verdict of the islanders as they stood round the fire, pronounced upon him with all the rapidity of popular inference, almost

[1] S. Luke vi. 26.

sums up the treatment which he experienced from the world. At one time they pronounce him a murderer, whom vengeance suffereth not to live; and then they change their minds, and say that he is a god.[1] At one time he is called Mercurius,[2] and with difficulty escapes the impiety of a sacrifice offered to him; at another time he is being stoned.[3] At one time he is the much-cherished Apostle, venerated by Churches, and cheered by solid marks of affection; at another time he is left almost to himself, to linger out the days which precede his martyrdom. "Only Luke is with me."[4] And every priest who enters on his ministry receives his commission from a hand that is pierced. The King Who accredits His ambassador is Himself "the outcast of the people." He remembers that God might have manifested His Son in glory; but, in the secrets of His providence, it was necessary that He should be manifested in shame. He remembers those scenes of rebuke and blasphemy, when such words as "Samaritan," and "devil," and "winebibber," and "blasphemer," were hurled about. He remembers that "at the last came two false witnesses,"[5] and that the ostensible reason for our blessed Lord's death was impiety combined with unpatriotism. He remembers that these false accusations came to the Son of man in His capacity as Representative of the race; in His profession, so to speak, as the Priest or the fallen. He remembers that these accusations came as the return for a devoted ministry of love;

[1] Acts xxviii. 4, 6.   [2] Acts xiv. 12.   [3] Acts xiv. 19.
[4] 2 Tim. iv. 11.   [5] S. Matt. xxvi. 60.

that men, when not actively opposing, were too often
unthankful, as were the nine lepers who had been
healed of their disease. He remembers how even His
brethren did not believe in Him, and how He died
under a false accusation. He notices also the kind of
people who remained faithful to Him, from whose
lips came the scanty honours which greeted His
actions. "The people who knew not the Law," ready
to veer round from "Hosannas!" to "Crucify!" Or
the closer band of fishermen, here and there a publican,
one or two of the wealthier sort, and a few women,
some of whom had a broken character. He remembers
how the infant Church was first frozen by calumny,
and afterwards scorched by patronage. Popularity,
unpopularity; evil report, good report; opposition,
flattery; disdain, approbation; starving out, pampering up;—it is a difficult atmosphere which surrounds
the priest; and certainly he will enter on his profession as one who does not seek to found a reputation or win renown, but prepared, whatever comes,
to commend himself as the minister of God.

I.

For, first of all, he is stepping down into the arena
to fight with sin—a fight which has been the grave of
many reputations. This is a factor which seems more
and more to be ignored in summing up the difficulties
which surround us—the presence of sin. It is this
that the priest has to make for and grapple with as
the very heart of the questions with which he has to

deal. The social, political, economical aspects of the case may be all very interesting, and may make a demand on his efforts as a man; as a priest he has to seek at once for the spiritual. And here people will not follow him; here he is denounced as a mystic, or gibbeted as a retrogressive mediævalist, if he has any motion at all; if not, he stagnates in sacerdotalism. He is accused of being out of sympathy with the best thought and highest aspirations around him. At times he almost thinks that he will be left as a voice in the wilderness; or he is tempted to earn a little popular applause by an appeal to a sentiment which his better self tells him is false. It is then that he has to show what manner of man he is; to show whether or not he can keep his weapons bright amidst the corroding fog and blackening vapour which showers down upon him in bad public opinion. It surely must be the part of the minister of God to show where religion comes in, for instance, in questions of the day. There is no doubt whatever that if nations and individuals all combined in carrying out the precepts of the Sermon on the Mount, that it might be made the basis of an international code far greater and nobler than that by which nations are governed now; that if rich and poor, employer and employed, high and low, all in their station, equally governed their actions by its precepts, many, if not all, of the more serious social difficulties would vanish. The man of wealth would regard his riches as a solemn trust, and not allow himself to fatten in selfishness while others starved through his neglect. Improvidence, prodigality, all poverty which waits on idleness, drunkenness, and other forms of sin, would vanish.

Surely the minister of God must not be afraid to proclaim this; to say to contending parties and opposing ranks and conflicting claims, "You, each of you in your turn, are wrong and need amendment. Seek political remedies and social cures, if you will, elsewhere; but from me learn first of all that it is sin which disturbs society where it is disturbed, and only a pure and undiluted Christianity which will permanently set it right." The minister of God will have nothing to do with a scheme of morality which supposes that a man can justify himself with God by his own efforts, or be holy by a negation of vice, or attain to human perfection by substitution of a scheme of respectability for the law of holiness. He will show that books of morality may be excellent for the statesman, and prudence be a proper lesson for the doctor; but that, as the servant of a religion which deals with the heart, and attends to motives, he can put up with nothing short of holiness. But where people need quick returns and outward results, and where fashions and modes of religion change almost as rapidly as the fashion of dress, this will not be popular. The law of holiness has always been a slow, difficult, and complicated thing. Those who insist on its integrity have been called at various times by names which signify the impatient scorn of those who despise the delicate intricacy which aims at producing the holiness of a perfectly Christian life. A rougher, simpler life will pass muster, there is no doubt about that; but when you come to look for the more delicate virtues—humility, gentleness, love—where are they? Character after character snaps in its effort to produce them out of the diluted religion which passes with the world for Christianity. It became necessary, some years ago, to produce a facsimile of some eighteenth-century ironwork in S. Paul's, when considerable difficulty was found in reproducing the sharpness of the old work, and in securing the necessary delicacy of workmanship in the foliated parts, owing to their splitting under the hammering required. It was then remembered that the original work was made of charcoal-smelted iron; and, accordingly, when iron which had been so prepared was imported from Norway, the difficulty ceased. And now the new is hardly to be distinguished, in beauty of workmanship and grace of ornamentation, from the old. A little thing neglected, a small ingredient in success, spoiled the perfect work. So the minister of God has to insist on petty details, as they seem, as necessary to the perfection of character; and it requires some patience and confidence in methods to risk the popular displeasure, and refuse to put up with inferior work which makes a show, rather than wait for work which is good.

II.

But if public opinion can bark at the heels of the messenger whom it despises, it can also fawn on the messenger whom it welcomes. Good report, as well as evil report, tries the stuff of which the minister of God is made. What a terrible danger there is in the publicity which waits on almost every servant of God now, in his sphere and station, and which he may so easily mistake for fame when it is only notoriety! "They have their reward."[1] These are ominous words which our Lord and Master has inscribed over the region of prayer, fasting, and alms. We did not think that the flattering account in the newspaper of an eloquent sermon was all that was to come to us; when we composed it, we meant it to do good. The newspaper praised us; we kept the praise. There is nothing more to come; the praise is forgotten, and the report also in a day or two. But the recording angel's tablet is blank. "They have their reward." The photograph in the shop-window, the flattering review, the biographical notice, all tickled us at the time. We thought it might do good; it might cheer a friend, it might be the means of disseminating profitable literature, it might make the Church popular. But we are proud of it; we are talked of, we are known; we keep the praise. And the life withers; the sun beats in on it; the leaves of modesty are gone, and the fragrance of humility vanishes. The shade which ministers to growth is withdrawn, and with it some distinctive grace. We thought we were only cheering passengers on the dusty road; but we are noticed. We are proud; we keep the praise; and the angel, who watches over our literary and our home-

[1] S. Matt. vi. 5.

life, flies away with blank tablets. The reward has been enjoyed; there is nothing more to come. There is a growing danger that we should seize the false jewels and the debased coin which the world can offer. Good taste prevents many a man from vulgar display and self-advertisement; but it is not humility. Modesty prevents an extravagant self-obtrusiveness, and dictates a yielding spirit; but it is not love. Refinement and delicacy of language may veil some very black thoughts. Honied words may conceal sentiments which in themselves are very swords. It has been said that there are two thoughts which maintain for the prophet of God a true and proper independence in the midst of popular applause and popular blame. The one is the sense of the future, and the other is the sense of the presence of God. The thought of the day of judgment may well correct an estimate founded on popular opinion. "As they that must give account."[1] The minister of God, when asked to give away religious truth, either to satisfy some popular development or to gratify some hostility to religious strictness, must remember that he has been put in trust with the gospel. A logical development may be all very well, but his instruction stopped short of that development. What seems unnecessary to us, would not seem unnecessary if we knew all the facts which lie at the bottom of the requirement. We shall have to face the Judge Who gave us our instructions; and this may well make us pause. And also we are conscious that we work in His immediate

[1] Heb. xiii. 17.

presence. S. Stephen, in the midst of a heated discussion, when men gnashed with the teeth and were carried away by fury, maintained on his face the radiance of an angel,[1] because the higher summit of his life caught the glow which was denied to his enemies. Popularity, applause, esteem, favour,—these may all be denied to us, or all be bestowed upon us in full measure. But the minister of God looks higher; he looks for a richer glow; he looks to see heaven open, in the confidence of an unerring judgment which will confirm his integrity, in the prospect of a brilliant glory which will show him a present Jesus, standing at the right hand of God.

III.

Has, then, public opinion no value? Must a man be always in the right who persistently despises it? No, by no means. There is a legitimate function for public opinion which we all recognize. A healthy public opinion is a great engine for good, which every parish priest who is in earnest will seek to produce in his own immediate sphere of life and activity. The public conscience is a rough-and-ready instrument, but in general it is the safeguard of principles of right and wrong; it has for the most part a solid idea of justice, and it has put its experience into the form of proverbs, which are the common axioms of elementary morality. To get a good public opinion in a place is a great step towards the creation of an

[1] Acts vi. 15.

atmosphere without which the feebler forms of religious life are unable to exist. And so, accordingly it will always be, with sorrow and even hesitation, that the minister of God first sets himself against the opinion of those among whom he is called to work. It is a serious thing to find yourself in opposition to the religious life and the best minds of your parishioners; and, therefore, it will require very earnest thought, and very fervent prayer, before any question of mere ritual, for instance, can be put in the same scale of importance as the church-going of a pious man. The prayers of a good man must of necessity be of more importance to the reverence of Divine service than a mere question of ritual. It is true that matters of principle do gather round questions of ritual; and then the battle must be fought out there, just as earnestly as a battle may rage about the possession of a flag, or the respect paid to an ambassador. But this does not apply to details of ritual, or mere self-pleasing, which self-importance or wilfulness magnify into the dignity of a principle. The minister of God cannot afford to be indifferent, in non-essentials, to the evil report and good report of those whom he hopes to raise to heaven, and bring to the full enjoyment of the privileges of the Church. But the matter runs deeper than this. How hard it is to fight against prejudice, the judgment which has been made on false premises, the false conclusion which has been raised into the position of an undisputed axiom! Shall the minister of God say that his duty, as a man of truth, is at all hazards to set forth the bare and absolute truth, and let prejudice alone? There are few things so irritating as prejudice. A particular line of thought has been handed on from father to son as an heirloom of error, unverified, unvalued, simply as a tradition of almost family honour. Or it has been merely taken up as an easy form of religious belief, where there is an intellectual incapacity, or a moral weakness, or a dislike to serious trouble; or, worse still, where a man has deliberately shirked his responsibilities as a thinking man, and merely says that he has too much to do, and has other things to think about, and must leave these questions to others to decide, and take on trust what good men tell him is true; or even worse, when the order has come from a party-leader that, truth or no truth, he must believe and think to order. What is the minister of God to do with prejudice?—with what people like which is wrong, with what people dislike which is right? There are rough-and-ready measures. The car of a fixed opinion may be dragged along, over and across the bodies of those whose only form of religion seems to be opposition; or for a long time progress must be stayed, while prejudice is being dispersed and the knots of error untied. There is no doubt that if public opinion can be respected, without sacrifice of principle, that a great gain has been effected. Should we not be very anxious not to break with the past? Not to make every incumbency the beginning of a new parish history, almost of a new religion? Should we not be careful to see what principles have been planted there by previous workers, who watched their steady growing up in carefully prepared soil, who saw them expand through sunshine and shower, braced by frost and softened by sunshine, and which have now become flourishing trees? Fruitless they seem to us; we know of better fruits and truer stocks. If so, cannot we graft on to these stems, which represent the labour of the past, the branches of richer fruit and more enlightened religion? Is it true wisdom to cut down and plant all over again? or to plant out hothouse trees and tender saplings from other lands, which will not grow in our ruder and harder climate? Impatience of public opinion means too often love of our own methods, impatience of being thwarted and not getting our own way! What a strong and vigorous stock, for instance, is the Englishman's love for the Bible! How he has been taught to love and venerate it, with a devotion bordering on superstition! It would be perfectly easy to point out a want of proportion here, a neglect of the true recognition of the position and functions of the Church. It would be quite possible delicately to insinuate some modern doubts, to suggest the existence of critical cobwebs spun across a supposed crack or flaw. A wiser method of procedure would surely suggest that here, at all events, is something which the people believe in; the true theory of the Church may more readily be grafted on to it, than a new tree be planted in a soil disturbed by the pulling up of an old and rightly cherished religious faith. Or the observance of Sunday may be grossly Puritanical, savouring more of Jewish legalism than Christian freedom; is the minister of God going to commend himself here again by running counter to public opinion? Here is a religious observance which people believe in, which cannot be said to involve any serious breach of principle, but, in view of modern laxity, to err rather on the side of safety. Is it his wiser course to pull it up, and encourage cricket and Sunday recreation? or rather to graft on to the simple reverence which venerates the Lord's day, truer ideas of Christian duty and Christian privilege? Or the people prefer sermons to sacraments, or sit loosely to ecclesiastical customs. He may either defy public opinion and pull up, or add to the stock of public opinion a richer slip of fruit-bearing doctrine in patience and hope.

A manly independence,—this, as we have seen, can only belong to him who is in close contact with God. "What will men say?" It becomes a potent cry, until it is superseded by another, more loud and more commanding—"I will hearken what the Lord God will say concerning me;"[1] "Lord, what wilt *Thou* have me to do?"[2]

[1] Ps. lxxxv. 8.   [2] Acts ix. 6.

CHAPTER XVII.

SUSPICION.

"All true opinions are living, and show their life by being capable of nourishment, therefore of change. But their change is that of a tree, not of a cloud."

'Ως πλάνοι, καὶ ἀληθεῖς
("As deceivers, and yet true.")

As the portrait of the ideal minister of God grows before us, coming out of the canvas, we are more and more struck with this ominous fact, that here, at all events, is no popular character. Touch after touch which gives the likeness, the likeness which we know so well and yet cannot quite catch, is painted with sombre colours. The minister of God is one who is hounded down through prisons and tumults. That we should expect; we learned it in the Sermon on the Mount. Dishonour is mixed up with his honour, evil report with his good report; defensive armour is needed as well as offensive. And now there settles on his fair fame that foul suspicion of deceit. "As deceivers." We English people, at all events, who pride ourselves on our bluntness and sincerity, we do not care to be thought impostors. "Differ from me as

they will, oppose me as much as they please, at least
I shall get the credit of sincerity, even if I be in
error; of straightforwardness, even if I give pain and
rouse displeasure." No! "As deceivers." The minister
of God will have to show how a man can behave
himself who is thought to be a deceiver. It has been
so always. "We remember that that deceiver said."[1]
It was a characteristic of our blessed Lord's life,
which His enemies thought to need no further
particularization—"That deceiver." "We have heard
him speak blasphemous words against Moses, and
against God."[2] The first martyr is only one more
fanatic, deceiving and being deceived. "When they
heard of the resurrection of the dead, some mocked:
and others said, We will hear thee again of this
matter."[3] Just as if a cultivated Athenian audience
was to be taken in by such nonsense! And a careful study of the literature of the Oxford Movement of
this century will show that it was more than suspected
in some quarters that the Tractarians were guilty of
evasion and underhand methods. "As deceivers."
We have to face this pain also—as we proclaim the
paradoxes of the gospel in the foolishness of preaching,
the offence of the Cross in the losing of life in order
to gain it; in setting forth a Church system which
cannot be hurried, which demands for its completeness sowing, maturing, reaping, extending over a
long time. Listen to the tone of incredulity waxing
louder and louder, and still more querulous: "What
have you done? What have you to show? What

[1] S. Matt. xxvii. 63. [2] Acts vi. 11. [3] Acts xvii. 32.

results can you tabulate?" Over and over again we can trace, only thinly covered by the conventional politeness of society, the firm conviction underneath, that strong common sense has unearthed a delusion, and blunt honesty unmasked a deceiver.

I.

"As deceivers." Do we not sometimes detect a lingering suspicion in those to whom we deliver our message, that we are doing so merely because it is part of our profession; that, like the augurs, we cannot meet each other without laughing; that we are delivering an impossible message, to which we do not ourselves attach credit, but are bound to proclaim with a wearisome monotony? It is a terrible phenomenon when we see it. We know it better in the shape of the libertine who does not believe in the possibility of morality; but it is also to be found in the man who, for one cause or another, has lost touch with God, and believes only in the impossibility of belief. Such a case has been described in the man who is "bribed to disbelieve things which his conscience tells him are true, by doing acts which his conscience tells him are wrong." We have to go out into the world to deal with men who have largely ceased to have a God at all; to whom the command appeals not so much in its negative form, "Thou shalt have none other gods but Me," but rather in a positive form, "Thou shalt have a God." Whether it be the study of secondary causes which has so largely circumscribed the horizon of our vision, or the great advance of material prosperity which stifles the higher aspirations; or whether it be the loss of the spiritual sense, which no longer is able to appreciate the refinements of spiritual facts;—the result is the same. The supernatural dies away. As in old days the Egyptian saw the Nile fertilizing his land, and spreading life and verdure around it, until in his gratitude and wonder it became his god—an easier and simpler belief than the presence of an unseen God, in a far-off heaven, so it is now: men see workshops and machinery worked by almost superhuman intelligence, and the provident adjustments of an ever-thoughtful science. They do not worship the chimneys, nor sacrifice to the machinery, but they stop there at what they see. They do not quite see where a God would come in. They are practical men, and they can do without Him. They are accustomed to hard facts and unyielding laws; they must be pardoned if the visionary does not appeal to them, if they do not go beyond that which they can appreciate and verify. Or the Egyptian, again, saw the crocodile devour his child. It had strength, it had malignity; it must be appeased. He worships it, and raises it on a pedestal of superhuman power. Again, it is an easier belief than to carry his eyes upwards to a God invisible in the highest heaven. And so now, when death mows down with his sharp scythe a man's nearest and dearest friends, medical science investigates, can interpose between it and its further prey, can shed abroad beneficent remedies and healing medicines; but we do not, therefore, worship the physician, nor decree an altar to the genius of medical science; but we content ourselves with accurately measuring the laws of sanitation, the principles of health, and the power of the healing art; and there we stop. Turn where you will, there is a shrinking from God; from a personal God; from the supernatural. It is as when a valley is invaded by machinery, the blue goes from the sky, the green from the grass, the beauty from the flowers, the tenderness from the landscape. There is clatter and activity and work. Man has come in as a new tenant, and at first sight it is not so easy to see the traces of God's majesty as it was when we considered the lilies, or watched the fowls of the air, or gazed at the spreading tree and the waving corn.

> "The world is too much with us; late and soon,
> Getting and spending, we lay waste our powers:
> Little we see in Nature that is ours;
> We have given our hearts away, a sordid boon!"

Go and tell an ordinary man of the world that you are going, for instance, to pray for rain; speak to him in words which show that you are the messenger of the supernatural. He will soon show you that religion is a thing which must be very definitely kept in its place; that, consciously or unconsciously, you are a deceiver; that you speak conventional words, from which modern science has emptied out all the meaning. The old face is there, but the illumination from on high is suited only to the old-fashioned dial of a clumsy age, which has given place to a clock of perfected and accurate machinery. The minister of the supernatural, he must face it before long that he appears as a deceiver.

Think, again, how often it comes to pass that we hear muttered in our ears the one word "tendencies." We have tried to carry out what we believe to be the doctrine of the Church of England as regards sacramental truth, and we have been met with surprise and coldness, and the proverbial unfairness of unproved assertion. There is something behind it all, men seem to say. You mean more than you affirm; we detect tendencies. Or it may be that we have tried to restore the old weather-beaten church, to make it once more in appearance what it is in reality, the house of God; and there has been the letter to the newspaper, or the indignation meeting, and still again the sound of "tendencies." Or we have tried to realize in our services the idea of worship, we have endeavoured to make the church a centre of life and prayer, which is awake throughout the week, and not only on Sundays; and people have looked on coldly, and muttered "tendencies." Daily service may conceal a dangerous Pharisaism, and the frequent Eucharist be a trusting to forms. "Deceivers!" We feel it—we feel that we are not trusted. Or it goes even further; it penetrates into our home. Our unguarded actions, our looks, our words, our friends, our pictures, our books, are all scrutinized. Oh, how the newspapers gloat over a clerical scandal! Or, short of that, how infinitely it amuses the world to be confronted with the irony of a worldly priest pointing towards heaven; of a luxurious priest announcing the fasts of the Church; of a careless priest using the highly-strung phraseology of Church worship! A fall from a high position, an inconsistency detected, a weakness exposed, are all tremendous victories for the world, because men jump to the conclusion that the whole life had been always a conscious sham; that the higher life was even dangerous; that to practise its precepts and to aim at its ideals denoted either a hypocrite or a fool.

II.

There have been deceivers, and there will be deceivers. But this is what the minister of God must be able to answer, "And yet true." As if an assassin had stabbed a furious thrust, only to find his knife shiver to atoms before the coat of mail underneath. We know how, over and over again, truth has shown its power to assert itself. Read the graphic touches in which Dean Church has described the unfairness of suspicion, and the bitterness of attack, which for two years silenced Dr. Pusey at Oxford; and compare with them the almost fulsome praise in which on his death the public newspapers vied with each other not to appear lacking in appreciation, or removed from the circle of admirers of one of the most remarkable men of this century. There is this power in every true life to win the homage of men sooner or later, even if it comes after the lapse of centuries, and from other generations. The fathers kill, and the children build the tombs of those tardily recognized as prophets of truth; over and over again the cloak has fallen away, and, instead of the impostor, there has stood out the true man. In some hour of awful trial, of plague or sickness, when the hireling has gone, flying from the post of danger, the true shepherd is seen, fearlessly facing death; in the presence of some sickening scandal, in dealing with some abandoned case, where for the moment rescued and rescuer seem involved in a common cloud of stifling smoke and lurid flame. at last the true man stands out untouched. In the midst of forebodings and muttered threats, amidst the gaunt ruin of failures, and the depression of false movements and misplaced enthusiasms, at last it comes out. Here at length we have not been deceived; we are on firm ground. "Yet true." And so it comes to pass that whatever else we can part with in our methods—beauty, refinement, popularity, applause, speedy returns, quick profits—at least we cannot afford to part with this. We must be true men, dealing with truth, and in everything we advocate, in everything we do, be at least careful about this, that we deal with true work.

"And yet true." Where shall we look for this truth? First of all, in our doctrines. The assertions now advanced, and the concessions as to the precise value of some of the narratives in Holy Scripture, cannot at least be received with indifference. We cannot stand by unmoved when weapons which we before thought to be of first-class importance, turn out in their true estimate to be of very modified temper and of very ordinary workmanship. We listen with gratitude to the glowing tribute of praise which is passed on the poetry and picturesqueness of the Bible records. We cannot refrain a passing wonder at the ingenuity which has enabled writers to palm off a composite mosaic of the most elaborate kind, as a contemporary record of precise fact. We rejoice to hear that, in the story of the Fall, we have a picturesque description of the collapse of the will; in the Deluge, a graphic account of an inundation in the Eastern valleys, as a sign of God's wrath. But we remember, when before now we have told a tale of wonder to a little child; when we have lodged, as we hope, the most sound and important moral lesson, wrapped up in suitable myth, in his tiny heart, the breathless cry, "Is it true?" And we know the sigh which greets the discovery that it is only another phantom in this phenomenal world. And also, we know, that we have recognized this also as a paramount duty, as part of the respect which we owe to the child's young mind, to say, if it be so, "No, my child, this is not true; it is only a story containing a moral which I wish you to remember." And surely it makes all the difference in the world whether or not we are dealing with facts or fancies. We cannot quite accept as unimportant (albeit we must accept it with sorrow if it is the fact) that an historical setting is quite unnecessary, provided that the main spiritual or typical truth is proclaimed thereby; that we need care no more for accuracy of detail and an historical fitness, than we do for the empty rocket-case and bare stick, which descend unseen amidst the blazing showers which sparkle in the sky at some display of fireworks. Still, we hear grown-up children say, not, "Is it a beautiful story, or a gorgeous myth?" but, "Is it true?" If it be merely an interesting vehicle for conveying truth, why should we not have the old mythology at once? Hercules and his labours, instead of Samson; Orpheus and Eurydice, Helen, and the fabled Tantalus, and the woes of Prometheus. These contain in their history deep moral truths; they are full of lessons, but do not strain our faith, at all events at the present day, by claiming to be true. More than this, Jesus Christ came into the world as a great Teacher; He retold some of these stories, or at least endorsed them. Have I been taken in, as a child might be, by a fairy story, which he was allowed to believe to be true; and who now walks in a world the colder and barer because fairies have left it, and trust in the teacher in graver matters is somewhat shaken? Can we be quite happy if a fabled pair of ancestors is paralleled with the primæval sanctity of the marriage law; a fabled flood with the day of judgment; an impossible Jonah with a necessary resurrection? When Plato was constructing his ideal republic, he took a definite line towards ancient mythology, and announced how the myths should be received or rejected in his model state. Are we to believe that the Incarnate God, when founding His Church, was silent; or, worse still, did not know; or, worse still, was driven to an accommodation? Are we to believe that He, when as God He knew, and must have known, the strain upon faith that there must always be in the supernatural, yet deliberately willed to sacrifice Celsus or Porphyry, or the eager youth of this and many other centuries, to the torture of doubt, which one word could have put right? Further, are we to believe it possible, as has been pointed out in words solemnized to us by the nearness of death, that the Holy Spirit of truth could be associated with error and literary fraud, or that there is such a thing as the inspiration of inveracity?[1] Surely, whatever else it may be, it cannot be a light and unimportant change that we should be asked to part with the absolute truth of our sacred documents, or to think that righteousness of purpose or beauty of expression make up for inveracity. A brilliant piece of metal-work in a shop-window ceases to interest us when an expert whispers in our ear, "It is a pretty pattern, but it is not real; it glitters, but it is not gold."

III.

"And yet true." There is a little word somewhat bandied about in controversy, which we need to keep steadfastly before us, and that is "loyalty." Loyalty to the Church of England, loyalty to the Prayer-book, loyalty to the great Catholic Church to which we belong. Our whole lives must give the lie to the unjust muttering of "tendencies." Certainly, if we have not made up our minds about the English Church; if we think that she is only one out of many conflicting

[1] "The Worth of the Old Testament," Dr. Liddon, pp. 19, 20.

sects; if we can trace in her grand history no right to the ancestry of the Catholic Church; if we think that there is any doubt that our mother is the Queen and Lady that she is; if we think that anything we do not fancy in the Prayer-book must be at once supplemented from the formulæ of the sects or from the missal, in all the private judgment of a personal reformation;—it is difficult to keep the ring of truth and consistency, which at the last rises clear above "tendencies." Surely, in days like this, of restless movement and ill-considered schemes of private ecclesiastical enterprise, we must sacrifice more and more of the individual to the welfare of the whole body. We owe a great debt to Christendom to commend the Church of England " as true."

And still we come back to this—whatever he believes, whatever he says, underneath must be the true man. The minister of God cannot acquiesce in being a Caiaphas or a Balaam. But how difficult this is! How long it takes! The Church of which we are the ministers puts upon our lips the phraseology of a life so high that it is difficult to live up to it. What a depth of repentance lies beneath its simplest strains! A miserable sinner, under an intolerable burden, unworthy to pick up the crumbs at the Royal Banquet, with piteous cries for mercy, and frequent pauses for forgiveness,—this is the normal attitude of the devout worshipper. How impossible to substitute the cadences of a well-trained choir, or the postures of a well-regulated ritual, for the sentiments of devotion, mingled with abasement, which ring through these tones! Certainly ritual without reality, and praise without penitence, the outward glory of the Church without her inner life, sits awkwardly upon the soul. Ritualism without devotion is like a ring on a dirty finger, or the adornment of an unwashed face; the contrast is repulsive, and the incongruity is intensified. The Psalter, again, with its impassioned utterances, may so easily become a numbing unreality. "One day in Thy courts is better than a thousand,"[1] comes in with awkward emphasis at the end of a week of closed doors and neglected worship; or in the mouth of a holiday priest at a watering-place, who, as he says, is "off duty." "Thy Word is a lantern unto my feet, and a light unto my paths,"[2] hardly runs off smoothly from lips which seldom seek guidance from God's Holy Book, and know little of the rich labour and fruitful research of systematic meditation. "The Catholic Faith," "our holy religion," "the sacramental life," "worship,"—people are always on the look out for cant, and for that startling discrepancy between words and their meaning, which when intentional is irony, when not intended is of the essence of cant. Can we say, out of the very high life which the phraseology of the Church presupposes, "We are true men"?[3] Most certainly again and again we come back to this—it is the life which makes itself felt. "What we are comes before what we teach." The life which is fed on realities expresses itself in truth. There is a sad story of a priest who is described

[1] Ps. lxxxiv. 10.   [2] Ps. cxix. 105.   [3] Gen. xlii. 11.

as exhibiting a relic of the consistency of a hair to the veneration of the people, in a gorgeous reliquary; who, on being asked to point out the relic to one who wished to inspect it more closely, was fain to confess that for years he had exhibited it without himself seeing it. Whatever credit we may attach to the truth of this as a fact, as a parable its importance is evident. How many priests there are who exhibit that which they have never seen, praise that which they have never appreciated, discuss that which they have never studied, condemn that which they have never verified! And then there comes a false ring about the utterance, a false tone about the life; an eloquence which does not convince, a rhetoric which does not satisfy, a display which does not command respect.

We shall all of us be looked upon as deceivers; our doctrines, our words, our lives, our very selves, will be called in question. God grant that we may be proved to be true! And in the homage which we pay to truth, in the loyalty of our efforts, and in the sincerity of our lives, here too commend ourselves as the ministers of God. "To know that we are His servants shall keep us meek; that we are held fast by His hand shall keep us calm; that His great laws are not abrogated shall keep us sane."[1]

[1] "The Book of Isaiah," Rev. J. Adam Smith, vol. ii. p. 306.

CHAPTER XVIII.

OBSCURITY.

*"The universal instinct of repose,
The longing for confirmed tranquillity,
Inward and outward, humble yet sublime,
The life where hope and memory are as one."*

'Ὡς ἀγνοούμενοι, καὶ ἐπιγινωσκόμενοι
("As unknown, and yet well known.")

SURELY S. Paul could not give us a mark of the minister of God which is more distasteful than this to our modern ideas and practices. To be regarded as "an unknown," to work out of sight, without advertisement, without praise,—this is rather to be the victim of a misfortune, and to belong to the great body of the unappreciated. A whole literature is devoted to making public the most trivial actions of any one who for any reason has a claim to notoriety. We know their thoughts, their schemes, their opinions, their very faces; their alms are paraded in printed lists, their good deeds are sown broadcast in the religious intelligence of the gossiping paper. Abuse is better than silence; a caricature will do, if not a portrait. Let the King of Babylon's ambassadors see all the treasures if they will, even the gold of our inner life, or the treasures which we have gathered round our religious worship. Anything to be known. To be an unknown priest seems next akin to being held in utter contempt; not a thing to be coveted, or regarded as a mark of God's minister. And yet many things combine to correct this impression; to give us a more just estimate of true worth, and to show us the real value of obscurity. It is certainly a characteristic expression, one of the lines which mark off the expression in Him Who is our great Example. We have already glanced at the important lesson which underlies the choice of Nazareth for the abode of the representative Son of man; there He lived for nearly thirty years, until the spirit of the place settled upon His fame. And it came to be regarded as a sufficient bar to any caprice of the unexpected, to quote the verdict of an unvaried experience, "Can there any good thing come out of Nazareth?"[1] Or we read again, when the life of God shone most persistently through the human nature, with its inevitable attraction and persistent strength, "Jesus had conveyed Himself away, a multitude being in that place."[2] Again and again, apart from any deeper meaning which the circumstances of each case suggested, "See thou tell no man;"[3] or, "Jesus straitly charged them, saying, See that no man know it,"[4] barred the way to any display of popular applause, or expenditure of feeling on merely surface

[1] S. John i. 46.
[2] S. John v. 13.
[3] S. Matt. viii. 4.
[4] S. Matt. ix. 30.

approbation. Again, in prophecy it was foretold of Him, as a characteristic mark, of that which few have the strength to resist, or the wisdom to avoid, "He shall not cry, nor lift up, nor cause His voice to be heard in the street."[1] A message which requires attention, and a summons which requires thoughtfulness, would need the atmosphere of quiet, and the environment of obscurity. His own words emphasize the same truth, "How can ye believe, which receive honour one of another, and seek not the honour that cometh from God only?"[2] It is not a mere harmless compliance with the spirit of an advertising age; it is a renouncing of the way of God for the way of the world, the quiet of the garden of the Lord for the toil and competition which follows the taste of the forbidden fruit, and an unchastened desire to be thought wise.

And so it must ever be; to seek for honour in the ministry is the way to lose it. To seek for fame and notoriety is the sure way to contempt and failure. To exhibit oneself is to come under the rules which regulate the competition of the world, and to bid farewell to the higher class of talents, which, as being lent by God, are not for competition. These are words which we do well to lay to heart, "We have no trace of evidence that Christ forbade this advertisement also for His own sake,—as a temptation to Himself, and fraught with evil effects upon His feelings. We know that it is for this reason we have to shun it. Even though we are quite guiltless of contributing

[1] Isa. xlii. 2.   [2] S. John v. 44.

to such publication ourselves, and it is the work of generous and well-meaning friends, it still becomes a very great danger to us. For it is apt to fever us, and exhaust our reserve force, even when it does not turn our heads with its praise,—to distract us, and to draw us more and more into the enervating habit of paying attention to popular opinion. Therefore, as a man values his efficiency in the service of man, he will not make himself to be heard in the street. There is an amount of making to be heard which is absolutely necessary for the works' sake, but there is also an amount which can be indulged in only at the works' expense."[1] Hence there comes a danger to the very busy man, who spends his life immersed in a round of meetings, and in the maze of a network of organizations, lest the inner life, "like that river of which Alexander broke the strength," spend itself in channels which only dissipate spiritual intensity, while they seem to extend a thin ripple of Church life. Hence, too, there comes a danger to the man who, as he tells you with absolute frankness, never opens a book. In other words, one fountain of supply is cut off, while the demand upon the gushing stream is increasing on every side. Day by day the tax and demand on strength increases, without any attempt to keep up its source of energy. Or, again, there is the same danger threatening the man who tells you he has no time to say his Daily Office, or who never can find leisure to meditate, or who only goes to church when he is obliged. It means, once more,

[1] "Isaiah," Rev. J. Adam Smith, vol. ii. pp. 304, 305.

that other and more important sources still are dried up, and that many of the institutions and departments of life are already beginning to look brown and dry, as they are no longer touched by prayer, or refreshed by thoughtfulness, or watered by devotion. A man may soon get to dread and dislike all times of obscurity, and to fence with them, and curtail them, like a child querulous at the approach of bedtime, which yet means to it life and growth. The absence of society, the humble nature of the task allotted to him, the uncongenial atmosphere, may become at last so utterly distasteful, that he only finds relief in occupations unworthy of him, in purely lay pursuits, or in starring it about the country to the neglect of his own immediate charge; while he becomes less and less self-contained, more and more dependent on surroundings, bound to talk rather than think, to turn retreats into clerical meetings, and clerical meetings into afternoon parties, as the highway of life engrosses more and more of his heart, which is swept by flocks of fowls, who make it increasingly impossible for a serious thought to take root, or for the lessons of life to grow. But obscurity is the time for growth. When S. John Baptist has gone into the deserts, he is preparing for his showing unto Israel. When our life is screened off, God is working at it. The unknown parts of the day—those times when, like General Gordon, we put the signal outside the tent, which is to show that on no account is our communing with God to be disturbed; the unknown periods of our life, when the would-be biographer is puzzled to find no record, or is driven to invent; the quiet parish, where life circles round and round in uneventful monotony; the life which offers no startling features, or stern experiences; the stagnation, as it seems, or the absolute failure;—all these might be, and in thousands of cases are, times of immense growth. Happy the man who has early learned the all-important lesson how to live alone; how to withdraw himself, even in the busiest and most public life, into the quiet of suspended conversation and intercepted business. It is certainly a mark of the minister of God to know how to conduct himself, how to live, during those days, and those hours in every day, which the wise man is content to label, " Unknown."

II.

"And yet." Here is another of those wonderful disjunctives—a disjunctive in appearance, but more really a conjunctive; the one being part of the other. At those times when the minister of God has passed out of sight of the world, he has really passed within sight of something far higher and far better. At the very time when he is unknown in one direction, he is well known in another. And our thoughts turn to the time when the Apostle first entered Rome; just another criminal, another Jewish fanatic. Cæsar supped that night no less madly and furiously. The Prætorian guard had no foreboding of transferred allegiance. The unknown, ignominious, "ugly little

Jew" passed in, well known, however, to the hosts of heaven as the advanced guard of European Christianity, and the beginning of the downfall of the empire of paganism.

Our thoughts turn to the same Apostle on shipboard, "giving advice both gratuitous and uncalled-for; not to be listened to where there is a master and owner of the ship, who can give professional advice worth hearing;" and yet to him the angel of salvation wings his way. Our thoughts go back to Lot in the midst of a wicked Sodom and a heedless household; to Noah in the midst of a reckless world, unknown, uncared for, unrecognized, yet in touch with all the dread machinery of God's vengeance—unknown to the world, well known to God. And it begins to dawn upon us what is the true meaning of the Apostle's words.

No, we are not called upon to live in obscurity; to circle round in a dull eddy of unprogressive motion, or to wear ourselves out by a reiteration of grinding toil. We are called upon rather to live in the fierce light of the glory that streams from the throne of God. We may see sometimes, in a shop-window, one of those puzzle pictures, arranged to deceive the eye. When we first gaze at it we see two young people seated at a Moorish window—a representation of youth and happiness. A slight alteration in the focus of gaze, without altering a line or stroke of the picture, will show us a skull, the image of death. So it is with the world around us. It is only a question of adjusting the sight. It may speak to us of God, of His presence, of His greatness and beauty. We may see all around us the supernatural—the heavens declaring the glory of God, the firmament showing His handiwork; or in the same surroundings and the same images we may see only the skull, death, worldliness, fleeting fashion, the honour which comes from one another.

"And yet well known." (1) Surely it would be a help to us if we tried to remember that we are the agents of God in our different parishes. What a wonderful thought that is, which sees in the angel who receives the Apocalyptic message the representative of God in the different Churches! "Unto the angel of the Church of Ephesus write;" "Unto the angel of the Church in Smyrna write."[1] What a wonderful privilege that man should be God's angel, God's accredited agent, even to one single soul—His angel, who cares for the one lost sheep, and who must therefore earnestly look for the salvation and well-being of a whole parish. Think of the despair which sometimes breathes in the complaint, "I have only two hundred people to look after!" whereas He, the Divine Wisdom, devoted Himself to twelve poor peasants. It would be something to be well known to God, as His angel in the parish; to be known, as our voice day by day beats at the door of heaven, in the psalms and prayers of the Daily Office; that it should be our voice which summons Him to the careless, the dying, and the dead, and brings Him to His altar-throne, where the sick and needy can lay

[1] Rev. ii. 1, 8.

their wants before His felt Presence; that it should be our voice which summons Him to lay His hand upon the poor penitent, which enables us to say, "By His authority committed to me, I absolve thee;" our voice, which at night lays before Him the report of our stewardship for the day, as we tell Him what we have done and what we have taught.[1] This would elevate our surroundings, and make the most trivial life full of importance. Here am I God's agent, God's angel, His representative, His ambassador, well known to Him. Even if I do not mount platforms, and seek to stamp my own individuality on public questions; even if I am not sent for here and there, or noticed in the papers, or followed with admiring gaze; I am known in heaven. I have changed the focus of my vision; its well-known lines bend and converge with a wider circle of a fuller responsibility. "Our conversation is in heaven."[2]

(2) And the same thought would help us in our own personal lives, where there is so much to tempt us to lower our standard, where in the yearning for sympathy the strictness of gospel precepts seem to fit us like the starched stiffness and sombre gloom of a profession of piety, which are a menace to ease, and a protest to the common ways of life; until one by one we lay aside the refinements of the inner life. What a help it is then to remember, "I am God's messenger, God's angel; I am known there"! The glory of heaven must be respected more than the

---

[1] S. Mark vi. 30.   [2] Phil. iii. 20.

loose fashions of the hour. It is not merely a question of the covered or the uncovered head; a little piece of ritual which called for the interference of the Apostle in the affairs of the Corinthian Church.[1] The presence of angels is a postulate of religious worship; it might be an uplifting recall in daily life. The same thought might help us wherever we go. Cannot I do some good to this house where I visit? to this parish where God has placed me? Ought not men to be better, or conscious of help, because I have been there? Ought they not to be able to say, "This is an holy man of God, which passeth by us continually,"[2] and to be nearer the desire of their hearts because they have entertained us? When a government official is staying in a place, his presence is known by the letters and telegrams which reach him on the Queen's service. So the man of God, wherever he goes, is in daily official communication with Heaven. And so Holy Scripture has said, "Be not forgetful to entertain strangers: for thereby some have entertained angels unawares."[3] If we are only known to God, we never can tell whither He will send us; where He may wish us to find His lost sheep, or to help His servants. He may send us to the receipt of custom to find out S. Matthew; to Simon's house to restore a penitent. He may raise us on the cross to find a thief; or bid us give up ourselves to martyrdom to rescue a Saul; or to preach on the desert road to find a person of influence, or to languish in confinement to reach the Prætorian guard. To be

[1] 1 Cor. xi. 10.   [2] 2 Kings iv. 9.   [3] Heb. xiii. 2.

God's representative is a great and noble privilege. We move then attended by a princely retinue. Then we are never out of the sight of His eye; always well known to Him. "Before that Philip called thee, when thou wast under the fig tree, I saw thee."[1] He will say, after a long experience of our imperfect service, which His infinite pity has crowned with His own gifts, "Come, ye blessed of My Father, inherit the kingdom prepared for you from the foundation of the world: for I was an hungred, and ye gave Me meat: I was thirsty, and ye gave Me drink." And we shall answer, "Lord, when?"[2] "Unknown, and yet well known." This is abundantly true even in this world. As the sailor beats up the channel, he looks out for light shooting forth its long pencil rays across the sea. He welcomes it, and steers on his way, while perhaps he seldom stops to bestow a thought on the man who is watching in loneliness through the night that he may pass in safety. Unknown, yet well known. The passing ships know nothing of the man; yet to miss his light would be to grope in a dangerous sea, and to follow on in a blind course.

(3) And yet once more, we may welcome these words as a message of homely truth. Do not let us seek the empty glory of fame; being known to the many for superficial excellences and mere attractiveness. Let us seek the real comfort and happiness of being well known to a few. Here is a joy and a privilege, a power of being useful, which belongs to

[1] S. John i. 48. [2] S. Matt. xxv. 34, 35, 37.

the incumbent of the smallest parish, the worker in the least known thoroughfare of life. We can make friends of those whom God has given us, and become known to them, each and all among whom God has placed us, however unknown we may be to the world outside. We can be well known to the children. The school is not that dull drudgery which we are apt to think it. Children, eager as they are for play, and restless in their movements and difficult to engross, are yet keenly sensitive to the growing power of knowledge. The world is opening up before them its capabilities and its history, and who but the parish priest can show them the misty crags of God's holy hill, and the bulwarks of the city of God, where the horizon-line of this world melts into the unknown glories which lie beyond? He should more and more protest against any divorce between so-called useful knowledge and religion. It is unfair to both. Religion is far too solemn and serious a thing to leave it to the haphazard of chance and inefficient teachers. Barred off already by the conscience clause, as if it were a dangerous subject, it would be fatal to its position, in the quick, sensitive apprehension of the child, to see it removed altogether to a separate system of education. And, on the other hand, the so-called useful knowledge is far too solemn and sacred a thing that the parish priest should ever acquiesce in the entire removal of that branch of teaching from his care and supervision, and the general circle of his parochial interests. The religious character of useful knowledge and the real usefulness of religious knowledge are both of them to be insisted on. And when the present mad rush has swept by, and our doctrinaires have leisure to study the ruins of patriotism, honour, and morality which strew the path of a godless education, a time of reformation will come, when religion will once more be allowed to permeate education, instead of being gathered off in a scum, to be reserved for those who are foolish enough to wish for it. But the question at the present moment becomes a pressing and an anxious one—Would there be the contented acquiescence in the suppression of clerical control, would there be even the demand for its abolition, which we can trace in growing volume and persistency, if the parish priest had been more careful of his few sheep; if he had been contented to be unknown elsewhere, if he were known at school, if he had made his daily presence there as much a matter of conscience as his daily presence in church; if he had remembered that in this busy age the same public opinion which had generously given him the first place in the education of the children, must inevitably turn round to demand the abolition of a mischievous sinecure?

What parish, again, is so small as not to have its young men? What parish is so blessed as not to find them a terrible difficulty? Here is a task demanding both skill, time, and tact to get well known to them. Not a mere question, surely, of driving them into a room where there are chessmen and dominoes and an illustrated paper; not, surely, a mere question of subscribing to a cricket club, or of organizing an annual treat of wearisome prolixity and doubtful pleasure. While, perhaps, the minister of God is mourning over his loneliness and want of society, there are minds around him full of interesting problems, hopes beating high, ambitions which will fall a prey to the first adventurer; and here and there some native genius, covered over with earth and stones, waiting for some one to get out the precious metal and discover its worth. There are few places so utterly bare as to be devoid of interests like these. And how subtle and how numerous are the channels which connect the quiet parish with the great world outside! A member of Parliament rises in his place, and adds the weight of his authority and vote to a measure antagonistic to the first principles of Christianity, or, at least, hostile to the real interests of the Church and the welfare of religion. Would he have done so, or would he have done so with such ease, had he known that there was a strong feeling in the country against it? or, better still, if he had known the true precepts of Church doctrine which made such a proposal distasteful to Christian instinct? And yet, perhaps, Sunday after Sunday he has been allowed to believe that a sermon was a good time in which to give advice to simple country people. His parish priest has strung a few platitudes together on Saturday morning which would pass muster as a sermon, but has never grappled with the real difficulty of conveying great truths in simple language, and in a telling way, or realized that the great test of a preacher's power is his ability to deliver a plain sermon—that is, a sermon which would appeal to the Christian sympathies of the educated few, while it would be eagerly welcomed by those who are ever ready to give an attentive ear to what they can understand—the simpler members of the flock.

To be well known to a few,—this, after all, is a solid treasure which lasts amidst the wreckage of enthusiasms and the fleeting of popularity. It is touching now to find in some quiet country village the memories still fresh and green of a parish priest who lived among his people, and shared their joys and sorrows where other things have passed over them and left them unmoved. The rush towards the towns has come as an impulse over the clergy as well as the labourer, where life is stronger and quicker, and each day has its adventures. And yet one who impartially surveys the town and country clergy would find it again true, that it is the man and not the place which makes the real difference. The same man who idled away his time in the country because there were so few people, is inactive in the town because there are so many. Town schools are not more attractive than those in the village; town churches, misty with fog and gas, are not more inviting than the bare walls of the cold country church. The despair of overwhelming numbers in a town population may paralyze activity as much as the uneventful lives of the scanty handful of a rural population. To know, and to be known,—this rolls away selfishness, and the morbid seeking for a self-pleasing which never comes. But to know closely, as a life's interest, has its counterpart, which must be resolutely faced. It means, as far as we are concerned, to be unknown to those towards whom God has not entrusted us with peculiar duties, or asked from us more than that love which we owe to our neighbour, the world.

CHAPTER XIX.

DEATH.

> "Thou, in the daily building of thy tower,
> Didst ne'er engage in work for mere work's sake;
> Hadst ever in thy heart the luring hope
> Of some eventual rest atop of it,
> Whence all the tumult of the building hushed,
> Thou first . . . might'st look out to the east.
> The vulgar saw thy tower—thou sawest the sun."

> Ὡς ἀποθνήσκοντες, καὶ ἰδοὺ ζῶμεν.
> ("As dying, and, behold, we live.")

THIS was a thought and an expression which frequently came to the lips of S. Paul—death; the act of dying, crucifixion, mortification. And when we recall the vigorous, active life which burned in the Apostle from his earliest years—the "Hebrew of the Hebrews; as touching the Law, a Pharisee; concerning zeal, persecuting the Church;"[1] pushing forward in his missionary enthusiasm to "the limit of the west;" never baffled, never still;—then, perhaps, we feel that he knew more than most men the secret of that dying, the agony through which he

[1] Phil. iii. 5, 6.

reached the calmness as of death, the pain, the shame, the lingering weariness of crucifixion, the ebbing vitality of all within him which had contact with the earth. "In deaths oft;"[1] "I die daily;"[2] "By Whom the world is crucified unto me, and I unto the world;"[3] "As dying, and, behold, we live;" as if he would say the minister of God must know how to shut off all correspondence with the lower things which surround him—that is, to die. He must learn to be in correspondence with the higher environment of his being—that is, in the truest sense of the word, to live.

I.

(1) "As dying." He had known all that was meant by death in the region of *the spirit*. There was a time when, in the darkness of an unspeakable crisis in his life, when he sat sightless and panting like an animal that had dashed out its eyes by frantically leaping against the bars of circumstance, Ananias had come to him in the Straight street of Damascus, had put his hands upon his eyes, and had poured upon him the water, which meant both death and life. Then and there the old nature had changed; the vigour that was rushing away into the barren shoot of fanaticism was arrested, and turned into the living branch of holy zeal; the hasty dialectical temper, smartened with the wisdom of Gamaliel, was checked in its course, where it was rushing to form a mere intellectual rabbi, and was poured into the groove

[1] 2 Cor. xi. 23.   [2] 1 Cor. xv. 31.   [3] Gal. vi. 14.

which makes an apostle. The same man, yet how different! The life arrested and turned from one set of correspondences into another. All his old impulses dying, yet strangely living again in another direction. He looks over the life of grace; it was death and life together. Is it not so with those who devote themselves to God now, for His own more especial service? Does not God lead them on in the life of grace, beginning at baptism, until they have been able to die, in order to live? The same education would, it may be, have opened up a profession more lucrative, more full of self-gratification, more acceptable to the world's standard of excellence; but they die to this, that they may live to that which is higher. The physical strength which God gives, the vigorous health, the endowment, the technical skill, which might have run to waste in mere recreation, or the busy idleness of a worldly life, are turned into the service of God, or stand them in good stead in many a hard day's work in the village, or the town, or in the stern experience of the mission-field. Yes, their very sins betray some good qualities which have run off into wrong grooves, or have been allowed to develop themselves without restraint. These, too, God has known how to use; the house of Israel possesses them in the land of the Lord for servants and handmaids; they take them captive whose captives they were, and they rule over their oppressors. Anger dies away, and becomes alive in a judicial resentment and spirit of discipline. Pride dies out, and lives again in an honest striving after the true, the beautiful, and the good. Cowardice dies, and mistrust of self lives. Sloth dies; calmness and peace spring out of its ashes. Envy dies; holy rivalry takes its place. The death unto sin and the new birth unto righteousness, which started with Baptism, go on, as it were, in the spiritual life. The old fever bursts up again from time to time, and is slowly killed back by absolution, until the life which was only in correspondence with the lower side of our nature dies off into life—that is, into correspondence with the higher, with the spirit. "To be carnally minded is death; but to be spiritually minded is life and peace."[1]

(2) Further, the Apostle knew what was meant by death in the *moral* life, as well as in the sphere of spiritual experience. There is a well-known legend attributed to S. Macarius, which tells us how that when a young man asked him what was meant by mortifying his pride and being dead to the world, he asked him to go into a churchyard, and there, among the memorials of the dead, to praise and call by every flattering name, and load with every glorious title of fame, those who there lay buried; and, when he had done this, to return and tell the saint how they had answered him. He came back, and said, "My father, I have done as thou hast commanded me; I have praised and flattered the dead while in the presence of their monuments." "And what did they answer thee?" said the saint. "Nothing," was the reply. "Go now, my son, once more," he replied, "and blame them; pour insult and contumely upon

---
[1] Rom. viii. 6.

those whose graves thou seest before thee, and come back and tell me what they answer thee." Once more he returned, and said, "My father, I have done as thou didst command me; I have blamed and insulted the dead, and poured contempt upon their memory." "And what answer did they make to thee, my son?" said the saint. "Nothing, father," said the youth; "they are dead, and cannot speak." "So," said the saint, "must thou be in the presence of the praise and blame of this world—dead alike to its caresses and insults; and this is what is meant by being mortified, being like a dead man when the world is speaking." One who aspires to be the minister of God has to learn this death also; to be like a dead man in the presence of temptation. He has to labour and pray that he may reach that state in which temptation, when it comes, may find him like his Lord and Master, with all inclination to what is evil absent—a wilderness around him, and all inclination dead within; acquiescence gone, no traitorous voice, no timid half-unbarring of the door of resolution, no balancing of loss and gain, no fear of consequence barely outweighing the longing for present gratification—dead in the presence of moral evil. "Likewise reckon ye also yourselves to be dead indeed unto sin, but alive unto God through Jesus Christ our Lord."[1] But S. Paul would be the first to tell us that this mortification does not come naturally, but only slowly and with an effort. "I keep under my body, and bring it into subjection;"[2] "I die

Rom. vi. 11.   [2] 1 Cor. ix. 27

daily;"[1] "In fastings often;"[2] "Mortify therefore your members which are upon the earth."[3] It is one of the disappointing features of the present Church revival, that where so much has been done for the feasts, so little has been done for the fasts; that where every week has its Easter Day, in the fuller recognition of what is meant by the feast of Sunday, that it still lacks too often its Good Friday, by reason of the scanty observance of the Friday fast.

(3) And yet in one more region still the Apostle had realized this dying. He had faced death more than once, at the hands of infuriated mobs, on the lonely deep, amidst the howling storm, amidst the weary inaction of his confinement at Rome, as it presented itself to him in its cruelest forms. We must not forget this, the first and most obvious meaning of his words. Any one who has offered himself to God as His minister must have learned this lesson also, "Whosoever shall lose his life shall preserve it."[4] It is possible to think too much about our health, or to shrink from hard work and difficult tasks; and even to make nervousness on the score of health, and a mere tenacity of life, a terrible scourge to our reason betrayed of its true succours; to forget that it is better to die than not to do our duty. For, parry the stroke as we will, the day will come when the blow must fall, and death will not be put off any longer. And it may be that some of us are disquieted already, and are beginning to wonder how we

---

[1] 1 Cor. xv. 31.
[2] 2 Cor. xi. 27.
[3] Col. iii. 5.
[4] S. Luke xvii. 33.

shall face it, and think, perhaps, that as wise men we ought to be practising death now, in advance, before its terrors are upon us. It may be so. But he who is training for some great adventure, does not commence with taxing his strength to the utmost limit of endurance. He who is endeavouring to accomplish a leap of unusual dimensions, does not seek at first to compass the utmost limit of his capacity, but rather leads up to it little by little. So it may be that the way to die is almost to reverse the precept—"As living, and, behold, we die." It is to keep very close to God. To do each day's work as it comes, "with God onwards." It is by missing days out of life, by prayerless days, by idle days, that we suffer ourselves to be taken by surprise. With God each day prepares for the next. Over and over again, in sudden death as we call it, He has given the warning in the way which He knows how to give. It is by going on with Him, by daily breaking with the world, by daily loosing our hold on it in little things, that we prepare for death. When dying—behold, we live!

II.

It is for those who are bound closest to God by a vow of consecration to make the fullest ventures, to reach out more than others into the deeper life which opens out through the regions of death.

(1) For many years the Church of England had, alas! been reversing the process; living in ease and luxury, and abundance of idleness, in close correspondence

with all that the world calls life. And common experience had traced up over its failure, "Thou hast a name that thou livest, and art dead."[1] Then, like pioneers of an expedition into a foreign land, where a past and almost forgotten experience had told them there was life, and there was treasure, here and there devoted souls embarked; leaving the world, leaving possessions, friends, and ease, to seek for themselves a higher life, a fuller life; to spend it not on self, but on the Church. And have they not found it? How little do we know about the possibilities of life, or, indeed, of that which is going on around us! If we take a child to see a picture-gallery, perhaps he will fasten his attention on the frames; if we take him to hear a concert, he may be captivated simply by the noise of a drum. Have we not all of us felt at times the poverty of our experience, when an antiquary has taken us through some of our most familiar haunts, and peopled them with moving figures out of the past; or a botanist has shown us the treasures stored in our common lanes, or the geologist the history written on the stones beneath our feet, or the astronomer the glory and beauty of the stars? Have we not felt at such times what treasures lie around the borderland of our familiar experience, unnoticed and unknown? And amidst the other duties of the ministerial life, more striking, more apparently useful, with a quicker and more obvious return, is there not still a wide field of rich treasure opening out before the contemplative

[1] Rev. iii. 1.

life—for those who, in a constant round of prayer and meditation and study, search for the things new and old in the great treasure-house of God? Is there not room for those who study God's mysteries on their knees; for those who would show us the highest flights of which human nature is capable in the spiritual life? Are we at home yet in the higher spirituality? Do we quite understand how human nature can be connected as it were with the Sermon on the Mount? How, for instance, meekness can possibly be a master virtue; how love of enemies can become practicable, natural, and salutary; how poverty and persecution may come to be regarded as blessed states, in possession already of the kingdom of heaven; how love is meant to be the ruling power in human life. Are there not yet great correspondences to be traced by those who have severed themselves from the lower life—correspondences with the high and noble things of God? An active age has always disliked contemplation. In looking back on an age when activity largely meant killing and plundering, we can still only speak of the lazy monks. In the ceaseless rush of the present day, when every one who is not a river, at least wishes to be a brook, if it be only to turn a millwheel, we find it difficult to distinguish between the repose of stored strength and the stagnation of arrested life; to distinguish between a lake and a pond, a river pool and a roadside puddle. So that, again, we are brought face to face with the beauty and the responsibility of a quiet life. From those to whom God gives a greater measure of outer repose, and whom He withdraws into the wilderness, we look for greater ventures into the spiritual world, for freer and fuller contributions to the science of the highest life. Some seek retirement, some are forced into it; but both may have larger opportunities than the restless activity of the world allows, to study that life so difficult to all, which is put before us by the Apostle as a life hid with Christ in God.[1]

(2) But besides ventures into the region of the contemplative life, it is for those who are consecrated to God to show us what can be done in the ascetic life as a power in the world. Asceticism is not a thing from which we ought to shrink as unreal and unpractical; nor, on the other hand, is it a mediæval toy to be played with: it simply means discipline and the life of rule. All sin, all the disorder of this fallen world, lie in the warping of the will towards the gratification of wrong desires—those things, that is, which God by His eternal law has forbidden; while it is by discipline of the will, by constant practice, by learning to submit the will to rule, and putting it under the constraint of thwarting precepts, that a man is able to pass through the world unscathed. Dying to sin, he lives only unto God. And in an age where there is so little discipline, where wilfulness penetrates to our very religion, where the field of human enjoyment gets ever wider and wider, where men are laid low all around us by disordered lives, unbridled wills, and unrestrained appetites, it is surely

[1] Col. iii. 3.

something that those struggling in the world should have examples to fall back upon, of the highest and purest morality, of a life regulated and guided by a well-trained will. We have already tried to see the value of a rule; it is valuable in what it secures for us, and it is also valuable in itself, because it helps us more and more to keep our lives under the influence of a will which has learned to submit itself to the direction of Almighty God. While to those who, like the ministers of God, have to grapple with sin in its most deadly forms, it is a simple necessity. The discipline of the soldier is not an ornament which will help him to make a display on the parade-ground; it is his safety in the hour of battle, or in the terror of some lonely outpost duty, or in the despair of an enforced retreat. So with the priest; it is in the strength of the disciplined life that, as from a higher vantage-ground, he is able to stretch out a helping hand to those who are struggling with sin; it is self-discipline which prevents him from quailing before the powers of darkness in his lonely watch, or consoles him in his apparent failure. For sin is not the simple thing we are apt to consider it to be, neither will it give way to shouts and disordered menaces, or the display of ill-regulated force. It requires to be dislodged by very serious tactics, and driven back by very vigorous measures. And in the ascetic life of those who live in obedience to discipline, and the restriction of rule, we have the training which is to help the Church to grapple with the forces brought to bear against it, in the deliberate effort of those who have taken their Lord and Master at His word, and, believing that this kind of evil spirit goes not out but by prayer and fasting, have submitted themselves to His guidance and discipline, while they strive to bring every thought into captivity to the obedience of Christ. It is a contrast, indeed—a contrast as strong as that between life and death which we see in the two forms of life which meet in our parishes, where the true minister of God is struggling to save the servant of sin. Here is the strong, well-disciplined life, where not a thought passes in unchallenged, where no region of life lies outside the domain of duty, no appetite roams abroad without its tether and well-defined limit. And, on the other hand, there is the poor struggling, fluttering life, crushed and bleeding, yet unable to avoid that which bruises and maims it. A soul groaning under cruel taskmasters, yet pretending it is free; driven back always by the iron wall of habit, which bars the road to freedom, which looms darkly behind the fringe of dancing flowers, which beguile it with the fantasy of freedom, and the delusion of an unfettered life.

Strong in the power of discipline, certain of his retreat, undismayed, undeceived, the minister of God advances to the rescue. Calmly and patiently he is striving to extricate the victim, impotent from long acquiescence in slavery, dazed and stupefied by the poisonous atmosphere which he has so long been breathing, scared by the very freedom to which he has been so long a stranger. We need more than good will in releasing sinners, more than a general philanthropy, and a wish to do good. Thousands of years of experience in a fallen world are against us; a power curbed by the Cross, which, however, can be made of none effect to those who despise it. Hard work like this needs hard men. As God said of old to Gideon, "By the three hundred men that lapped will I save you,"[1] so He says now Not by those who go down on their knees to drink, and forget the eagerness of the warfare, and the fierce nature of the struggle, but by the three hundred that lapped, by those who simply taste of life's pleasures as a refreshment in warfare, in absolute self-restraint, unhindered in pursuit, unwearied in the struggle, will I drive back the hosts of Midian who prowl around the camp of Israel.

(3) There yet remains the region of the active life, to which the ascetic life has already partially introduced us. There were regions of unexplored wealth, which opened up through the spirit; the restraint of the ascetic life, which bound a man to higher things, seemed necessary to one so perilously occupied, and enabled him to reach further, by means of the discipline which seemed death to freedom, but which really secured a wider range of power. The minister of God still must feel that his powers and his opportunities have not been given him selfishly to enjoy; that he is in no sense his own; that the self within him which would pile up power, or build a tower of Babel, or sit down and contemplate full barns, and think only of building and filling bigger;

[1] Judg. vii. 7.

—that all this must die within him, and that his life must expand in activity and usefulness around him. It is one of the saddest sights of the present day to notice not only the idleness, but the acquiescence in idleness; or in the fixed idea of their own helplessness, which characterizes so many lives. Schools and universities pour out their thousands of educated or semi-educated scholars; and what becomes of them? How little realization is there of a duty towards the world! The minister of God should at least set the highest example in this, of a life which is not his own; which is dead to all self-pleasing or mere selfish enjoyment—dead to self; which is at the disposal of others, at the beck and call of their numerous needs; he must show that "a man's life consisteth not in the abundance of the things which he possesseth;"[1] he must be ready to go off to the mission-field if God so orders; he must feel, when tempted to take his ease, "There are those of my brethren who are failing for want of support; how can I help them?" he must check any thought of luxury, by the vision of the starving multitude around him; or any repining at the hardness of his lot, by the thought of sorrow as being an elevating cross, rather than a blow to happiness. Self is always trying to push up its mushroom growth, out of all manner of circumstances, and self must be resolutely killed down by the thought of our mission to the world, and all the consequences involved in it. The life which opens out before us all, has its correspondences of death and its

[1] S. Luke xii. 15.

correspondences of life. Let the minister of God meet it by the high spiritual life, which kills off all that connects itself with the lower and the base; which has mortified everything that is bad; which is like a dead man in the presence of sin, or of anything which is lower than the highest. Let him meet it by a spirit of detachment, which sits loosely to the things of this world; which values something more than health, ease, reputation, or self-pleasing; which chooses death because it is assured of this, that all along the line *mors janua vitæ*.

CHAPTER XX.

CHASTISEMENT.

"The joy of an accepted sorrow."

'Ως παιδευόμενοι, καὶ μὴ θανατούμενοι.
("As chastened, and not killed.")

IT must surely be one of the hardest tasks which a surgeon is called upon to perform, to operate upon a very little child. The piteous appeal, the terror, the wild apprehension, the belief that the pain inflicted is wilful, and to no purpose or ultimate good,—all this to a sensitive mind must be very hard to bear. The same sort of feeling in its degree is felt in doctoring any of the lower animals; they do not understand it, and at the best patiently accept it as a mysterious pain inflicted from a quarter which they have habitually learned to trust and love. And in like manner, in us who are grown-up children, and think we know something of the ways of God, it requires a considerable amount of faith, assurance, and certainty, to enable us to talk with sincerity about chastisement. S. Paul, even when he had died to the old Saul, did not always find it easy; the long list of spiteful inflictions, of scourgings and stonings, and hardship and peril, show us scars cut deep into a nature in itself sensitive and proud. He did not recognize in the unmannerly roughness of officials, or the coarseness of the presiding high priest, the hand of a chastisement. Human nature, even in him, cries out in its sense of failure, loneliness, and weariness which sometimes press upon him. And oftentimes we fear lest we pain the heart of the all-loving God, when He sees how little we still understand chastisement. All around us men are chafing and groaning, blaspheming or snapping off under His punishment. They feel the hardness of sorrow, the bitterness of pain, and they see no reason for it nor correction in it. Here the intellect strains and groans under its restrictions, and injures itself as it bends before the wind in its chafing against the prop of faith. We wish to stand alone and bear the brunt of every blast of error which sweeps across the world, without being held firmly erect by a prop, which indicates weakness, and which prevents a full opposition to the rising storm. In our petulance we cry out—What do we care for faith? Give us freedom; a firm hold in the earth which we have made for ourselves, not a dependence on cut-and-dried dogmas of an abstract faith. The old moral sore has healed up so long, and remains only as a weakness or a scar. Why, then, is it necessary to reopen the wound, and cut away in pain and anguish to the root, that which we find hard to believe is there rankling into disease? Life is so easy, so peaceful, so happy, that we can only writhe and groan, and grovel in despair, as the wind of trial snaps here, and loosens there the cords, which would make it impossible for us to leave this earth without too grave a wrench. We are familiar enough with the pages in the world's vocabulary which deal with these things; "trouble," "misfortune," "affliction," "bad luck," are all terms which we know. But the minister of God has to show what he is in trouble as in joy; he is as one chastened. To him it is remedial, retributive punishment, not death.

I.

Now, chastisement in the ministerial life will take many forms, and we shall have in many ways to set the example of bearing it. And it is difficult to avoid repetition in dealing with just another stroke in those series of sombre lines which have given us the portrait of the minister of God, sad even when powerful. And it would not be true to nature if we did not recognize in this dark line, first of all, the mark of professional chastisement—the chastisement which comes to us in so far as we are priests, rather than in so far as we are men. How an earnest man grows to his profession, how its joys and sorrows are among the keenest which sweep across men! Holy Scripture, as it is always so minutely true to nature, shows this professional sensitiveness in the touching character of Eli, with its strange mixture of strength and weakness. He endured the news of Israel's defeat, the news of the death of both his sons; but when he heard of the loss of that sacred trust, which was dearer to him than life, he fell backwards and died.[1] Dearer than patriotism, dearer than home affection, dearer than life, was the ark of God, once his glorious charge, now his irreparable loss. And what minister of God is there who has not before now listened anxiously for news from the battle, where his cherished schemes are bandied about in the throes of political strife; to hear whether the scanty endowments which are to him the sinews of war in his conflict with sin are to be taken from him to satisfy the greed of some political exigency; to hear whether the children whom he has loved and taught are to be taken out of his care, because she who is not the true mother of the child is ready to say, "Let it be neither mine nor thine, but divide it"[2]—let it be brought up without religion at all rather than be brought up in the doctrines of the Church? Many can still remember the bitterness of the sorrow, when newspapers brought in records of ecclesiastical proceedings in the law courts, to be discussed at public-houses, and to be piled up as fuel on the fires of controversy, when brother went to law with brother before the unbelievers, and the most solemn verities of our faith, or the simple exponents of religious worship, were held up to execration and contempt. Many an Eli has been tempted to despair during the last fifty years, and still the battle rages. And things which are discussed as abstract questions elsewhere, press on the servant of God as being matters of life and death. With much labour and difficulty he has taught his people the truth enshrined in the Church Catechism;

[1] 1 Sam. iv. 18.   [2] 1 Kings iii. 26.

by the next post his people may read that it is doubtful, or at the best an open question. With infinite trouble he has secured the outward decencies of worship in his church; his people have begun to like it, and enter into it. Some party paper whispers, "Superstition!" and a blight falls on his efforts. Or he is dealing with souls—so delicate, so difficult, so disappointing. He has prayed, and laboured, and taught, and braced up, when a sudden twist, an unlooked-for turn, snaps the flower away, or an unseen influence sweeps over them. One morning all seemed so fair, and now a night's frost has nipped off all the bloom, and all apparent hope of fruit is gone. There is the choir with whom he has taken so much trouble, whom he has trained to be the mouthpiece of Divine worship, and the pattern of reverence. It comes upon him with the shock of a blow, shattering his methods, and shaking his very principles of action, to find out that one of the men has been living in deadly sin, which most people knew except himself. To see the policeman come for one of the boys; to become conscious that they are quite unimpressed by the awe which clings to holy things; unmoved by the greatness of religious worship; asleep at the Transfiguration, asleep at the Agony, unheeding during the most awakening appeals; at the end uninstructed, with no definite hold on Church belief;—this is no uncommon experience in choirs. Or, again, he takes the list of his Confirmation candidates. They all seemed in earnest once; what are they now? Some have drifted off altogether into careless lives; some are opposing the Church

T

in which they promised to believe; some few are regular communicants. But it falls like a sharp blow to find that so much of the seed which was sown in severe self-denial, in the coldness of a winter's night, or in the interval snatched from a very wearying day, the product of thought and prayer, has fallen on stony ground, or has been choked with thorns, or has been devoured by birds. It strikes right across his self-respect; it makes him feel, "Am I fit to teach?" It drives him away into a feeling of despair and a faithless forsaking of a discredited trust. Or who is there who has not before now smarted under the pain of being taken in, either by hypocrisy which has traded on religion, or by the many ramifications of a mendicancy which respects neither honour nor religion? When these blows beat down on our self-respect, and we feel ourselves humiliated in our powers, or in our discernment, or practical wisdom, then there is a better chance for asking ourselves that searching question of self-examination, to which every priest should be able to give an answer—the question which Satan with his keen perception asked about Job, "Doth Job fear God for nought?"[1] Are we quite sure that we are disinterested? Are we quite sure that it was not the quiet life that attracted us, or the love of authority, or the learned profession, or a sense of our own power? These blows, in so far as they fall across us, serve to take the self out of our work, and mercilessly cut away all the self-sufficiency which too often underlies

[1] Job i. 9.

"*my* choir," "*my* communicants," "*my* people," "*my* parish," which have become to us the very measure of the universe, the puff of platforms, and the advertisement of the journal. But these chastisements incident to our profession we feel to be salutary to our souls; we must expect them. We are dealing with men and women; we must not look for a rigid uniform result as following of necessity from well-known causes. This rigidity may be a failure, even where you find it to exist. The firm, well-ordered parish, hedged in by statistics, may be, after all, like the arrangement of artificial flowers: they are perfectly correct, perfectly stiff, they don't even want water; whereas the real ones hang down their heads, and snap, and fall, and drop, and go all awry, and need looking to, and constant refreshing. But they have this merit, that they are alive. This parochial, professional chastisement is one which we are bound to expect, hard to bear, and galling to our pride.

II.

It is more obvious to turn to personal chastisements those punishments which come to us as men; and there is one which all have to bear at some time, but some more than others, and that is bad health. It is touching to notice how patiently this is submitted to very often by the poor, to whom it means so much. "It is all what pleases God," is their simple comment of complete resignation. But to the minister of God also ill health means a good deal. There are two dangers attending it: the one seems to be, not to know when he ought to give in; the other, not to know when he ought to keep on. That is to say, there are times when God interferes, and tells us in ways which we cannot misunderstand that He will take charge of the parish for us; when we can no longer go to school, or go into choir, or visit the people, or minister in the Church; when we have simply to let things go, or rather resign them into God's hand. Then, what a difference there is between the man who recognizes God's chastisement and one who does not! If God withdraws us, it is that He may take our place; it is that He may tell us, and tell our people, that He has no need of us. Perhaps at the very time when work was becoming too personal, or too much of an advertisement, or people were beginning to lean on the man rather than on the realities of the faith to which he pointed them, then God withdrew the agent, and taught Himself in his place with little or no human intervention. Whereas, on the other hand, the chastisement consists sometimes in going on beneath the Cross, in speaking words which are emphasized by pain, in making visits which have defied the impediment of sorrow, in teaching with manifest difficulty, in labouring under a distressing weight. It is told of Francis Borgia "that he was asked to preach at a certain church in a distant city, and that on his arrival he was too ill to speak, and requested some one to occupy his place. 'No,' said the priest who had summoned him, 'only mount the pulpit, say nothing, and come away.' He did so; hearts were touched, people burst into tears, and the confessionals were filled with penitents; he was a man of prayer," and therefore God spoke through his silence.[1] It may be that this also is God's will for us, that the shadow of the Cross should be shed abroad from our lives by the fierce glow of sorrow within; that the pain which burns there, consuming our strength, should throw out into strong relief the message of the sombre Cross, and the message be the message of our lives rather than the message of our lips.

III.

Yet, once more, besides the chastisement which reaches us through our profession, and the chastisement which corrects us through our personal lives, there are the blows and buffeting which smite us in the region of the spirit, where the priest is most obnoxious to the strokes of sorrow. There comes upon us, with a persistence sometimes little short of a pain, the smart of temptation. We are conscious at such times of the terrible affinity of our weak nature to many forms of sin, or to a lower life, which startles and frets us; and yet we feel that these very twinges and pains are merciful monitors speaking to us, in tones which cannot be misunderstood, the warning message, "Let him that thinketh he standeth take heed lest he fall."[2] The death of a scientific man which was chronicled a few years ago in the newspapers, contains for us a significant parable. He

---

[1] Baring-Gould, "Post-Mediæval Preachers," pp. 132, 133.
[2] 1 Cor. x. 12.

was, we are told, investigating the origin of a plague of locusts in the East, and he was found suffocated by millions of them, which had settled upon him, it is supposed, as he had fallen asleep, in the midst of his labour. So, as we move in the midst of sins, which we are striving to eradicate, we must expect to feel from time to time the smart of temptation. The pain and the shame and the difficulty we feel are all merciful chastisements; they make us feel how close we are to dangerous foes, and how slight is the barrier between us and destruction. Or the same sort of trouble comes to us in our devotions. What a scourge is spiritual dryness, when our prayers, our thanksgivings, our very communions, are all unmeaning to us! When He makes as though He would go further,[1] and we seem hardly able to constrain Him to stay, —this, too, is a chastisement, a correction of our spiritual life, a correction of the past wastefulness, urging us to a closer communion with Him. Has our life of devotion hitherto been any mere self-pleasing? Has it been only to satisfy feeling, or a simple luxury of the imagination? Have we learned to reach out to God? As one by one all the outposts are driven in, we are constrained to fall back upon Him. And we find that the spiritual deadness has in itself helped us; it has enabled us to feel His overshadowing Presence. No, not killed! It is wonderful to find the vitality which still remains beneath the heaviest chastisement. The enemy may burn us, cut us down to the ground, shave off the locks of our consecration,

[1] S. Luke xxiv. 28.

and yet there remains a strong power of life within. "There is hope of a tree, if it be cut down, that it will sprout again, and that the tender branch thereof will not cease. Though the root thereof wax old in the earth, and the stock thereof die in the ground; yet through the scent of water it will bud, and bring forth boughs like a plant."[1] Only let us learn to bear God, to practise *sustinentia*—the power of bearing—and then pain will help us, where misfortune only slays the ungodly. God knows best what He is obliged to put upon us, if we are to carry the weight of His exceeding great glory. Boyish troubles and boyish discipline made ready the heart for the grace of God in Confirmation. The discipline of penitence prepared our hearts for the mighty gift of our communions; and now are we strong enough to bear the full grace which awaits us in the priesthood? God never builds a graceful superstructure on a crumbling base. If we will let Him, He cuts and carves away until He gets down to the rock. Natural aptitude, untiring energy, powers of organization, powers of command, eloquence, teaching, skill of different kinds,—these may be only so much sand, which support a fair-weather structure, when the air of popular applause breathes softly, and life's sea smiles without a ripple; and God levels them to the ground, and sweeps the sand away that He may get down to the rock, where the house may be built on the love of God, not on the applause of men. Or there is some virtue lacking in us which He wills to give us, which as yet we are not able to

[1] Job xiv. 7-9.

bear; some little thing which means perfection, some little thing which weighs us down. S. Christopher carries people over the stream all day long without feeling it; it is the little child which weighs him down. Perhaps now it is just some little weight which we refuse to carry, for which God has to prepare us, that we may offer to Him the entire sacrifice of self-surrender, of perfect self-discipline, and absolute self-denial. If we are holding back any one thing from Him, He will correct us until we yield it up.

So, once more, must the minister of God exhibit himself as not killed by the chastisement which so many seem unable to bear. Alas! we know something of men who have given up in failure, who sit mournfully in their boats as dawn succeeds night, tossing on the sullen sea, which hitherto has mocked all effort, and has yielded no return to labour. They read in the papers of vigorous efforts crowned with success, of methods hitherto untried by them, of the dawn of better things, of Jesus pointing to the right side of the ship, with new hopes and new promises; but they have lost their vitality, and lost their hope. They do not believe in the sacramental system—it is sacerdotalism; nor in multiplied services—it is formalism. They do not believe in parochial agencies—it is spoiling the people; they do not believe in clergy interfering in education—it is the province of the State. All these methods will have their day, and fail like their predecessors. And yet there was a time, when they first came to their parishes, when they put forth into the deep with alacrity and eagerness; and the persistent chastisement of failure has killed out hope. It is a terrible thing to despair of the power which God has put into our hands, or to read our own inactivity into the barrenness of the unyielding sea. We know something also of lives which have bowed before the strokes of pain and personal sorrow; who have shrunk from bearing the cross, until the cross has ceased to bear them. The valetudinarian, the slave to comfort, the man who has his eye only on the temporal advancement of the ministry,—misfortune can only too easily slay such an one. There is a good deal of the spirit of Ananias and Sapphira still among us, which crops up in the great surrender of ordination. Men cannot forget the long years of expensive education, or the rich prizes which seem to be dangling within their reach. They keep back part of the price; they make a reservation in their sacrifice, and the chastisement of God is the death-blow to their hopes, and they become melancholy, discontented, dead while they live, as those who have failed in a commercial speculation.

But harder still is it to keep alive the spiritual life under the repeated blows which are necessary to work out its perfection. Never for one moment are we able to relax our efforts, never for one moment can we leave our spiritual life to itself. To relax our efforts is to drift back on a strong tide. To relax our vigilance is to find ourselves surrounded by a masterful enemy, while over our best actions comes the film of imperfection, which has to be removed in pain and discipline. Truly the portrait of God's minister almost repels us by its very sternness; and we feel that, as we leave it, there are finishing strokes still darker, which must come in yet. It is told of Cardinal Bellarmine that, when asked by a friend for his portrait, he replied, "Which portrait do you want? The likeness of the old man, or of the new man?" The old man, he said, was not worth having, whereas the new one was not yet finished. This is the end of all chastisement—"let patience have her perfect work, that ye may be perfect and entire, wanting nothing."[1] But there are times in a man's life when he finds it hard to say, "The Lord hath chastened and corrected me: but He hath not given me over unto death."[2]

---

[1] S. James i. 4.   [2] Ps. cxviii. 18.

CHAPTER XXI.

SORROW.

"There are wounds of the spirit which never leave us, and are intended in God's mercy to bring us nearer to Him, and to prevent us leaving Him by their very perpetuity. Such wounds, then, may be almost taken as a pledge, or at least as a ground for humble trust that God will give us the great gift of perseverance to the end."

'Ως λυπούμενοι, ἀεὶ δὲ χαίροντες.
("As sorrowful, yet alway rejoicing.")

A MAN was once asked if he saw any difference in the faces of two very striking sisters who had just passed before the window out of which he was gazing into the street, and he answered, "I think I detect in the one a sort of *arrière pensée de douleur*."[1] An undertone of sorrow—is not this what we detect in so many whom we meet in the world? With some it is an undertone; a kind of moan of sadness, which is never quite absent. In others it is the dominant tone which pervades their utterance. It is an inner presence which has stamped itself on the lines and

[1] I am indebted to Canon Knox-Little for the above illustration; it occurred in a speech made at Worcester some years ago, the impression of which is still vivid in my memory.

wrinkles of their face; it has weighed down their figure and weighted their footsteps; it has taken off their chariot-wheels so that they drive them heavily. It is to be noticed sometimes in people whom we have not met for a long time. Experience has been writing a history on their face, and some of its lines are cut very deep.

Whatever may have been the road by which God has hitherto led us, whether through dancing sunshine or hard pitiless storms, and hours of desolating darkness, the time comes sooner or later to all, when we are so thankful that we can look up to a face marred more than the sons of men, and crowned with thorns, instead of parading our gaunt sorrows before an unheeding god, of smooth unruffled beauty, and lapped in voluptuous ease, tossing aside pain from his limbs of perfect symmetry, unmoved by even a passing care, untouched by the smart of a passing pain. With the merciless irony of unconscious truth, the Epicurean poet portrays the absolute gulf which must exist between the gods as the heathen conceived them, and the troubles of men as they experimentally knew them.

> "Omnis enim per se Divum natura necesse est
> Immortali ævo summâ cum pace fruatur,
> Semota ab nostris rebus, sejunctaque longe;
> Nam privata dolore omni, privata periclis,
> Ipsa suis pollens opibus, nihil indiga nostri
> Nec bene promeritis capitur, nec tangitur irâ."[1]

And yet under these splendid lines we detect the forlorn despair of humanity forsaken of its natural

[1] Lucretius, i. 45.

protectors. After centuries of Christian tenderness and love we can but say, this god is not our God. "Their rock is not as our Rock, even our enemies themselves being judges."[1] The time comes to us all, sooner or later, when we see more the deep meaning of sorrow as it comes from the hand of God, and recognize the possibility of a state which can be described as "sorrowful, yet alway rejoicing." And we do well to remind ourselves, first of all, of the attitude of our blessed Lord towards sorrow and pain, the great problem of the thinking world, when it tries to adjust its path to the strange vicissitudes of suffering that threaten to overwhelm it. "Fly from it," said the Epicurean; "Ignore it," said the Stoic; but Christ said, "Use it." "Sorrow, like the ravens which fed the prophet, will come charged with blessing to the soul." He went further; He distributed sorrow around Him, as a kind of royal *largesse,* wherever He went. His infancy was surrounded by the wailing of babes at Bethlehem. His death was associated with the martyrdom and sorrow of His dearest friends. All suffered who came near Christ; nay, more, we may say now, all whom the King delighteth to honour are called upon to suffer still. We, the ministers of God, entered on our service as priests of the King of Sorrows, prepared to meet them in His strength, and to scatter their gloom by the consolations by which we ourselves are comforted of God.

[1] Deut. xxxii. 31.

I.

"Sorrowful." Whither does this word take us? Perhaps, first of all, to Gethsemane; to the scene of the Agony and Bloody Sweat, where the Soul and Body of the Incarnate God were weighed down, crushed and bleeding, beneath the weight of sin. It must be so for us priests, as we stand at the Altar to plead the great Sacrifice; as we go before God to offer up the prayers of the people; as we come forth, perhaps in our youth and untouched strength, as yet inexperienced in many of the hardest struggles of life, to speak to grey-headed men, to the sinful, to the sorrowing, to those who are torn and lacerated by the awful tragedies of life. If our actions are not to be a hopeless mockery, if our words are to be anything else than empty platitudes,—it must be so. We must have gone out into the night, and over the brook, and knelt down in the garden, and there felt that load of sin, which, whether we know it or not, has been upon us with its dread weight and stifling embrace.

"My God! my God! and can it be
 That I can sin so lightly now,
And think no more of evil thoughts
 Than of the wind that waves the bough?

"I sin, and heaven and earth go round,
 As if no dreadful deed were done,
As if God's Blood had never flowed
 To hinder sin, or to atone.

"I walk the earth with lightsome step,
 Smile at the sunshine, breathe the air,
Do my own will, nor ever heed
 Gethsemane, and Thy long prayer.

"Shall it be alway thus, O Lord?
　　Wilt Thou not work this hour in Me
The grace Thy Passion merited,
　　Hatred of self, and love of Thee?

"O by the pains of Thy pure love,
　　Grant me the gift of holy fear;
And give me of Thy Bloody Sweat
　　To wash my guilty conscience clear!

"Ever when tempted, make me see,
　　Beneath the olives' moon-pierced shade,
My God, alone, outstretched, and bruised,
　　And bleeding, on the earth He made.

"And make me feel it was my sin,
　　As though no other sins there were,
That was to Him Who bears the world
　　A load that He could scarcely bear."

"Sorrowful." Does it mean sorrowful because of our sins? Alas! it is a sad and humiliating sight. If we see them, we can do nothing else but mourn. We look back on the fair tree of our life, so fresh and vigorous, opening up its leaves to the light, and spreading its shoots towards heaven. And the seed of evil was dropped; it came flying in on the breeze and took root, and gradually a growth of evil shot up beneath our growth. At first its leaves looked fair and fresh, and then by little and little it coiled itself, outwardly green, even covered with flowers, round the stem of our life; and its tendrils of habit bound us down like cords, and cut into our very heart; blackness and blight began to gather, the leaves became shrivelled and died; we shot up, still struggling to be free, still bound, until the severance came; and with it were stripped off many of the leaves and flowers of our former vigour. And we felt all the time that the root of evil was still there beneath us, ready to blossom again; ready once more to bind us with its flowery cords, and reach up over the blackened past; to strangle the new life which had crowned the bare stem of a withered life. And still the thought will cross our minds—is the root of bitterness still there? Will the sunshine that makes my life smile and expand draw this poisonous growth up still? This distaste in prayer, these hateful thoughts, this weariness in well-doing,—are they the creeping tendrils of past sin, springing up once more from a hidden root? Perhaps that is the sorrow which we ought to face— the rooting up of the sources of sin far back in the recesses of our life; not the sorrow for its more prominent results, which circumstance or shame have torn away, but a patient digging up of the root of sin, far back in life, far back in childhood, in youth or manhood. Here is a sorrow, indeed, but a sorrow that brings healing with it; as we feel that the painful digging up and untwining of sinful principles, which lie about the sources of our spiritual life, have helped us to eradicate a deadly growth, which, having its root in the past, has been hitherto rather disentangled than destroyed. This is a sorrow in the ministerial life which has in it much of pain, but nothing of regret.

II.

But this word "sorrowful" may take us still further, to the grave of Lazarus, to the side of Olivet, where the tears are the tears of sympathy, and the sorrow is the sorrow for others. The priest has to learn this lesson among the very earliest; it is the very message which God gives him, to rejoice with them that do rejoice, and weep with them that weep.[1] Once more we are face to face with sympathy, one of the peculiar virtues necessary to the priestly life. Once more we remind ourselves that sympathy cannot be put on, assumed like a cheerful manner, or as a feigned interest in something which is really unpalatable. Sorrow is a sacred thing, a terrible experience, a secret agony: every sorrow that we see is a reminder to us that we are on Calvary, and present at the Crucifixion. We cannot put on sympathy; to do so, if nothing worse, would be to show ourselves hollow in our affections, and provoking in our interference. Sometimes God will send to us His priests sorrows in our own lives, that we may the better learn the diagnosis of sorrow. Doctors will sometimes submit to painful and dangerous operations in their own persons, that they may be the better able to snatch a relief for some terrible form of disease. There are flowers which only grow in the dense fever jungles of oppressive sorrow—flowers of patience, kindliness, gentleness, refinement, tenderness, which they bring forth to charm the hard and trodden thoroughfares of the world, who have plucked the bloom, or extracted the root, amidst the stifling poison of a life's sorrow. It may be God's will that we should exhibit what can be done in illness, or He may wish to refine our

[1] Rom. xii. 15.

influence by some secret virtue which comes from the subdued vigour of feeble health. He may will simply to put us on the Cross, to show the world what can be done by suffering, and how close it runs in efficacy to the idolized activity of its myriad workings. Sir Joshua Reynolds, with his keen appreciation of colour and form, dying blind! Beethoven, with his exquisitely attuned ear, to whom beauty of sound was life and happiness, dying deaf! These are marvellous mysteries, which we cannot explain. But experience does tell us this, that sorrow will help us to gain that sensitiveness of touch which will stand us in good stead in dealing with the troubles of the world. It will help us, as we remember how we magnified little things into great afflictions, to be patient and thoughtful, as our sympathy is very much tried by the pettiness and exacting nature of those who make demands upon it. We are sent for, it may be, to see people at most unreasonable and inconvenient times, to find at the end of it that our labour has been thrown away; that the trouble is only an exaggerated apprehension, or has to do with the death of a domestic animal, or arrears of rent, or the spitefulness of a neighbour, or some problem which needs no Solomon to unravel it; things so mean and petty, so trifling to us. And then we remember how some of our greatest troubles had been those of our own making, and products of our own imagination, and we were able to sympathize in the sorrow, in the dark shade which even a tiny object is able to throw upon our lives, when the sun of our vitality is low on the horizon.

And when we have learned true sympathy, we feel we must beware of selfishness in our love; we must sacrifice self at every turn, and strive to be like our Master before us, Who died for all. We feel that we must try and sympathize with men naturally repugnant to us—the unfortunate, the outcast, the uninteresting. We remember how patiently our blessed Lord laboured with those who showed no capacity for understanding Him. We remember that an Apostle must have gone out to the gospel-field with Judas, as He sent them out two and two to preach, and no record survived of suspicion and dislike, to suggest any other answer to our Lord's sorrowful prediction of His betrayal, saving "Lord, is it I?"

And true sympathy, again, we feel, must be practical. What do the people really need? What does this sorrow mean to them? It is this which throws up that hard manner which I mistake for rudeness. It is weakness which breaks through resolution after resolution, not hypocrisy, as I am tempted to think. Suppose God had treated me as a hypocrite when I received His gifts only to sin once more, and went from church into sin, and from communion back to my carelessness, as resolution after resolution gave way beneath me! Shall I give him up before God gives him up; or get tired before his guardian angel gets tired? Or begin to count up my hundred pence, when God has never said a word to me about my ten thousand talents? Sympathy carries us a long way—sympathy which does not patronize, but grieves; which does not scold, but sorrows; which does not wait for satisfaction, but perseveres until there is a result. This is a sorrow of which the minister of God is bound to know a great deal—the reflected sorrow of others.

III.

But we must go further still. "Sorrowful" has not exhausted its meaning. It takes us to the road which leads down to our ministry; and there, where the ways of our life converge, we see a crucifix overhanging the path, and looking up to it, we see this legend traced over it, "A Man of sorrows, and acquainted with grief."[1] And we feel that here is something which we may not forget; that our message must come from Calvary; that the hands of our working are pierced, the feet of our activity are pierced, our heart riven, by the sorrows of the Crucified. Our message, our theme, our contemplation, is a message of holy sorrow, at least of seriousness. Here is another call to us to part with the life of mere easiness, to remember that what is good and innocent in lay-people may be a hindrance to our message. We have to do more than take the sting out of lay opposition to clericalism by letting them show we have a layman's heart under a clerical coat; we want rather to bring the lay-mind to see that serious things must be included within the daily scope of their earthly life, and that the things connoted by clericalism cannot be put aside by simply ignoring them. If people come and find us idling away our time at some

[1] Isa. liii. 3.

frivolous amusement, or know that we spend large
parts of our time in theatre-going, or have to fetch us
out of the hunting-field, it is quite possible that they
may not say much, but there is an unconscious revul-
sion of feeling which they find it difficult to resist.
The clerical costume, the black dress, are not the
unwelcome livery which kills out joy, and exercises
an unwholesome restraint; they might be a constant
recall to us, as they certainly are to our people, of the
dark form of death which is never far away; of
visitants from another world which are all around us.
Brightness, joy, humour, these are all excellent; they
help to make' people remember that when S. Paul is
on board, for all his prayers and serious talk, there
is yet one at hand full of resource, full of courage,
able to speak, and entitled to warn, and at the end
they are glad he should be there, as the ship breaks
up, and planks and boards are the only things left, for
a precarious life to cling to. The priest, however,
must not hesitate to let it be seen that there is of
necessity about him that undertone of sorrow of which
we have been thinking. He has been at Gethsemane
himself; the lines of anguish are still there. He has
been hearing confessions, and face to face with the
deepest sorrows of a man's life; he cannot be frivolous.
He has just come down from Calvary, where the
anguish of life's pathos has been pouring down in
streams of bitterness; he cannot be light and foolish.
He has been on the Mountain of Transfiguration; he
has been meditating on mysteries, and handling sacraments; he cannot mix in the curious throng of idlers

which surround the mount. He has been on the Mount of Teaching, on the Hill of the Beatitudes; out of the same mouth cannot proceed blessing and cursing; those who have been listening to the earnest flow of his pleading exhortation, do not expect to hear the multitude of words in a conversation which lacks not the elements of sin. The world has two weapons, like Jeroboam of old. It first tries to put forth its hand, and seize the prophet of the higher life; when that withers up and fails, it will silence him with dinner-parties, or entrap him into a symposium of worldly priests, or mix him up with the priests of Baal, or at least break down the light restrictions which to the man of God are part of the mysteries of proportion, only to be parted with at peril; to the world, the badges of an irreconcilable hostility. We have passed through many dangers in the clerical life. We have still a hard fight to wage with frivolity. We must refuse to part with a sorrow which once was real when the world was more hostile, which must equally be retained in the shape of seriousness now that the world is more flattering.

IV.

"Yet alway rejoicing." This comes at the end, bursting out of the cloud, which it has illuminated all along with a subtle light. We know something of that exceeding great joy which awaits those who mourn over their old sins. Fresh beauties covering the old scar with verdure, a growth of new leaves in the old dead places. The very awful experience of sin becoming itself a help in dealing with others. We know from experience the joy which breaks over that pit of repentance, over the rooted-up malice of sin, in the words of peace and power, " I absolve thee from all thy sins." We know and we yearn to impart to others the blessing of penitence; it prevents us from ever thinking of such things in the spirit of controversial bitterness, or with the patronizing contempt of those who have never tried the remedy; who talk of imaginary horrors, and hypothetical weakness, in a matter where the experience of one who has tried, counteracts the testimony of a hundred who have not.

And sympathy has its joys as well; there are few bonds so sacred as those which bind a priest to his people in the ties of a common sorrow. The comfort indeed is blessed, the joy is indeed real, which comes to him who has been enabled in any way to share the burden of a fellow-creature, to relieve the oppressed, to bear the cross after another when it was weighing him down. Nor is seriousness without its joys as well; gradually and surely a deeper happiness succeeds to the more surface-pleasures of our earthly life. When we have gathered flowers at the foot of the Cross, when we have climbed the Mount of Transfiguration, when we have sat upon the Mount of the Beatitudes, then we shall wonder how lower things could have so long detained us. The mournful climb up the mountain-side has landed us in the joy of heaven, which is never far absent from the keenest sorrow.

CHAPTER XXII.

POVERTY.

> "Hark how birds do sing,
> And woods do ring !
> All creatures have their joy, and man hath his
> Yet if we rightly measure,
> Man's joy and pleasure
> Rather hereafter than in present is.
> Not that he may not here
> Taste of the cheer;
> But as birds drink and straight lift up their head,
> So must he sip, and think
> Of better drink
> He may attain to after he is dead."

> Ὡς πτωχοὶ, πολλοὺς δὲ πλουτίζοντες.
> ("As poor, yet making many rich.")

THE sayings of our blessed Lord about poverty were, and continue to be, some of the hardest for His followers to accept. The rich young ruler could not stand such an injunction; anything else but that. Poverty and utter renunciation of all worldly power came in direct conflict with his most cherished plans of doing good. "What shall we have therefore?"[1] There lingered deep down in apostolic minds, even

[1] S. Matt. xix. 27.

after the great sacrifice of all that made up life, a sense of recompense, of a bargain, one side of which remained to be adjusted. And now, when we read the Beatitudes, the Beatitude of poverty is emptied most frequently of half its force, by the undue insistence on humility, as being the essence of our blessed Lord's precept. Whereas, in the account given us by S. Luke[1] of the same or a similar saying, the modifying words "in spirit" find no place; and a dread counterpart is added, a monitory clause to this effect, "Woe unto you that are rich!" If we pass from the precepts to the example of our blessed Lord, it is possible that we do not sufficiently consider the example which He set us. "Though He was rich, yet for your sakes He became poor."[2] The manger at Bethlehem, the ignominy of Nazareth, the homeless wanderings, the Divine self-emptying, are mysteries which demand attention. Regard it as we may, there is no doubt that Jesus Christ, both by word and example, inculcated poverty, praised poverty, enjoined it upon His Apostles, held it up as a standard of perfection. Poverty being possible in three states:[3] first, in a state of actual poverty, without poverty of spirit; secondly, in a state where actual poverty and poverty of spirit are combined; and thirdly, in a state of poverty of spirit, where actual poverty does not exist. And so, we may say, without watering

---

[1] Cp. S. Matt. v. 1, etc., with S. Luke vi. 20.
[2] 2 Cor. viii. 9.
[3] See Fr. Coleridge, "The Public Life of our Lord," vol. ii. chap. x. p. 154.

down the force of our blessed Lord's words, that the poverty which He praised is not necessarily mere abnegation of this world's goods, but the emptying out of self, and of all purely earthly enjoyment, in a spirit which either in poverty or riches could still be called poor. And this poverty S. Paul sketches in as part of the portrait of the minister of God. "As poor" (ὡς πτωχοί).

Certainly, as a profession, the clergy of the present day seem favourably placed towards securing the rough material, at all events, which forms this excellence, towards realizing at least the matter out of which this virtue may be formed—actual poverty standing, as has been shown, almost in the same relation to poverty of spirit, as humiliation does to humility.[1] The hard times, the depreciated benefices, the diminished tithes, the hungry looks cast upon the pittance that remains, the responsibilities which surround the posts of greater endowments leaving in many cases the incumbent virtually poor,—all this opens up before the clergy the matter out of which true poverty is formed, or, alas! the material for a crippling discontent.

I.

"As poor." We must not shrink from it. It is a question which, in view of the past, and with our eye upon Church history, we must anxiously ask ourselves—Is there any danger from luxury in our

[1] Fr. Coleridge, "The Public Life of our Lord," vol. ii. chap. x., p. 155.

profession? The comfortable home, the absorbing garden, the sense of possession; the growing breach between ourselves and the poor of the parish; the dinner-hour at which we may not be disturbed; the breakfast, when the working man's day is already well advanced; the parish room, when, pressed from its legitimate purpose, it means keeping the poor at arm's length; the inability to enter into their joys and sorrows, combined sometimes with even roughness and imperiousness, shown in a want of courtesy in entering their homes, or respecting the privacy of their domestic economy;—all these things need watching. A spirit which is removed from the poverty of the gospel is liable to misunderstanding even when it fancies itself to be humble. And innocent actions suggest things which we never meant, and mean things which we never suspected. More and more at the present day God seems to be laying this burden on the Church of England; more and more does He seem to be impressing this truth upon us, that hard times require hard men; a missionary harvest is cropping up all round and within our civilization, and hard men are wanting who can reap it. Over and over again, as the population in our large towns becomes heathenized by godless education, or brutalized by utter neglect, or stupefied by material progress, missionaries have to reconquer the ground which the Church has lost, and needs its hard men to do it. Work in the villages is waiting for those who can work and wait, in patient exhausting toil; for men who can act as mediators between the selfishness of classes, exaggerated and inflamed by interested politicians. The parish priest has an immense work to do, if he be nothing more than the quiet bridge which spans the various chasms which keep men apart, and binds in a Christian unity the conflicting elements of his parish. He is in sympathy with the poor; he understands the rich; he knows that social difficulties are not to be adjusted in a moment, or by revolutionary processes, or by a reconstruction out of ruin. He, from his study of life, as God has shown it to him illuminated by the light of Revelation, knows that life is not a mere confused and tangled skein, which a benevolent fairy can disentangle from the outside, but that it is rather an elaborate network of causes and effects, of effects working themselves out from causes which must run their course. A disputed succession, and the horrors of civil war link themselves back to an act of perfidy and sin in the person of David.[1] The horrors of famine, year after year,[2] are bound up in the breach of a solemn covenant with treacherous enemies. The mistakes and sins of past generations leap down on the children to the third and fourth generation; and so, in the presence of wrong and injustice, of sorrow and misery, it is the province of the minister of God to find the clue, the end of the tangle which tends to righteousness, to undo the complications of sin, and untwine the selfishness of the human heart, and recognize the need of patience, the slow working of religious solvents, the reassertion of principles which

[1] 2 Sam. xv.   [2] 2 Sam. xxi.

have been lost sight of amidst the cries of contending interests aggravated by the party cries of opposing factions. The parish priest has an unique position if he does not throw it away, or barter it for self-importance. He is not tenacious of his position, while he refuses to lower himself; he is accepted and welcomed by the great majority; he works for all. What might he not do, if there were not that miserable percentage which he is ever claiming for self—the reward of dignity, or comfort, or ease? How many sermons are preached in the pulpits of the Church on the publicans, and their unjust extortions, in exacting the tax from the people, and with the tax an unjust addition for themselves! And yet how many of those who condemn others are really condemning the same spirit in themselves, which makes religious duties, already burdensome to the people, ten times more burdensome, by the claims which are urged for self! "As poor." Would that there were with us more of the spirit of the great S. John Baptist, "He must increase, but I must decrease."[1]

> "God's fashion is another; day by day
> And year by year He tarrieth: little need
> The Lord should hasten: whom He loves the most
> He seeks not oftenest, nor wooes him long,
> But by denial quickens his desire,
> And in forgetting best remembers him,
> Till that man's heart grow humble, and reaches out
> To the least glimmers of the feet of God,
> Grass on the mountain-tops, or the early note
> Of wild birds in the hush before the day—
> Wherever sweetly in the ends of earth
> Are fragments of a peace that knows not man."

---

[1] S. John iii. 30.

"As poor." A contribution towards this poverty would be to acquiesce in whatever God sends us. People who are not kindly disposed towards the clergy, and also some who are, tell us that self-pleasing is a characteristic of that profession at the present day. That there is no discipline in their ranks, a dislike for authority, a seeking after a religion which catches the passing fancy or fashion of the moment, where the music is attractive, or the ritual interesting, or the work congenial to their tastes; if this be so—

"Fas est et ab hoste doceri."

Let the virtue of poverty recall us to our better selves. One great characteristic of the state of poverty is this, that the poor man is of necessity, in a large measure, dependent. He cannot go where he likes, nor do as he likes. So God will hold us down to uncongenial work, if we will let Him; so He deprives us of those things that would hurt us, if we will let Him; so He will elevate us through trouble upon the saving cross, if we will let Him. But this blessing of poverty can easily be dispersed by discontent, by fretting and grumbling, as, like the impenitent thief, we are crucified and yet blaspheme. We suffer and are not softened; we are marked out by suffering, yet not elevated. We need not go far to study poverty as a mark of the minister of God. It means a life which has accepted as its motto, "Here have we no continuing city, but we seek one to come."[1] It means a life which has taken as its model the lives of those

[1] Heb. xiii. 14.

whose whole existence was shaped by a promise. They " confessed that they were strangers and pilgrims on the earth."[1] It means a yearning looking forward, as strong as theirs of whom it is written, " But now they desire a better country, that is, an heavenly: wherefore God is not ashamed to be called their God: for He hath prepared for them a city."[2] Poverty is not the mean thing we take it to be; a disease which God may send, to be shunned as long as possible, and to be dreaded when it comes. It is rather a virtue, or a series of virtues clad in a homely dress, and wrapped in a sad garb. Watchfulness over creatures, acquiescence in God's will, produce at last the attitude of mind which S. Paul is here really insisting upon; detachment—that spirit which makes a possession of nothing in this world; whose home is a moving tent; whose possessions are loans; whose cherished likes and dislikes can and will be all thrown to the winds at the call of duty. So God is ever gently detaching us, by trouble, sorrow, losses of all kinds, failures, disappointments, that He may loose our hold upon this world. Just as when a balloon is being prepared to soar into the air, it pulls and tears at the ropes which keep it down, and one by one they are loosened and cast off, and it sails away lightly into the sky; so we are bound down to earth by many ties which must be loosened before we go. Some people have such a capacity for earthly happiness, drink in such joy from the simplest things, settle down so firmly where God places them, that they would leave the

[1] Heb. xi. 13.   [2] Heb. xi. 16.

world at last with difficulty, did not God Himself gently loose the hampering cords, and set free the heart in detachment. Hard and sharp as the wrench is, we feel that afterwards it will be easier to go, out of a life which He has made poor. Yet even more, He bids us make ourselves poor; to cast out with our own hands the corn which weighs down the ship; to part with the tackling as we toss up and down in Adria, storm-swept by temptation. We have seen already that the priest must know something of the poverty of fasting. And even more than this, we must not shrink from stripping ourselves in voluntary almsgiving, in making ourselves to that extent poor, that others may be made rich; cheerfully recognizing that God has stored with us money for distribution, greater wealth, that may help others' poverty; not that we should enjoy up to the very last penny our own superfluity, but be ministers to our brothers' want. Here is a poverty which we recognize as a mark of the minister of God, in a humble acquiescence in what God sends to us, in detachment, in fasting, in almsgiving, in whatever accepted trouble or self-imposed burden we shake ourselves free from the weight of worldly encumbrance.

II.

And then there follows as a consequence, as a blessing growing out of poverty, the power of "making many rich." Being poor, we are so much the more ready to give; having made ourselves poor, we have more that we can put at the disposal of others, for their comfort, consolation, and advantage.

We find this to be true all through the different parts of our ministry. Out of the time which we have snatched from sleep, we find that we have been able to gather together those stores of learning which are able to steady the doubtings of some wavering soul; out of the time which we snatched from self, and devoted to our morning meditation, we find that we have a message ready, a word in season to him that is weary; out of the peculiarity as the world counted it, the patient refusal of the lower life, the quiet acceptance of the rule imposed upon ourselves which at the time seemed to cut us off from so much honest pleasure, we have been able to bring forth riches which can help the many who are starving around us. The service in church persevered in day after day, the drudgery of the morning lesson at school, the choir practice never pretermitted, the visiting undertaken as a duty, regardless of inclination or disinclination, all have brought with them unlooked-for opportunities and unexpected sources of help. The very regularity, while it has tied us down, has proved a source of blessing to us. And we remember how Anna, who never departed from the temple, was privileged to be one of the few witnesses when the Lord, Whom men sought, suddenly came to His temple,[1] and how the absence of S. Thomas from the Christian assembly on one night caused him the pangs of doubt, a week of uncertainty, and the shame of a loving reproof.[2]

[1] S. Luke ii. 36, etc.   [2] S. John xx. 24, etc.

These are striking examples which emphasize the value of regularity in Christian duty. But, beyond all this, it is the higher atmosphere in which we live which helps us to make others rich. Why do our people complain that they listen to our sermons and receive no good; that they welcome our pastoral visits and are not edified; that we live among them and they are not lifted up by our example? It is that we have nothing in our hands; that we are preaching from an empty heart, an ill-stored mind, a spirit which no grace from on high has enriched. But by the ascetic life, by poverty, by the life of discipline and rule, by a will trained to submit and obey, we are lifted up into a higher region of blessing and power. The poverty we have thought of is the ladder which carries us up into the lonely watch-tower, where we can study and think and compare; from which we descend with knowledge, power, and blessing; with riches not for ourselves, but for others; for God has rich gifts in store for those who have learned His lesson of poverty. It is in these refinements of Christianity that the minister of God shows more especially his true worth; he knows, and is willing to produce as far as he may, the finer virtues of Christian character. It is the fashion in some quarters to speak of the simplicity of Christian life; in one sense it is simple, in another it is infinitely complex. It is possible that a stranger, entering a town in the Potteries, might admire the simplicity of texture in the china displayed in the shop-windows, on which the artist has expended his skill in design and his wealth of colour. But let him go through the factory, and there see the variety of processes which are necessary to produce that simplicity; let him be told that the absence of any one of these processes would be fatal to the integrity of that surface which he so much admired; let him be told, further, that any flaw in the working, or any defect, albeit cognizable only to the eye of an expert, would so damage the value of the product, that the same piece which unimpaired would cost several pounds, can, now it is damaged, be bought from a travelling pedlar for a mere song,—he will see that in some cases simplicity and complexity go together. It is so with the Christian character. It is so pre-eminently with that perfection of life which the minister of God is bound to aim at; it is not possible to neglect any one precept without running the risk of damaging the whole. If we shrink from what is meant by poverty, there is all the more reason why we should face it. The absolute poverty of our Master stands before us; without possessions, without a fixed home, with His last earthly property, such as it was, raffled for beneath the Cross, with an association with the poor so strongly impressed on His life, that it was made a subject of special prophecy that He should be with the rich in His death.[1] The utter self-surrender of His first followers, who forsook all to follow Him, appeals to us; the power of self-denial in all ages calls to us with no uncertain tone, that if we would do the work of the great leaders in the past, we must not shrink

[1] Isa. liii. 9.

from their methods. Poverty in its dependence on God, poverty in its want of self-satisfaction, poverty in its detachment, will make us useful servants of Jesus Christ, Who has His lost sheep among the mountains, where only they can climb who are lightly equipped; Who has His banished among all the allurements of the world, where only they can venture who are impervious to the poisonous atmosphere of worldliness and sensual ease; Who has to bid us seek His wanderers in the very jaws of death. Over and over again, in the history of the Church, God's people have gone forth to battle, and have returned routed and disgraced before their enemies, and the secret of the overthrow has been found to be this: Achan, who professed to be the servant of God, has buried beneath his tent the Babylonish garment and the wedge of gold.[1] God's army marches to defeat, because those who should fight for it, and those who should lead it, have given their hearts away to the spoils and the forbidden treasures of a captivating world, and have forgotten the lesson of poverty.

[1] Josh. vii.

CHAPTER XXIII.

SELF-SURRENDER.

"It is said that Satan, who can transform himself into an angel of light, has before now come to tempt men in many seeming appearances of Christ, but he has never shown himself as upon the Cross."

'Ως μηδὲν ἔχοντες, καὶ πάντα κατέχοντες.
("As having nothing, and yet possessing all things.")

"HAVING nothing." This has a sad ring about it, coming at the end; as if one were to ask, What, then, is left, when afflictions, necessities, distresses, ignominy, degradation, hardness of every sort, have done their work? When the hold is loosened on much which seemed so necessary; when the grasp is almost roughly unclasped from so much which seemed pleasant; when every tender fibre of our being seems sore and bruised with disappointment, failure, and trial; the old question seems to rise once more unbidden to our lips, "What shall we have therefore?" Where are the milk and honey which we were promised? Where is the land of delight to which we have been tending? S. Paul gives us the answer, simple and stern. If we speak of having, we must be prepared to go on as having nothing;

if we seek for a land of promise, we are really in possession of all things. "All things are lawful for me, but I will not be brought under the power of any."[1] The minister of God passes through all things without retaining any, but at the same time he has a firm possession of all that is good and true.

> "Much have I seen and known;
> I am a part of all that I have met."

As with the tribe of Levi of old, so with the priesthood now—"Levi hath no part nor inheritance with his brethren; the Lord is his inheritance."[2] Removed from earthly cares and earthly interests, he yet possesses Him Who is the Author and Giver of life, from Whom all good things do come.

I.

"Having nothing." It may be that far back in life, when our aspirations began to shape themselves, that we were drawn towards the priesthood as one of the learned professions, in which there was a good deal to attract; where, removed from the fierce struggle of competitive life, we might look for a settled home, a recognized position, a fair competence, and the delights of leisure; while, quite unconsciously, these thoughts usurped the place of higher aims, and quenched the more worthy longings. They wound themselves round our souls, and our work was done tending towards an aim lower than the highest. We were competing with our fellows; we were candidates

---

[1] 1 Cor. vi. 12.   [2] Deut. x. 9

for a prize, and working towards a post of mere earthly advantage, with an eye on the distinctions, as we thought them, of our profession. And then came the long wandering in the wilderness, the protracted life as a curate (as we contemptuously put it), the dreary lodgings, the daily routine. Or we got our desire; we became what is known as beneficed, and we found things harder than before— less freedom, more responsibility; the hard times beat down heavily upon us, and we found that the inheritance of Levi was not here; not in the settled home, nor the comfortable income, nor in the freedom from care, but in higher things which give home its value and money its importance; so that the very disappointment came to us as the hand of God, and lifted us up into the higher possession of life. Or, on the other hand, all came to us, and even more than we had anticipated. Life was full of comfort and happiness; things smiled on us, and we grew to the place and expanded in the sunshine of prosperity, And then God smote us with a sharp bereavement; our vitality hung withered on the wall, severed from the stem, and snapped by the fall of the props over which it had trained its luxuriant growth, and we *had it* no more. But we were lifted by the blow into a higher region of real possession. Or we felt ourselves able to do useful work; we had begun to think ourselves necessary to the parish or to the diocese; we went along our way exulting in our strength, and confident in our powers. And God put forth His hand and snapped them off; we had not even our strength, but we were constrained to preach from a cross, and were elevated into a higher region of possession than we had as yet known. And so it was that in all these, and in many more ways, God drove back the sap which was expending itself simply in fruitless blossom and in blossomless leaves, until we possessed what was true life, until we could lay hold of and assimilate what was Divine, permanent, and true, in sorrow as well as gladness, in failure as well as in success. And we realized that the golden background of our life was meant to be not a mere glitter, a shadeless mass, but rather to be broken up with bits of black and brown, of blue and grey, until it shone with a deeper splendour, instead of an even mass of unrelieved glare; golden, it is true, but with the gold which comes from the combination of broken colours blended into a depth of mystery. "I see that all things come to an end," in my shattered life, which stands "having nothing." "But Thy commandment is exceeding broad,"[1] as it is found at the end "possessing all things."

> "And this it is that links together as one
> The sad continual companies of men;
> Not that the old earth stands, and Ararat
> Endureth, and Euphrates till to-day
> Remembers where God walked beside the stream:
> Nay, rather that souls weary and hearts afire
> Have everywhere besought Him, everywhere
> Have found, and found Him not, and age to age,
> Though all else pass and fail, delivereth
> At least the great tradition of their God."

---

[1] Ps. cxix 96.

II.

If comfort and ease are unworthy ends, which slipped in almost before we were conscious of their presence, to thrust out higher aims, at least we may feel an honest pride in a profession of admitted distinction and well-earned respect. The priesthood we feel we may regard as the greatest of all professions, and at least we shall not do wrong if we magnify our office. And we picture to ourselves the ambassador, the honoured bearer of credentials from the imperial court, which ensure him a welcome, and secure to him respect. Or we feel that the priest is the keeper of a peculiar knowledge, on which the spiritual life of many depends. Or we picture ourselves as the glittering occupants of hierarchical thrones of greater or less degree. And we do not feel how quickly the thin barrier which separates the personal from the official is broken down, and that ambition, the last infirmity of noble minds, has taken up its restless abode within. We do not pause to remember the bold request advanced by the two sons of Zebedee, through the mouthpiece of a mother's blinded love, for a place on the right hand and on the left in their Master's kingdom. We do not realize that the request, if it had been granted in the earthly sense in which it seems to have been preferred, would have served to raise them only to the position afterwards occupied by the two thieves on either side of the throne of the cross.[1] We do not stop to listen to the

---

[1] See Archdeacon Farrar's "Life of Christ," vol. ii. p. 180.

laws of His kingdom, or to hear our Lord and Saviour say to His servants, "Blessed are the meek: for they shall inherit the earth."[1] Or if at times we praise meekness and admire humility in others, we look upon it rather as a special gift, or as an ornament which can be put on to relieve the glare of an exaggerated individuality, which blesses the too prominent self with the delicate softness of faint blame. And we never stop to ask Moses how he became meek; we never stay to hear him tell us that it was by beating down in the hottest fire the strong impetuosity of a hasty nature, that he developed in his spiritual life this ornament, by the help of the grace of God. We never stop to ask S. John how Boanerges melted into the apostle of love; or S. Paul how he could contentedly acquiesce in his own estimate of himself, as "of one born out of due time," the least of the apostles, unworthy to be called an apostle,[2] the chief of sinners. Reputation is a thing which the minister of God tightly clings to, while he succeeds in persuading himself that it is for his office, and not for himself, that he is careful. If it be but the notice in the newspaper, to say that there is such a work going on, to be encouraged, recognized, yes, praised. But his better self rises up and tells him that he must not stop to have this, to gather this, but that he must press on to possess a wider, a more blessed circle of good, which comes to the meek. There is an ominous compound which gathers round the word ἔχοντες which we have already considered, ἀπέχουσι τὸν μισθον

---

[1] S. Matt. v. 5. [2] 1 Cor. xv. 8, 9.

αὐτῶν. It becomes all too easy to live for praise, and to sacrifice higher things to reputation, and to shut the gates against the advancing hosts of the Lord as they sweep to battle, in fear of compromised interests and of endangered possessions. Reputation, position, glory, a selfish pinnacle of isolated power,— these are not things to *have;* these are the first fruitless buds which gather on work, and which must be ruthlessly nipped off to make way for meekness, humility, gentleness, simplicity, which are the true fruits of heaven, reared on the same plant, which would throw up pride, ambition, self-importance. These have a momentary triumph, but they do not possess the abiding glories of the higher life.

III.

"Having nothing." At least, if reputation is denied me, I can do a work for God and offer myself to Him. Here, too, we must learn sooner or later to strip off our individuality, and know that we cannot *have* the satisfaction of serving God in our own way. We all of us feel from time to time that we have let our own will or our own fears, or the gusts of popular fashion, come between us and the integrity of our message; that we, as a matter of fact, have shunned to declare unto the people all the counsel of God; that we have felt the gospel message to be unsuited to the age, or we have persuaded ourselves that our people will remain babes to the end, and incapable of assimilating meat; or the new doctrines, so much in vogue, seem so much simpler, easier, and quicker in their effects. It is then that we have to remember the Apostle's words which still echo around us, " having nothing. The minister of God dare not interpose his private feelings or methods, which have not the sanction of Divine authority. Look at the fierceness with which the great Apostle denounces any attempt to impose Judaism on the Church, braving thereby the scorn and opposition of his former friends. See him boldly insisting on unpopular doctrines, proclaiming the doctrine of the resurrection of the body before cultivated sceptics; the gospel, with a passionate assertion of his confidence in its power, at Rome, the seat of the haughtiest despotism that the world has ever seen. " Having nothing." Can we still go out brave beneath the offence of the Cross, to meet those who laugh at our antiquated doctrines and old-fashioned methods; who will tell us that Moses' place is down in the valley to lead the combatants, not on the mountain-top, in the powerlessness of his multiplied Eucharists, and oft-repeated services; who will tell us that "Dearly beloved brethren," and a repetition of the service day by day, when there is no congregation worth ministering to, can do good to nobody; who will remind us that "the Athanasian Creed" is not suitable to the mental habits of the present day; and that we need a new Reformation, or, until that can be attained, every one must reform in his own way, and carry out his own methods? "Having nothing." the minister of God is content to abide by his instructions, and do as he is told; and he finds, if he waits long enough, that in the end he is possessing all things. The Church, when she is true, and content to wait, may not always *have* the immediate triumph which follows the effervescent novelty, but she possesses any residuum of vitality which is found to belong to it.

So the image of the minister of God has been carefully sketched out for us by the Apostle. It would be well for us if from time to time we corrected ourselves by the portrait, and rectified our ideal. To miss any one of these marks so carefully drawn, we feel is to run the risk of spoiling the likeness. If the priest degenerates into the official, or the servant of the State, or the paid instructor, or the moral policeman, if he severs his connection with court, and is seldom seen at the altar, spends little time in prayer, and sinks as far as may be the cleric in the layman, it is difficult to see how he is to secure the expression which marks the features of the minister of God. If he quails before afflictions, his life will miss the heat of the furnace which is to give to him the permanence of the image; if he fails beneath it, patience will have lost its perfect work. Idleness will at once destroy a distinctive feature in the servant of the God Who never slumbers nor sleeps in the ceaseless working of His beneficence. Watchfulness will bring to him opportunities golden in their importance; fastings will keep down the rebellion of the lower life, which is ever threatening his usefulness. Purity is the atmosphere of his higher life, at once a privilege and a necessity. Knowledge will help him to remember that he is one who has been accredited by a special influx of spiritual gifts. Long-suffering keeps him from giving in, and helps him to bear long with his own infirmities, and with the trials which others bring upon him. Kindness is an atmosphere which makes all his voices of exhortation audible. The Holy Ghost is the central store of strength on which, as outwork after outwork is stormed, he falls back in the battle of life. Love unfeigned carries him forward, on his missionary journeys, towards imprisonments and martyrdom itself. The Word of truth is on his lips, as the deposit of truth is in his heart; it has come to him with all the power of a tradition which he dare not betray. The power of God is ever at hand to support him with the sense of a strength which is not his own, in supernatural gifts, in Divine help, in accredited agencies. He knows of an armour which he needs. He does not shrink from controversy if the truth so demands; but he knows that his real strength is in a holy life, and in the protection of God's almighty arm. Honour and dishonour come to him alike, and both find him prepared; he is neither to be frightened into forgetting his message, nor coaxed out of delivering it. If, like Daniel, he is promoted, he accepts the honour; if, like him, he is degraded to the den of lions, he still holds fast his integrity. He remembers that the most honoured names in the Church now, were despised in their life, and were martyred in their death, and therefore he thinks little of evil report or of good report, knowing the frequent reversal of the world's verdict, and the weakness of its praise and the powerlessness of its blame. Among the first who are last, he can look back to the favoured of the world; among the last who are first, he can recognize those who endured its persecution. He is content to be counted as a deceiver, if his heart within convict him of no want of truth. He appeals to time as the justifier of his methods; he traces the principles of his actions back to God, and he can confidently await their result. He dreads most of all unreality, and any appearance of inconsistency between the words which he takes on his lips and the actions in which he carries them out. If it be God's will, he is content to remain unknown to the world, if known to Him "unto Whom all hearts be open, all desires known, and from Whom no secrets are hid." Obscurity has no terrors for him; it is not

> "To rust unburnished, not to shine in use
> As tho' to breathe were life."

It is rather to live the life "hid with Christ in God," and when the side turned to the world is most dark, to be brightened on the other with the full glory of God's presence. And so he meets death by dying daily, by making a study of mortification, by killing out all the lower desires, and dying to what is base, that he may live to what is noble, and by recognizing something higher than the mere life which he shares with the rest of the animal world, in the fuller development by contemplation and asceticism of that which is truly life. If chastisement comes to him, he bears it without flinching; disappointment, bad health, spiritual difficulties, fail to kill him, while they wither up in him all that is not of God. Sorrow is a characteristic of his life, but it is lit up by an inner brightness of joy. He can scarcely avoid sorrow, who is so frequently reminded of his own sad past; he lives in an atmosphere of sorrow which sympathy with others brings about him, while his own seriousness reflects the life of Him Who "reigns from the tree;" Who, while He is "the Son of man," the Representative of our humanity, is known to us as "a Man of sorrows, and acquainted with grief." Poverty, again, marks him as her own, but a poverty which is full of resource, and which leaves a rich store of help for others. Poverty which is at once the mark of the good soldier, ready for hard warfare, and the sign of a life ready to place itself at the disposal of others. He has nothing: as all the wealth of God's mercy passes through his hands, he seeks to retain nothing for himself, no percentage of earthly ease, reputation, or power. He seeks to sink self and magnify God, and so possesses all things. Such is the character which is here put before us for our study and imitation; here is a mirror in which the priest can prepare himself for the great liturgy of his life. So may he be offered upon the sacrifice and service of the faith of the people; so may he be able to discern whether there is that purity of intention which befits those who draw near to the service of the sanctuary, and to the ministration of that holy rite which is "an extension of the Incarnation." So may he feel sorrow for the many sins and infirmities which baffle his efforts after holiness, and distort the image which he fain would produce; while, behind the example of the Apostle, he knows there is the faultless image of Christ, the sense of whose beauty never leaves him. If the lives of the saints are flowers which hide the bareness of the earth, they are also clouds which veil for us the brilliancy of heaven.[1] While we dread the very thought of any mediation other than that of the Eternal Son, we feel that following their bright examples, we shall best follow Him; and that in the life of the great Apostle, which glowed with the reflected radiance of Christ, we cannot do wrong in seeing a *speculum sacerdotum* at which to remedy the defects which mar our priestly life, from which to add to the poverty of our spiritual character those graces which are the gift of Christ.

[1] See Ruskin, "Modern Painters," vol. v. p. 105.

A Selection of Works
IN
THEOLOGICAL LITERATURE
PUBLISHED BY
Messrs. LONGMANS, GREEN, & CO.
39 PATERNOSTER ROW, LONDON, E.C.

Abbey and Overton.—THE ENGLISH CHURCH IN THE EIGHTEENTH CENTURY. By CHARLES J. ABBEY, M.A., Rector of Checkendon, Reading, and JOHN H. OVERTON, D.D., Canon of Lincoln and Rector of Epworth. *Crown 8vo. 7s. 6d.*

Adams.—SACRED ALLEGORIES. The Shadow of the Cross—The Distant Hills—The Old Man's Home—The King's Messengers. By the Rev. WILLIAM ADAMS, M.A. *Crown 8vo. 3s. 6d.*
The four Allegories may be had separately, with Illustrations. *16mo. 1s. each.*

Aids to the Inner Life.
Edited by the Rev. W. H. HUTCHINGS, M.A., Rector of Kirby Misperton, Yorkshire. *Five Vols. 32mo, cloth limp, 6d. each; or cloth extra, 1s. each.*
With red borders, *2s. each. Sold separately.*
OF THE IMITATION OF CHRIST. By THOMAS À KEMPIS.
THE CHRISTIAN YEAR.
THE DEVOUT LIFE. By ST. FRANCIS DE SALES.
THE HIDDEN LIFE OF THE SOUL.
THE SPIRITUAL COMBAT. By LAURENCE SCUPOLI.

Barry.—SOME LIGHTS OF SCIENCE ON THE FAITH. Being the Bampton Lectures for 1892. By the Right Rev. ALFRED BARRY, D.D., Canon of Windsor, formerly Bishop of Sydney, Metropolitan of New South Wales, and Primate of Australia. *8vo. 12s. 6d.*

Bathe.—Works by the Rev. ANTHONY BATHE, M.A.
A LENT WITH JESUS. A Plain Guide for Churchmen. Containing Readings for Lent and Easter Week, and on the Holy Eucharist. *32mo, 1s.; or in paper cover, 6d.*
AN ADVENT WITH JESUS. *32mo, 1s.; or in paper cover, 6d.*
WHAT I SHOULD BELIEVE. A Simple Manual of Self-Instruction for Church People. *Small 8vo, limp, 1s.; cloth gilt, 2s.*

A SELECTION OF WORKS

Benson.—THE FINAL PASSOVER : A Series of Meditations upon the Passion of our Lord Jesus Christ. By the Rev. R. M. BENSON, M.A., Student of Christ Church, Oxford. *Small 8vo.*

Vol. I.—THE REJECTION. 5*s.*
Vol. II.—THE UPPER CHAMBER. Part I. nearly ready. Part II. in the Press.
Vol. III.—THE DIVINE EXODUS. Parts I. and II. 5*s.* each.
Vol. IV.—THE LIFE BEYOND THE GRAVE. 5*s.*

Bickersteth.—YESTERDAY, TO-DAY, AND FOR EVER: a Poem in Twelve Books. By EDWARD HENRY BICKERSTETH, D.D., Bishop of Exeter. *One Shilling Edition*, 18mo. *With red borders*, 16mo, 2*s.* 6*d.*
The Crown 8vo Edition (5*s.*) *may still be had.*

Blunt.—Works by the Rev. JOHN HENRY BLUNT, D.D.
THE ANNOTATED BOOK OF COMMON PRAYER: Being an Historical, Ritual, and Theological Commentary on the Devotional System of the Church of England. *4to.* 21*s.*
THE COMPENDIOUS EDITION OF THE ANNOTATED BOOK OF COMMON PRAYER: Forming a concise Commentary on the Devotional System of the Church of England. *Crown 8vo.* 10*s.* 6*d.*
DICTIONARY OF DOCTRINAL AND HISTORICAL THEOLOGY. By various Writers. *Imperial 8vo.* 21*s.*
DICTIONARY OF SECTS, HERESIES, ECCLESIASTICAL PARTIES AND SCHOOLS OF RELIGIOUS THOUGHT. By various Writers. *Imperial 8vo.* 21*s.*
THE BOOK OF CHURCH LAW. Being an Exposition of the Legal Rights and Duties of the Parochial Clergy and the Laity of the Church of England. Revised by Sir WALTER G. F. PHILLIMORE, Bart., D.C.L., and G. EDWARDES JONES, Barrister-at-Law. *Crown 8vo.* 7*s.* 6*d.*
A COMPANION TO THE BIBLE: Being a Plain Commentary on Scripture History, to the end of the Apostolic Age. *Two Vols. small 8vo. Sold separately.*
THE OLD TESTAMENT. 3*s.* 6*d.*   THE NEW TESTAMENT. 3*s.* 6*d.*
HOUSEHOLD THEOLOGY: a Handbook of Religious Information respecting the Holy Bible, the Prayer Book, the Church, etc., etc. *Paper cover*, 16mo. 1*s.* *Also the Larger Edition*, 3*s.* 6*d.*

Body.—Works by the Rev. GEORGE BODY, D.D., Canon of Durham.
THE LIFE OF LOVE. A Course of Lent Lectures. *Crown 8vo.* 4*s.* 6*d.*
THE SCHOOL OF CALVARY; or, Laws of Christian Life revealed from the Cross. 16mo. 2*s.* 6*d.*
THE LIFE OF JUSTIFICATION. 16mo. 2*s.* 6*d.*
THE LIFE OF TEMPTATION. 16mo. 2*s.* 6*d.*

IN THEOLOGICAL LITERATURE. 3

Boultbee.—A COMMENTARY ON THE THIRTY-NINE ARTICLES OF THE CHURCH OF ENGLAND. By the Rev. T. P. BOULTBEE, formerly Principal of the London College of Divinity, St. John's Hall, Highbury. *Crown 8vo. 6s.*

Bright.—Works by WILLIAM BRIGHT, D.D., Canon of Christ Church, Oxford.
- WAYMARKS IN CHURCH HISTORY. *Crown 8vo. 7s. 6d.*
- MORALITY IN DOCTRINE. *Crown 8vo. 7s. 6d.*
- LESSONS FROM THE LIVES OF THREE GREAT FATHERS: St. Athanasius, St. Chrysostom, and St. Augustine. *Crown 8vo. 6s.*
- THE INCARNATION AS A MOTIVE POWER. *Crown 8vo. 6s.*

Bright and Medd.—LIBER PRECUM PUBLICARUM ECCLESIÆ ANGLICANÆ. A GULIELMO BRIGHT, S.T.P., et PETRO GOLDSMITH MEDD, A.M., Latine redditus. *Small 8vo. 7s. 6d.*

Browne.—AN EXPOSITION OF THE THIRTY-NINE ARTICLES, Historical and Doctrinal. By E. H. BROWNE, D.D., formerly Bishop of Winchester. *8vo. 16s.*

Campion and Beamont.—THE PRAYER BOOK INTERLEAVED. With Historical Illustrations and Explanatory Notes arranged parallel to the Text. By W. M. CAMPION, D.D., and W. J. BEAMONT, M.A. *Small 8vo. 7s. 6d.*

Carter.—Works edited by the Rev. T. T. CARTER, M.A., Hon. Canon of Christ Church, Oxford.

- THE TREASURY OF DEVOTION: a Manual of Prayer for General and Daily Use. Compiled by a Priest. *18mo. 2s. 6d.*; *cloth limp, 2s.*; *or bound with the Book of Common Prayer, 3s. 6d.* Red-Line Edition *2s. 6d. net.*
    Large-Type Edition. *Crown 8vo. 3s. 6d.*

- THE WAY OF LIFE: A Book of Prayers and Instruction for the Young at School, with a Preparation for Confirmation. Compiled by a Priest, *18mo. 1s. 6d.*

- THE PATH OF HOLINESS: a First Book of Prayers, with the Service of the Holy Communion, for the Young. Compiled by a Priest. With Illustrations. *16mo. 1s. 6d.*; *cloth limp, 1s.*

- THE GUIDE TO HEAVEN: a Book of Prayers for every Want. (For the Working Classes.) Compiled by a Priest. *18mo. 1s. 6d.*; *cloth limp, 1s. Large-Type Edition. Crown 8vo. 1s. 6d.*; *cloth limp, 1s.*

[continued.

Carter.—Works edited by the Rev. T. T. CARTER, M.A., Hon. Canon of Christ Church, Oxford—*continued.*
SELF-RENUNCIATION. 16mo. 2s. 6d.
THE STAR OF CHILDHOOD: a First Book of Prayers and Instruction for Children. Compiled by a Priest. With Illustrations. 16mo. 2s. 6d.
NICHOLAS FERRAR: his Household and his Friends. With Portrait engraved after a Picture by CORNELIUS JANSSEN at Magdalene College, Cambridge. *Crown 8vo.* 6s.

Carter.—MAXIMS AND GLEANINGS FROM THE WRITINGS OF T. T. CARTER, M.A. Selected and arranged for Daily Use. *Crown 16mo.* 1s.

Conybeare and Howson.—THE LIFE AND EPISTLES OF ST. PAUL. By the Rev. W. J. CONYBEARE, M.A., and the Very Rev. J. S. HOWSON, D.D. With numerous Maps and Illustrations.
LIBRARY EDITION. *Two Vols. 8vo.* 21s.
STUDENTS' EDITION. *One Vol. Crown 8vo.* 6s.
POPULAR EDITION. *One Vol. Crown 8vo.* 3s. 6d.

Copleston.—BUDDHISM—PRIMITIVE AND PRESENT IN MAGADHA AND IN CEYLON. By REGINALD STEPHEN COPLESTON, D.D., Bishop of Colombo. 8vo. 16s.

Devotional Series, 16mo, Red Borders. *Each* 2s. 6d.
BICKERSTETH'S YESTERDAY, TO-DAY, AND FOR EVER.
CHILCOT'S TREATISE ON EVIL THOUGHTS.
THE CHRISTIAN YEAR.
FRANCIS DE SALES' (ST.) THE DEVOUT LIFE.
HERBERT'S POEMS AND PROVERBS.
KEMPIS' (À) OF THE IMITATION OF CHRIST.
WILSON'S THE LORD'S SUPPER. *Large type.*
*TAYLOR'S (JEREMY) HOLY LIVING.
*———   ———   HOLY DYING.
    * *These two in one Volume.* 5s.

Devotional Series, 18mo, without Red Borders. *Each* 1s.
BICKERSTETH'S YESTERDAY, TO-DAY, AND FOR EVER.
THE CHRISTIAN YEAR.
FRANCIS DE SALES' (ST.) THE DEVOUT LIFE.
HERBERT'S POEMS AND PROVERBS.
KEMPIS (À) OF THE IMITATION OF CHRIST.
WILSON'S THE LORD'S SUPPER. *Large type.*
*TAYLOR'S (JEREMY) HOLY LIVING.
*———   ———   HOLY DYING.
    * *These two in one Volume.* 2s. 6d.

IN THEOLOGICAL LITERATURE. 5

Edersheim.—Works by ALFRED EDERSHEIM, M.A., D.D., Ph.D., sometime Grinfield Lecturer on the Septuagint, Oxford.

THE LIFE AND TIMES OF JESUS THE MESSIAH. *Two Vols.* 8vo. 24s.

JESUS THE MESSIAH: being an Abridged Edition of 'The Life and Times of Jesus the Messiah.' *Crown 8vo.* 7s. 6d.

PROPHECY AND HISTORY IN RELATION TO THE MESSIAH: The Warburton Lectures, 1880-1884. 8vo. 12s.

Ellicott.—Works by C. J. ELLICOTT, D.D., Bishop of Gloucester and Bristol.

A CRITICAL AND GRAMMATICAL COMMENTARY ON ST. PAUL'S EPISTLES. Greek Text, with a Critical and Grammatical Commentary, and a Revised English Translation. 8vo.

1 CORINTHIANS. 16s.	PHILIPPIANS, COLOSSIANS, AND PHILEMON. 10s. 6d.
GALATIANS. 8s. 6d.	THESSALONIANS. 7s. 6d.
EPHESIANS. 8s. 6d.	

PASTORAL EPISTLES. 10s. 6d.

HISTORICAL LECTURES ON THE LIFE OF OUR LORD JESUS CHRIST. 8vo. 12s.

Epochs of Church History.—Edited by MANDELL CREIGHTON, D.D., LL.D., Bishop of Peterborough. *Fcap. 8vo.* 2s. 6d. each.

THE ENGLISH CHURCH IN OTHER LANDS. By the Rev. H. W. TUCKER, M.A.

THE HISTORY OF THE REFORMATION IN ENGLAND. By the Rev. GEO. G. PERRY, M.A.

THE CHURCH OF THE EARLY FATHERS. By the Rev. ALFRED PLUMMER, D.D.

THE EVANGELICAL REVIVAL IN THE EIGHTEENTH CENTURY. By the Rev. J. H. OVERTON, D.D.

THE UNIVERSITY OF OXFORD. By the Hon. G. C. BRODRICK, D.C.L.

THE UNIVERSITY OF CAMBRIDGE. By J. BASS MULLINGER, M.A.

THE ENGLISH CHURCH IN THE MIDDLE AGES. By the Rev. W. HUNT, M.A.

THE CHURCH AND THE EASTERN EMPIRE. By the Rev. H. F. TOZER, M.A.

THE CHURCH AND THE ROMAN EMPIRE. By the Rev. A. CARR, M.A.

THE CHURCH AND THE PURITANS, 1570-1660. By HENRY OFFLEY WAKEMAN, M.A.

HILDEBRAND AND HIS TIMES. By the Rev. W. R. W. STEPHENS, M.A.

THE POPES AND THE HOHENSTAUFEN. By UGO BALZANI.

THE COUNTER REFORMATION. By ADOLPHUS WILLIAM WARD, Litt. D.

WYCLIFFE AND MOVEMENTS FOR REFORM. By REGINALD L. POOLE, M.A.

THE ARIAN CONTROVERSY. By H. M. GWATKIN, M.A.

Fosbery.—Works edited by the Rev. THOMAS VINCENT FOSBERY, M.A., sometime Vicar of St. Giles's, Reading.

VOICES OF COMFORT. *Cheap Edition. Small 8vo.* 3s. 6d.
The Larger Edition (7s. 6d.) may still be had.

HYMNS AND POEMS FOR THE SICK AND SUFFERING. In connection with the Service for the Visitation of the Sick. Selected from Various Authors. *Small 8vo.* 3s. 6d.

Gore.—Works by the Rev. CHARLES GORE, M.A., Canon of Westminster.

THE MINISTRY OF THE CHRISTIAN CHURCH. 8vo. 10s. 6d.

ROMAN CATHOLIC CLAIMS. *Crown 8vo.* 3s. 6d.

Goulburn.—Works by EDWARD MEYRICK GOULBURN, D.D., D.C.L., sometime Dean of Norwich.

THOUGHTS ON PERSONAL RELIGION. *Small 8vo.* 6s. 6d. *Cheap Edition,* 3s. 6d.; *Presentation Edition,* 2 *vols. small 8vo,* 10s. 6d.

THE PURSUIT OF HOLINESS: a Sequel to 'Thoughts on Personal Religion.' *Small 8vo.* 5s. *Cheap Edition.* 3s. 6d.

THE GOSPEL OF THE CHILDHOOD: a Practical and Devotional Commentary on the Single Incident of our Blessed Lord's Childhood (St. Luke ii. 41 to the end). *Crown 8vo.* 2s. 6d.

THE COLLECTS OF THE DAY: an Exposition, Critical and Devotional, of the Collects appointed at the Communion. With Preliminary Essays on their Structure, Sources, etc. 2 *vols. Crown 8vo.* 8s. *each.*

THOUGHTS UPON THE LITURGICAL GOSPELS for the Sundays, one for each day in the year. With an Introduction on their Origin, History, the modifications made in them by the Reformers and by the Revisers of the Prayer Book. 2 *vols. Crown 8vo.* 16s.

MEDITATIONS UPON THE LITURGICAL GOSPELS for the Minor Festivals of Christ, the two first Week-days of the Easter and Whitsun Festivals, and the Red-letter Saints' Days. *Crown 8vo.* 8s. 6d.

FAMILY PRAYERS, compiled from various sources (chiefly from Bishop Hamilton's Manual), and arranged on the Liturgical Principle. *Crown 8vo.* 3s. 6d. *Cheap Edition.* 16mo. 1s.

IN THEOLOGICAL LITERATURE. 7

Harrison.—Works by the Rev. ALEXANDER J. HARRISON, B.D., Lecturer of the Christian Evidence Society.

PROBLEMS OF CHRISTIANITY AND SCEPTICISM; Lessons from Twenty Years' Experience in the Field of Christian Evidence. *Crown 8vo. 7s. 6d.*

THE CHURCH IN RELATION TO SCEPTICS: a Conversational Guide to Evidential Work. *Crown 8vo. 7s. 6d.*

THE REPOSE OF FAITH, IN VIEW OF PRESENT DAY DIFFICULTIES. *Crown 8vo. 7s. 6d.*

Holland.—Works by the Rev. HENRY SCOTT HOLLAND, M.A., Canon and Precentor of St. Paul's.

GOD'S CITY AND THE COMING OF THE KINGDOM: *Crown 8vo. 7s. 6d.*

PLEAS AND CLAIMS FOR CHRIST. *Crown 8vo. 3s. 6d.*

CREED AND CHARACTER: Sermons. *Crown 8vo. 3s. 6d.*

ON BEHALF OF BELIEF. Sermons preached in St. Paul's Cathedral. *Crown 8vo. 3s. 6d.*

CHRIST OR ECCLESIASTES. Sermons preached in St. Paul's Cathedral. *Crown 8vo. 2s. 6d.*

LOGIC AND LIFE, with other Sermons. *Crown 8vo. 3s. 6d.*

INHERITANCE OF THE SAINTS; or, Thoughts on the Communion of Saints and the Life of the World to come. Collected chiefly from English Writers by L. P. With a Preface by the Rev. HENRY SCOTT HOLLAND, M.A. *Crown 8vo. 7s. 6d.*

Jameson.—Works by Mrs. JAMESON.

SACRED AND LEGENDARY ART, containing Legends of the Angels and Archangels, the Evangelists, the Apostles. With 19 Etchings and 187 Woodcuts. *Two vols. 8vo. Cloth, gilt top, 20s. net.*

LEGENDS OF THE MONASTIC ORDERS, as represented in the Fine Arts. With 11 Etchings and 88 Woodcuts. *8vo. Cloth, gilt top, 10s. net.*

LEGENDS OF THE MADONNA, OR BLESSED VIRGIN MARY. With 27 Etchings and 165 Woodcuts. *8vo. Cloth, gilt top, 10s. net.*

THE HISTORY OF OUR LORD, as exemplified in Works of Art. Commenced by the late Mrs. JAMESON; continued and completed by LADY EASTLAKE. With 31 Etchings and 281 Woodcuts. *Two Vols. 8vo. Cloth, gilt top, 20s. net.*

Jennings.—ECCLESIA ANGLICANA. A History of the Church of Christ in England from the Earliest to the Present Times. By the Rev. ARTHUR CHARLES JENNINGS, M.A. *Crown 8vo.* 7s. 6d.

Jukes.—Works by ANDREW JUKES.

    THE NEW MAN AND THE ETERNAL LIFE. Notes on the Reiterated Amens of the Son of God. *Crown 8vo.* 6s.

    THE NAMES OF GOD IN HOLY SCRIPTURE: a Revelation of His Nature and Relationships. *Crown 8vo.* 4s. 6d.

    THE TYPES OF GENESIS. *Crown 8vo.* 7s. 6d.

    THE SECOND DEATH AND THE RESTITUTION OF ALL THINGS. *Crown 8vo.* 3s. 6d.

    THE MYSTERY OF THE KINGDOM. *Crown 8vo.* 2s. 6d.

    THE ORDER AND CONNEXION OF THE CHURCH'S TEACHING, as set forth in the arrangement of the Epistles and Gospels throughout the Year. *Crown 8vo.* 2s. 6d.

Knox Little.—Works by W. J. KNOX LITTLE, M.A., Canon Residentiary of Worcester, and Vicar of Hoar Cross.

    SACERDOTALISM, WHEN RIGHTLY UNDERSTOOD, THE TEACHING OF THE CHURCH OF ENGLAND. *Crown 8vo.* 6s.

    SKETCHES IN SUNSHINE AND STORM: a Collection of Miscellaneous Essays and Notes of Travel. *Crown 8vo.* 7s. 6d.

    THE CHRISTIAN HOME. *Crown 8vo.* 3s. 6d.

    THE HOPES AND DECISIONS OF THE PASSION OF OUR MOST HOLY REDEEMER. *Crown 8vo.* 2s. 6d.

    CHARACTERISTICS AND MOTIVES OF THE CHRISTIAN LIFE. Ten Sermons preached in Manchester Cathedral, in Lent and Advent. *Crown 8vo.* 2s. 6d.

    SERMONS PREACHED FOR THE MOST PART IN MANCHESTER. *Crown 8vo.* 3s. 6d.

    THE MYSTERY OF THE PASSION OF OUR MOST HOLY REDEEMER. *Crown 8vo.* 2s. 6d.

    THE WITNESS OF THE PASSION OF OUR MOST HOLY REDEEMER. *Crown 8vo.* 2s. 6d.

[continued.

IN THEOLOGICAL LITERATURE. 9

Knox Little.—Works by W. J. KNOX LITTLE, M.A., Canon Residentiary of Worcester, and Vicar of Hoar Cross.—*continued*.

THE LIGHT OF LIFE. Sermons preached on Various Occasions. *Crown 8vo.* 3s. 6d.

SUNLIGHT AND SHADOW IN THE CHRISTIAN LIFE. Sermons preached for the most part in America. *Crown 8vo.* 3s. 6d.

Lear.—Works by, and Edited by, H. L. SIDNEY LEAR.

FOR DAYS AND YEARS. A book containing a Text, Short Reading, and Hymn for Every Day in the Church's Year. 16mo. 2s. 6d. Also a *Cheap Edition*, 32mo. 1s.; or *cloth gilt*, 1s. 6d.

FIVE MINUTES. Daily Readings of Poetry. 16mo. 3s. 6d. Also a *Cheap Edition*, 32mo. 1s.; or *cloth gilt*, 1s. 6d.

WEARINESS. A Book for the Languid and Lonely. *Large Type. Small 8vo.* 5s.

THE LIGHT OF THE CONSCIENCE. 16mo. 2s. 6d. 32mo. 1s.; *cloth limp*, 6d.

CHRISTIAN BIOGRAPHIES. *Nine Vols. Crown 8vo.* 3s. 6d. each.

MADAME LOUISE DE FRANCE, Daughter of Louis XV., known also as the Mother Térèse de St. Augustin.

A DOMINICAN ARTIST: a Sketch of the Life of the Rev. Père Besson, of the Order of St. Dominic.

HENRI PERREYVE. By PÈRE GRATRY.

ST. FRANCIS DE SALES, Bishop and Prince of Geneva.

THE REVIVAL OF PRIESTLY LIFE IN THE SEVENTEENTH CENTURY IN FRANCE.

A CHRISTIAN PAINTER OF THE NINETEENTH CENTURY.

BOSSUET AND HIS CONTEMPORARIES.

FÉNELON, ARCHBISHOP OF CAMBRAI.

HENRI DOMINIQUE LACORDAIRE.

DEVOTIONAL WORKS. Edited by H. L. SIDNEY LEAR. *New and Uniform Editions. Nine Vols.* 16mo. 2s. 6d. each.

FÉNELON'S SPIRITUAL LETTERS TO MEN.

FÉNELON'S SPIRITUAL LETTERS TO WOMEN.

A SELECTION FROM THE SPIRITUAL LETTERS OF ST. FRANCIS DE SALES.

THE SPIRIT OF ST. FRANCIS DE SALES.

THE HIDDEN LIFE OF THE SOUL.

THE LIGHT OF THE CONSCIENCE.

SELF-RENUNCIATION. From the French.

ST. FRANCIS DE SALES OF THE LOVE OF GOD.

SELECTIONS FROM PASCAL'S 'THOUGHTS.'

Liddon.—Works by HENRY PARRY LIDDON, D.D., D.C.L., LL.D., late Canon Residentiary and Chancellor of St. Paul's.

LIFE OF EDWARD BOUVERIE PUSEY, D.D. By HENRY PARRY LIDDON, D.D., D.C.L., LL.D. Edited and prepared for publication by the Rev. J. O. JOHNSTON, M A., Principal of the Theological College, and Vicar of Cuddesdon, Oxford; and the Rev. ROBERT J. WILSON, D.D., Warden of Keble College. *With Portraits and Illustrations. Four Vols.* 8vo. *Vols. I. and II.*, 36s. *Vol. III.*, 18s.

CLERICAL LIFE AND WORK : Sermons. *Crown 8vo.* 5s.

ESSAYS AND ADDRESSES : Lectures on Buddhism—Lectures on the Life of St. Paul—Papers on Dante. *Crown 8vo.* 5s.

EXPLANATORY ANALYSIS OF PAUL'S EPISTLE TO THE ROMANS. 8vo. 14s.

SERMONS ON OLD TESTAMENT SUBJECTS. *Crown 8vo.* 5s.

SERMONS ON SOME WORDS OF CHRIST. *Crown 8vo.* 5s.

THE DIVINITY OF OUR LORD AND SAVIOUR JESUS CHRIST. Being the Bampton Lectures for 1866. *Crown 8vo.* 5s.

ADVENT IN ST. PAUL'S. Sermons bearing chiefly on the Two Comings of our Lord. *Two Vols. Crown 8vo. 3s. 6d. each. Cheap Edition in one Volume. Crown 8vo.* 5s.

CHRISTMASTIDE IN ST. PAUL'S. Sermons bearing chiefly on the Birth of our Lord and the End of the Year. *Crown 8vo.* 5s.

PASSIONTIDE SERMONS. *Crown 8vo.* 5s.

EASTER IN ST. PAUL'S. Sermons bearing chiefly on the Resurrection of our Lord. *Two Vols. Crown 8vo. 3s. 6d. each. Cheap Edition in one Volume. Crown 8vo.* 5s.

SERMONS PREACHED BEFORE THE UNIVERSITY OF OXFORD. *Two Vols. Crown 8vo. 3s. 6d. each. Cheap Edition in one Volume. Crown 8vo.* 5s.

THE MAGNIFICAT. Sermons in St. Paul's. *Crown 8vo.* 2s. 6d.

SOME ELEMENTS OF RELIGION. Lent Lectures. *Small 8vo.* 2s. 6d.; or *in paper cover*, 1s. 6d.
The Crown 8vo Edition (5s.) may still be had.

SELECTIONS FROM THE WRITINGS OF H. P. LIDDON, D.D. *Crown 8vo.* 3s. 6d.

MAXIMS AND GLEANINGS FROM THE WRITINGS OF H. P. LIDDON, D.D. Selected and arranged by C. M. S. *Crown 16mo.* 1s.

DR. LIDDON'S TOUR IN EGYPT AND PALESTINE IN 1886. Being Letters descriptive of the Tour, written by his Sister, Mrs. KING *Crown 8vo.* 5s.

Luckock.—Works by HERBERT MORTIMER LUCKOCK, D.D., Dean of Lichfield.

THE HISTORY OF MARRIAGE, JEWISH AND CHRISTIAN, IN RELATION TO DIVORCE AND CERTAIN FORBIDDEN DEGREES. *Crown 8vo.* 6s.

AFTER DEATH. An Examination of the Testimony of Primitive Times respecting the State of the Faithful Dead, and their Relationship to the Living. *Crown 8vo.* 6s.

THE INTERMEDIATE STATE BETWEEN DEATH AND JUDGMENT. Being a Sequel to *After Death. Crown 8vo.* 6s.

FOOTPRINTS OF THE SON OF MAN, as traced by St. Mark. Being Eighty Portions for Private Study, Family Reading, and Instructions in Church. *Two Vols. Crown 8vo.* 12s. *Cheap Edition in one Vol. Crown 8vo.* 5s.

THE DIVINE LITURGY. Being the Order for Holy Communion, Historically, Doctrinally, and devotionally set forth, in Fifty Portions. *Crown 8vo.* 6s.

STUDIES IN THE HISTORY OF THE BOOK OF COMMON PRAYER. The Anglican Reform—The Puritan Innovations—The Elizabethan Reaction—The Caroline Settlement. With Appendices. *Crown 8vo.* 6s.

THE BISHOPS IN THE TOWER. A Record of Stirring Events affecting the Church and Nonconformists from the Restoration to the Revolution. *Crown 8vo.* 6s.

LYRA GERMANICA. Hymns translated from the German by CATHERINE WINKWORTH. *Small 8vo.* 5s.

MacColl.—Works by the Rev. MALCOLM MACCOLL, M.A., Canon Residentary of Ripon.

CHRISTIANITY IN RELATION TO SCIENCE AND MORALS. *Crown 8vo.* 6s.

LIFE HERE AND HEREAFTER: Sermons. *Crown 8vo.* 7s. 6d.

Mason.—Works by A. J. MASON, D.D., Hon. Canon of Canterbury and Examining Chaplain to the Archbishop of Canterbury.

THE FAITH OF THE GOSPEL. A Manual of Christian Doctrine. *Crown 8vo.* 3s. 6d.

THE RELATION OF CONFIRMATION TO BAPTISM. As taught in Holy Scripture and the Fathers. *Crown 8vo.* 7s. 6d.

Mercier.—OUR MOTHER CHURCH: Being Simple Talk on High Topics. By Mrs. JEROME MERCIER. *Small 8vo.* 3s. 6d.

Molesworth.—STORIES OF THE SAINTS FOR CHILDREN: The Black Letter Saints. By Mrs. MOLESWORTH, Author of 'The Palace in the Garden,' etc, etc. *With Illustrations. Royal 16mo.* 5s.

Mozley.—Works by J. B. MOZLEY, D.D., late Canon of Christ Church, and Regius Professor of Divinity at Oxford.

ESSAYS, HISTORICAL AND THEOLOGICAL. *Two Vols. 8vo.* 24s.

EIGHT LECTURES ON MIRACLES. Being the Bampton Lectures for 1865. *Crown 8vo.* 3s. 6d.

RULING IDEAS IN EARLY AGES AND THEIR RELATION TO OLD TESTAMENT FAITH. Lectures delivered to Graduates of the University of Oxford. *8vo.* 10s. 6d.

SERMONS PREACHED BEFORE THE UNIVERSITY OF OXFORD, and on Various Occasions. *Crown 8vo.* 3s. 6d.

SERMONS, PAROCHIAL AND OCCASIONAL. *Crown 8vo.* 3s. 6d.

A REVIEW OF THE BAPTISMAL CONTROVERSY. *Crown 8vo.* 3s. 6d.

Newbolt.—Works by the Rev. W. C. E. NEWBOLT, M.A., Canon and Chancellor of St. Paul's Cathedral, Select Preacher at Oxford, and Examining Chaplain to the Lord Bishop of Ely.

COUNSELS OF FAITH AND PRACTICE: being Sermons preached on various occasions. *New and Enlarged Edition. Crown 8vo.* 5s.

SPECULUM SACERDOTUM; or, the Divine Model of the Priestly Life. *Crown 8vo.* 7s. 6d.

THE FRUIT OF THE SPIRIT. Being Ten Addresses bearing on the Spiritual Life. *Crown 8vo.* 2s. 6d.

THE MAN OF GOD. Being Six Addresses delivered during Lent at the Primary Ordination of the Right Rev. the Lord Alwyne Compton, D.D., Bishop of Ely. *Small 8vo.* 1s. 6d.

THE PRAYER BOOK: Its Voice and Teaching. Being Spiritual Addresses bearing on the Book of Common Prayer. *Crown 8vo.* 2s. 6d.

IN THEOLOGICAL LITERATURE.

Newman.—Works by JOHN HENRY NEWMAN, B.D., sometime Vicar of St. Mary's, Oxford.
PAROCHIAL AND PLAIN SERMONS. *Eight Vols. Cabinet Edition. Crown 8vo. 5s. each. Cheaper Edition. 3s. 6d. each.*
SELECTION, ADAPTED TO THE SEASONS OF THE ECCLESIASTICAL YEAR, from the 'Parochial and Plain Sermons.' *Cabinet Edition. Crown 8vo. 5s. Cheaper Edition. 3s. 6d.*
FIFTEEN SERMONS PREACHED BEFORE THE UNIVERSITY OF OXFORD *Cabinet Edition. Crown 8vo. 5s. Cheaper Edition. 3s. 6d.*
SERMONS BEARING UPON SUBJECTS OF THE DAY. *Cabinet Edition. Crown 8vo. 5s. Cheaper Edition. Crown 8vo. 3s. 6d.*
LECTURES ON THE DOCTRINE OF JUSTIFICATION. *Cabinet Edition. Crown 8vo. 5s. Cheaper Edition. 3s. 6d.*

** *A Complete List of Cardinal Newman's Works can be had on Application.*

Osborne.—Works by EDWARD OSBORNE, Mission Priest of the Society of St. John the Evangelist, Cowley, Oxford.
THE CHILDREN'S SAVIOUR. Instructions to Children on the Life of Our Lord and Saviour Jesus Christ. *Illustrated. 16mo. 2s. 6d.*
THE SAVIOUR KING. Instructions to Children on Old Testament Types and Illustrations of the Life of Christ. *Illustrated. 16mo. 2s. 6d.*
THE CHILDREN'S FAITH. Instructions to Children on the Apostles' Creed. *Illustrated. 16mo. 2s. 6d.*

Overton.—THE ENGLISH CHURCH IN THE NINETEENTH CENTURY, 1800-1833. By the Rev. JOHN H. OVERTON, D.D., Canon of Lincoln, Rector of Epworth, Doncaster, and Rural Dean of the Isle of Axholme. *8vo. 14s.*

Oxenden.—Works by the Right Rev. ASHTON OXENDEN, formerly Bishop of Montreal.
PLAIN SERMONS, to which is prefixed a Memorial Portrait. *Crown 8vo. 5s.*
THE HISTORY OF MY LIFE: An Autobiography. *Crown 8vo. 5s.*
PEACE AND ITS HINDRANCES. *Crown 8vo. 1s. sewed, 2s. cloth.*
THE PATHWAY OF SAFETY; or, Counsel to the Awakened. *Fcap. 8vo, large type. 2s. 6d. Cheap Edition. Small type, limp, 1s.*
THE EARNEST COMMUNICANT. *New Red Rubric Edition. 32mo, cloth. 2s. Common Edition. 32mo. 1s.*
OUR CHURCH AND HER SERVICES. *Fcap. 8vo. 2s. 6d.*

[continued.

A SELECTION OF WORKS

Oxenden.—Works by the Right Rev. ASHTON OXENDEN formerly Bishop of Montreal—*continued.*
FAMILY PRAYERS FOR FOUR WEEKS. First Series. *Fcap. 8vo.* 2s. 6d. Second Series. *Fcap. 8vo.* 2s. 6d.
    LARGE TYPE EDITION. Two Series in one Volume. *Crown 8vo.* 6s.
COTTAGE SERMONS; or, Plain Words to the Poor. *Fcap. 8vo.* 2s. 6d.
THOUGHTS FOR HOLY WEEK. 16mo, *cloth.* 1s. 6d.
DECISION. 18mo. 1s. 6d.
THE HOME BEYOND; or, A Happy Old Age. *Fcap. 8vo.* 1s. 6d.
THE LABOURING MAN'S BOOK. 18mo, *large type, cloth.* 1s. 6d.

Paget.—Works by FRANCIS PAGET, D.D., Dean of Christ Church.
STUDIES IN THE CHRISTIAN CHARACTER: Sermons. With an Introductory Essay. *Crown 8vo.* 6s. 6d.
THE SPIRIT OF DISCIPLINE: Sermons. *Crown 8vo.* 6s. 6d.
FACULTIES AND DIFFICULTIES FOR BELIEF AND DISBELIEF. *Crown 8vo.* 6s. 6d.
THE HALLOWING OF WORK. Addresses given at Eton, January 16-18, 1888. *Small 8vo.* 2s.

PRACTICAL REFLECTIONS. By a CLERGYMAN. With Prefaces by H. P. LIDDON, D.D., D.C.L., and the BISHOP OF LINCOLN. *Crown 8vo.*

THE BOOK OF GENESIS. 4s. 6d.	THE HOLY GOSPELS. 4s. 6d.
THE PSALMS. 5s.	ACTS TO REVELATIONS. 6s.
ISAIAH. 4s. 6d.	

PRIEST (THE) TO THE ALTAR; or, Aids to the Devout Celebration of Holy Communion, chiefly after the Ancient English Use of Sarum. *Royal 8vo.* 12s.

Prynne.—THE TRUTH AND REALITY OF THE EUCHARISTIC SACRIFICE, Proved from Holy Scripture, the Teaching of the Primitive Church, and the Book of Common Prayer. By the Rev. GEORGE RUNDLE PRYNNE, M.A. *Crown 8vo.* 3s. 6d.

Puller.—THE PRIMITIVE SAINTS AND THE SEE OF ROME. By F. W. PULLER, M.A., Mission Priest of the Society of St. John Evangelist, Cowley, Oxford. *Crown 8vo.* 7s. 6d.

Pusey.—LIFE OF EDWARD BOUVERIE PUSEY, D.D. By HENRY PARRY LIDDON, D.D., D.C.L., LL.D. Edited and prepared for publication by the Rev. J. O. JOHNSTON, M.A., Principal of the Theological College, Vicar of Cuddesdon, Oxford, and the Rev. ROBERT J. WILSON, D.D., Warden of Keble College. *With Portraits and Illustrations. Four Vols.* 8vo. Vols. *I.* and *II.*, 36s. Vol. *III.*, 18s.

Pusey.—Works by the Rev. E. B. PUSEY, D.D.
PRIVATE PRAYERS. With Preface by H. P. LIDDON, D.D. 32mo. 1s.
SELECTIONS FROM THE WRITINGS OF EDWARD BOUVERIE PUSEY, D.D. *Crown 8vo.* 3s. 6d.

IN THEOLOGICAL LITERATURE.

Sanday.—Works by W. SANDAY, D.D., Dean Ireland's Professor of Exegesis and Fellow of Exeter College, Oxford.
  INSPIRATION: Eight Lectures on the Early History and Origin of the Doctrine of Biblical Inspiration. Being the Bampton Lectures for 1893. 8vo. 16s.
  THE ORACLES OF GOD: Nine Lectures on the Nature and Extent of Biblical Inspiration and the Special Significance of the Old Testament Scriptures at the Present Time. *Crown 8vo.* 4s.
  TWO PRESENT-DAY QUESTIONS. I. Biblical Criticism. II. The Social Movement. Sermons preached before the University of Cambridge. *Crown 8vo.* 2s. 6d.

Seebohm.—THE OXFORD REFORMERS—JOHN COLET, ERASMUS, AND THOMAS MORE: A History of their Fellow-Work. By FREDERICK SEEBOHM. 8vo. 14s.

Stanton.—THE PLACE OF AUTHORITY IN MATTERS OF RELIGIOUS BELIEF. By VINCENT HENRY STANTON, D.D., Fellow of Trinity Coll., Ely Prof. of Divinity, Cambridge. *Cr. 8vo.* 6s.

Williams.—Works by the Rev. ISAAC WILLIAMS, B.D.
  A DEVOTIONAL COMMENTARY ON THE GOSPEL NARRATIVE, *Eight Vols. Crown 8vo. 5s. each. Sold Separately.*
  THOUGHTS ON THE STUDY OF THE HOLY GOSPELS.
  A HARMONY OF THE FOUR GOSPELS.
  OUR LORD'S NATIVITY.
  OUR LORD'S MINISTRY (Second Year).
  OUR LORD'S MINISTRY (Third Year).
  THE HOLY WEEK.
  OUR LORD'S PASSION.
  OUR LORD'S RESURRECTION.
  FEMALE CHARACTERS OF HOLY SCRIPTURE. A Series of Sermons, *Crown 8vo.* 5s.
  THE CHARACTERS OF THE OLD TESTAMENT. *Crown 8vo.* 5s.
  THE APOCALYPSE. With Notes and Reflections. *Crown 8vo.* 5s.
  SERMONS ON THE EPISTLES AND GOSPELS FOR THE SUNDAYS AND HOLY DAYS. *Two Vols. Crown 8vo. 5s. each.*
  PLAIN SERMONS ON CATECHISM. *Two Vols. Cr. 8vo. 5s. each.*
  SELECTIONS FROM ISAAC WILLIAMS' WRITINGS. *Cr. 8vo.* 3s. 6d.
  THE AUTOBIOGRAPHY OF ISAAC WILLIAMS, B.D., Author of several of the 'Tracts for the Times.' Edited by the Venerable Sir GEORGE PREVOST, as throwing further light on the history of the Oxford Movement. *Crown 8vo.* 5s.

[continued.

A SELECTION OF THEOLOGICAL WORKS.

Wordsworth.—Works by the late CHRISTOPHER WORDSWORTH, D.D., Bishop of Lincoln.

THE HOLY BIBLE (the Old Testament). With Notes, Introductions, and Index. *Imperial 8vo.*
    Vol. I. THE PENTATEUCH. 25*s*. Vol. II. JOSHUA TO SAMUEL. 15*s*. Vol. III. KINGS to ESTHER. 15*s*. Vol. IV. JOB TO SONG OF SOLOMON. 25*s*. Vol. V. ISAIAH TO EZEKIEL. 25*s*. Vol. VI. DANIEL, MINOR PROPHETS, and Index. 15*s*.
    Also supplied in 12 Parts. Sold separately.

THE NEW TESTAMENT, in the Original Greek. With Notes, Introductions, and Indices. *Imperial 8vo.*
    Vol. I. GOSPELS AND ACTS OF THE APOSTLES. 23*s*. Vol. II. EPISTLES, APOCALYPSE, and Indices. 37*s*.
    Also supplied in 4 Parts. Sold separately.

LECTURES ON INSPIRATION OF THE BIBLE. *Small 8vo.* 1*s*. 6*d*. cloth. 1*s*. sewed.

A CHURCH HISTORY TO A.D. 451. *Four Vols. Crown 8vo.*
    Vol. I. TO THE COUNCIL OF NICÆA, A.D. 325. 8*s*. 6*d*. Vol. II. FROM THE COUNCIL OF NICÆA TO THAT OF CONSTANTINOPLE. 6*s*. Vol. III. CONTINUATION. 6*s*. Vol. IV. CONCLUSION, TO THE COUNCIL OF CHALCEDON, A.D. 451. 6*s*.

THEOPHILUS ANGLICANUS: a Manual of Instruction on the Church and the Anglican Branch of it. *12mo.* 2*s*. 6*d*.

ELEMENTS OF INSTRUCTION ON THE CHURCH. *16mo.* 1*s*. cloth. 6*d*. sewed.

ST. HIPPOLYTUS AND THE CHURCH OF ROME. *Cr. 8vo.* 7*s*. 6*d*.

ON UNION WITH ROME. *Small 8vo.* 1*s*. 6*d*. Sewed, 1*s*.

THE HOLY YEAR: Original Hymns. *16mo.* 2*s*. 6*d*. *and* 1*s*. Limp, 6*d*.
    ,,   ,, With Music. Edited by W. H. MONK. *Square 8vo.* 4*s*. 6*d*.

GUIDES AND GOADS. (An English Edition of 'Ethica et Spiritualia.') *32mo.* 1*s*. 6*d*.

MISCELLANIES, Literary and Religious. *Three Vols. 8vo.* 36*s*.

ON THE INTERMEDIATE STATE OF THE SOUL AFTER DEATH. *32mo.* 1*s*.

Younghusband.—Works by FRANCES YOUNGHUSBAND.

THE STORY OF OUR LORD, told in Simple Language for Children. With 25 Illustrations on Wood from Pictures by the Old Masters, and numerous Ornamental Borders, Initial Letters, etc., from Longmans' New Testament. *Crown 8vo.* 2*s*. 6*d*.

THE STORY OF THE EXODUS, told in Simple Language for Children. With Map and 29 Illustrations. *Crown 8vo.* 2*s*. 6*d*.

Printed by T. and A. CONSTABLE, Printers to Her Majesty,
at the Edinburgh University Press.

www.ingramcontent.com/pod-product-compliance
Lightning Source LLC
Chambersburg PA
CBHW032359230426
43672CB00007B/760